Scholars and Gentlemen

Shakespearian textual criticism and representations of scholarly labour,
1725–1765

SIMON JARVIS

CLARENDON PRESS · OXFORD
1995

Oxford University Press, Walton Street, Oxford OX2 6DP

Oxford New York
Athens Auckland Bangkok Bombay
Calcutta Cape Town Dar es Salaam Delhi
Florence Hong Kong Istanbul Karachi
Kuala Lumpur Madras Madrid Melbourne
Mexico City Nairobi Paris Singapore
Taipei Tokyo Toronto
and associated companies in
Berlin Ibadan

Oxford is a trade mark of Oxford University Press

Published in the United States
by Oxford University Press Inc., New York

British Library Cataloguing in Publication Data
Data available

Library of Congress Cataloging in Publication Data
Jarvis, Simon.
Scholars and gentlemen: Shakespearean textual criticism and
representations of scholarly labour, 1725–1765 / Simon Jarvis.
Includes bibliographical references and index.
1. Shakespeare, William, 1564–1616—Criticism and interpretation—
History—18th century. 2. Shakespeare, William, 1564–1616—
Criticism, Textual. 3. Great Britain—Intellectual life—18th
century. 4. Shakespeare, William, 1564–1616—Editors.
5. Criticism, Textual—History—18th century. 6. Editing—
History—18th century. I. Title.
PR2968.J37 1995 822.3'3—dc20 94–38660
ISBN 0–19–818295–3

1 3 5 7 9 10 8 6 4 2

Typeset by Best-set Typesetter Ltd., Hong Kong
Printed in Great Britain
on acid-free paper by
Biddles Ltd.,
Guildford and Kings Lynn

Acknowledgements

MARILYN BUTLER, Jonathan Bate, Alun David, Ernst Honigmann, John Mullan, and Fred Parker all helped to make this book much better than it would have been without their advice; participants in the Literary Theory and Textual Editing Group of the Centre for Cultural and Theoretical Studies in the School of English at Newcastle University also made useful comments on a draft of the Introduction. I wish to thank the following for their financial support: the Master and Fellows of Sidney Sussex College for the Junior Research Fellowship which enabled me to complete work on the dissertation; the British Academy for the Major State Studentship which supported the first three years of research; the University of Newcastle for the Postdoctoral Research Fellowship which I have held whilst completing this book. My thanks are due to the staffs of the Cambridge University Library, the British Library, the Special Collection of Nottingham University Library, the Library of the University College of Wales in Aberystwyth; to the Librarian of St John's College, Cambridge; and to the Librarian of Lincoln College, Oxford. I would like to thank the following friends for their indispensable support and advice: Yoram Gorlizki, Drew Milne, Simon Parker, Sean Allan, Garry Kelly, Nick Walker, Haydn Downey, Fenella Cannell, Alun David, Charlotte Grant, and Tim Jarvis. My greatest debt is to my parents.

Contents

Abbreviations

The following abbreviations have been used to refer to frequently cited works. Eighteenth Century Short-Title Catalogue numbers are given where relevant.

1637   *The Tragedy of Hamlet Prince of Denmark* (London, 1637).

1676   *The Tragedy of Hamlet Prince of Denmark. As it is now Acted at his Highness the Duke of York's Theatre* (London, 1676; repr. 1969).

1709   *The Works of Mr. William Shakespear*, ed. Nicholas Rowe and Charles Gildon (7 vols., London, 1709–10; repr. New York, 1967).

1714   *The Works of Mr. William Shakespear*, ed. Nicholas Rowe, 3rd edn. (8 vols., London, 1714) [ESTC n025981].

1723–5   *The Works of Shakespear*, ed. Alexander Pope (6 vols., London, 1723–5) [ESTC n026060].

1728   *The Works of Shakespear*, ed. Alexander Pope (8 vols., London, 1728) [ESTC t138594].

1733   *The Works of Shakespear*, ed. Lewis Theobald (7 vols., London, 1733–4) [ESTC t138606].

1740   *The Works of Shakespear*, ed. Lewis Theobald (8 vols., London, 1740) [ESTC t054701].

1744   *The Works of Shakespear*, ed. Sir Thomas Hanmer (6 vols., London, 1743–4) [ESTC t138604].

1747   *The Works of Shakespear*, ed. William Warburton (8 vols., London, 1747) [ESTC t138851].

1757   *The Works of Shakespear*, ed. Lewis Theobald (8 vols., London, 1757) [ESTC n026030].

1765   *The Plays of William Shakespear*, ed. Samuel Johnson (8 vols., London, 1765) [ESTC t138601].

1767–8   *Mr. William Shakespear his Comedies, Histories, and Tragedies*, ed. Edward Capell (10 vols., London, 1767–8) [ESTC t138599].

1785   *The Plays of William Shakespear*, ed. George Steevens and Isaac Reed (10 vols., London, 1785) [ESTC t138853].

1790   *The Plays and Poems of William Shakespear*, ed. Edmond Malone (10 vols. in 11, London, 1790) [ESTC t138858].

Allen and Muir   *Shakespeare's Plays in Quarto*, ed. Michael J. B. Allen and Kenneth Muir (Berkeley, Calif., 1981).

ESTC	Eighteenth Century Short-Title Catalogue
Furness	*A New Variorum Edition of Shakespeare: Hamlet*, ed. H. H. Furness (Philadelphia, 1877).
Hinman	*The Norton Facsimile: The First Folio of Shakespeare*, ed. Charlton Hinman (New York, 1968).
Mic.	*The Eighteenth Century on Microfilm* (Woodbridge, Conn., 1983–).

Lexicon ad finem longo luctamine tandem
Scaliger ut duxit, tenuis pertaesus opellae
Vile indignatus Studium, nugasque molestas
Ingemit exosus, scribendaque lexica mandat
Damnatis poenam pro poenis omnibus unam. . . .
  Fallimur exemplis; temere sibi turba scholarum
Ima tuas credit permitti, Scaliger, iras.

When Scaliger after long struggle finally finished his dictionary,
thoroughly bored with the slender achievement, indignant at the
worthless study and the troublesome trifles, he groaned in hatred,
and prescribed writing dictionaries for condemned criminals, one
punishment in place of all other punishments.

  We are deceived by examples; the lowest mob of scholars rashly
believes that your anger is allowed to them also, Scaliger.

Introduction

WHEN EDMUND WILSON came to review 'The Fruits of the MLA' towards the end of the 1960s he found them a poor harvest.[1] Wilson complained that his own plan to find a publisher willing to market a series of relatively inexpensive and uncluttered, yet reliable, texts of classic American authors, too many of whose works were at the time not in print, had been supplanted. In its place had emerged a series of 'approved texts' stamped with the seal of the Center for Editions of American Authors and prepared by what Wilson took to be a cartel of professional editors more interested in whether Mark Twain wrote 'ssst' or 'sssst', 'aunt Polly' or 'Aunt Polly', than in critical appreciation of or informative commentary on their chosen authors. Wilson conceded that textual-critical matters could on occasion be of interest to the general reader: where it was a case of rescuing a text from wholesale adulteration by publishers, censors, or revisers, detailed attention to editorial matters might be justified. In most cases, however, an excessive preoccupation with such details had led merely to the provision of grossly inflated apparatuses and textual prefaces dwarfing the contracted space given to critical assessment or biographical information. Wilson's attack was notable less for any attention to the epistemological presuppositions of its target discipline (its arguments were entirely extra-, indeed anti-philological) than for the sharpness with which it put the case against professional editors. Wilson wrote with the urbane contempt of a man of letters for what he took to be their narrow and provincial professionalism; in a characteristic aside he remarked that it 'does perhaps seem unfortunate that so many of these MLA volumes should be products of the Middle West'.[2] Professional scholars were not slow to reply that Wilson had a no less vested interest in *not* caring about philological minutiae than they had themselves in making such minutiae their business: Wilson's dilettantism, they responded, needed to regard all such scholarly minutiae as trifling in order to defend the necessary ignorance of detail incident to a literary-critical career of the diversity and scope of his own. Gordon Ray remarked that 'this attack derives in part

---

[1] Edmund Wilson, 'The Fruits of the MLA', *New York Review of Books* (26 Sept. 1968), 7–10; (10 Oct. 1968), 6–16.

[2] Ibid. (26 Sept. 1968), 9.

from the alarm of amateurs at seeing rigorous professional standards applied to a subject in which they have a vested interest' before concluding reassuringly that 'In the long run professional standards always prevail.'[3] It is a central contention of this book that the pattern of argument at work in the dispute between Wilson and the editors is one which has structured debate about vernacular textual criticism since its inception— both as an external framework for disagreement about the merits and utility of editing and as a set of internal criteria within epistemological and practical arguments about editorial procedures themselves. Men (less often women) of letters have spoken on behalf of a general reader against the supposedly interested and intellectually narrow depredations of professional pedants upon texts which are a public inheritance; professional scholars have lamented the incompetence in exact philology of dilettante critics, leisured or otherwise, and have insisted that all literary criticism rests on a base of minute editorial labours. The altercation is not one among inalterably fixed camps, but rather among divergent professional personae within a division of literary labours: ideally critics and scholars alike strive to be neither the ignorant dilettante nor the narrow pedant, to be both competent specialists and rounded generalists, or—to give the terms an eighteenth-century cast—at once scholars *and* gentlemen.

This book attempts to illuminate this contest of literary faculties by immersing itself in the detail of its earliest history. The antagonisms whose rhetoric and whose consequences for the reproduction of literary texts it traces are impelled less by theoretical disagreement than by a division of intellectual labour which has for good and ill become steadily more extensive since it caused such anxiety in the early eighteenth-century world of letters. That anxiety is a central interest of this study: not merely as an apologetic device for protecting ignorance or for depriving the many of access to the public sphere (although it could certainly be put to both those ends) but also as registering dismay at the advancing conversion of all cultural goods into inert and saleable material. I do not wish, that is, to champion Bentley against Boyle, Theobald against Pope, Tanselle against Wilson, nor vice versa. Instead, my interest is in how apparently purely epistemological and philological issues are perennially entangled in, although not reducible to, representations and self-representations of the disputants' labour, and of the world of literary labour in which those disputes are presented. What a study of the history of such questions can begin to suggest is the impossibility of reconciling such

---

[3] Ray is quoted in G. Thomas Tanselle's *Textual Criticism since Greg: A Chronicle 1850– 1985* (Charlottesville, Va., 1987), 34–5.

antagonisms as though they testified only to theoretical contradictions or empirical deficiencies. From such a perspective we can begin to see how the terms in which 'theoretical' discussion of the relations between textual and literary criticism is sometimes framed—what is the editor's *task*? what is the *function* of criticism?—would already concede as a given just what any critical theory needs to reflect critically upon.[4] The possibility that 'the function of criticism is the criticism of function',[5] to adopt Drew Milne's chiasmus, would already have been overlooked. The present work cannot make good such a possibility.[6] Yet it does seek to contest demands for the limits and tasks of textual criticism to be prescribed as functions once and for all, by illustrating some of the historical contexts in which such demands are embedded.

I

The last decade has seen a dramatic expansion of scholarly interest in the history of what has variously been regarded as the 'appropriation', 'reinvention', or 'reconstitution' of Shakespeare and his work, not only in print or on the stage but also in film and television, caricature, political satire, painting, and sculpture.[7] Interest in the history of Shakespeare's text after the publication of the First Folio in 1623, meanwhile, has also experienced a modest revival.[8] Such interest is clearly more than a mere echo of the wider interest in the reconstitution or reappropriation of all things Shakespearian. The re-evaluation of the afterlife of Shakespeare's text cannot be separated either from the transformation of Shakespearian

---

[4] 'Critical theory' is here to be understood not as a synonym for 'literary theory' but in Max Horkheimer's sense. 'Traditionelle und kritische Theorie', *Zeitschrift für Sozialforschung*, 6 (1937), 245–94; *Critical Theory: Selected Essays*, tr. Matthew J. O'Connell *et al.* (New York, 1972).

[5] Drew Milne, 'The Function of Criticism: A Polemical History', *Parataxis: Modernism and Modern Writing*, 1 (1991), 30–50 (p. 30).

[6] For a fully developed critique of methodologism in general see Gillian Rose, *Hegel contra Sociology* (London, 1981); for further discussion see Simon Jarvis, *Adorno* (Cambridge, forthcoming).

[7] For some examples see Jonathan Bate, *Shakespearean Constitutions* (Oxford, 1989); Gary Taylor, *Reinventing Shakespeare* (London, 1989); Michael Dobson, *The Making of the National Poet* (Oxford, 1992); Jean Marsden, ed., *The Appropriation of Shakespeare* (London, 1991).

[8] See, for examples, Arthur Sherbo, *The Birth of Shakespeare Studies* (East Lansing, Mich., 1986); Margreta de Grazia, *Shakespeare Verbatim* (Oxford, 1991); Peter Seary, *Lewis Theobald and the Editing of Shakespeare* (Oxford, 1990); Colin Franklin, *Shakespeare Domesticated* (Aldershot, 1991).

textual criticism itself which has taken place over the last fifteen years, or from the (still vehemently contested) reconsideration of the theoretical grounding of textual criticism which has accompanied it. Here I want briefly to sketch some of the reasons for the collapse of any consensus as to the proper aims and methods of textual criticism, before going on to consider the implications of this collapse for historians of editing.

Grounds for a thoroughgoing reconsideration of the edited afterlife of Shakespeare's text have been offered by the disintegration of what had by the mid-1970s become a widely accepted New Bibliographical consensus on the aims and methods of textual criticism: a consensus based most importantly on the work of Sir Walter Greg and Fredson Bowers, and whose most tenacious polemicist has in recent years been G. Thomas Tanselle. A wide variety of New Bibliographical tenets has come under attack, for equally various reasons. On the one hand, a new generation of textual bibliographers have for some time found reason in the course of detailed empirical inquiry to question some of the New Bibliography's most widely accepted procedures: Paul Werstine's work on the idea that 'Bad' Quartos were memorially reconstructed by rogue actors, and D. F. McKenzie's demonstration that widely agreed-upon assumptions about patterns of work in printing-shops in the hand-press period simply could not be squared with the available empirical evidence, are especially trenchant examples.[9] At the same time, a new interest amongst editors in the possibility that Shakespeare revised many of his plays has clearly left the pivotal New Bibliographical concept of 'final authorial intentions' looking like a rather uncertain help to the editor. The idea had always raised problems of application, especially in the eyes of those working outside the Anglo-American tradition of textual criticism: Hans Zeller once put the case against the canon of 'final authorial intentions' at its bluntest by pointing out that the literal application of such a principle would leave any conscientious editor of Virgil seeking out extant copies of the *Aeneid* in order to destroy them.[10] But the possibility (to put it no more strongly) that Shakespeare revised some of his plays means that it is now especially unclear, even to those who have no doubts about making 'authorial intention' the determining criterion for editorial procedure, 'why final versions or latest substantives, merely because they are latest,

[9] Paul Werstine, 'Narratives about Printed Shakespearean Texts: "Foul Papers" and "'Bad' Quartos"', *Shakespeare Quarterly*, 41 (1990), 65–86; D. F. McKenzie, 'Printers of the Mind: Some Notes on Bibliographical Theories and Printing-House Practices', *Studies in Bibliography*, 22 (1969), 1–75.

[10] Hans Zeller, 'A New Approach to the Critical Constitution of Literary Texts', *Studies in Bibliography*, 28 (1975), 231–64 (p. 243).

should be considered more authoritative than any other that carry the writer's authority', as Jack Stillinger has put it.[11]

That this Pandora's box is not closed simply by settling on final authorial intentions for what are taken to be discrete versions of a particular text, however, is sufficiently demonstrated by the predicament of the recent Oxford *Complete Works*, in which the decision to present separate texts of the Quarto and Folio *Lear* had to be followed by a decision to emend the Folio with reference to the Quarto, and vice versa.[12] Rather, any attempt to edit a revising writer indicates how vulnerable the attempt to reconstruct even temporarily settled authorial intentions must be; Dieter Sattler's criticisms of Friedrich Beissner's edition of Hölderlin, for example, offer a salutary warning as to the difficulties of closing down such a disintegrative process once it has been started.[13] Such revisionary editorial practice has prompted a re-examination of some aspects of the history of Shakespeare editing: scholars have returned to earlier editors in order to trace the roots of those fallacies which are now to be overcome, or to trace hitherto neglected pioneers of the new methods.[14]

Such empirically and editorially grounded challenges to the New Bibliographers, and in particular to the concept of 'final authorial intentions', have been paralleled by the theoretical inquiries into the logic of textual criticism whose most widely influential statement has been Jerome McGann's *Critique of Modern Textual Criticism* (1983).[15] McGann has insisted that, since printed books are the products of collaborative labour, their apparently non-authorially intended features may not be treated as the accidentals which are to be cleared away to reveal authorial substantives. This insistence is partly a belated appearance in the field of textual criticism of a scepticism as to the decisive hermeneutic role of any idea of authorial intention, a scepticism which has, of course, long been pervasive in literary criticism. But McGann's way of putting such an insistence—

[11] Jack Stillinger, 'Multiple Authorship and the Question of Authority', *Text*, 5 (1991), 283–93 (p. 289).

[12] As David Bevington pointed out in his review of the Oxford text, *Shakespeare Quarterly*, 38 (1987), 501–24 (p. 506).

[13] For an account of the debate over Hölderlin's text, see Klaus Hurlebusch, 'Conceptualisations for Procedures of Authorship', *Studies in Bibliography*, 41 (1988), 100–35 (pp. 123–4).

[14] For examples, see Steven Urkowitz, 'The Base shall to th' Legitimate: The Growth of an Editorial Tradition', in Michael Warren and Gary Taylor, eds., *The Division of the Kingdoms* (Oxford, 1983), 23–43; Grace Ioppolo, ' "Old" and "New" Revisionists: Shakespeare's Eighteenth-Century Editors', *Huntington Library Quarterly*, 52 (1989), 347–61.

[15] See also J. J. McGann, ed., *Textual Criticism and Literary Interpretation* (Chicago, 1985); Margreta de Grazia, 'The Essential Shakespeare and the Material Book', *Textual Practice*, 2 (1988), 69–86.

and his corollary to it, that the literary critic should not feel free to set textual criticism aside as a matter for others—has seemed more important as more work has appeared on the contribution made to the meaning of any book by features often assumed to be non-authorial. D. F. McKenzie's *Bibliography and the Sociology of Texts* (1986), as well as a series of articles by the brilliantly destructive Randall McLeod, and, in a more traditional vein, the work of D. F. Foxon and James McLaverty on typography in early texts of Pope, have shown what a range of meanings is lost when supposedly non-authorial features of typographical detail are considered as dispensable to the reproduction of texts.[16] Such a reconsideration of the relationship between textual and literary criticism offers more fundamental reasons for a new interest in the history of Shakespeare's printed texts: from such a perspective, that history would no longer be a contingent, but a constitutive element of the 'Shakespeare' addressed by literary critics.

2

The opponents of the school now represented by Bowers and Tanselle have by no means won the day: a clamorous dialogue has ensued, in which, however, the opposing parties (and would-be moderators between them) have sometimes failed to engage with each others' positions.[17] But the collapse of any consensus as to the aims and methods of editing and of textual criticism must lead historians of these practices to reflect anew on their own procedures. The New Bibliographical approach to editorial history is well illustrated by a survey such as McKerrow's 1937 article on Shakespeare's early eighteenth-century editors.[18] McKerrow's article, impressively informative given its brevity, assesses the editors discussed from the vantage point of his own settled convictions about the necessary procedures of Shakespearian textual criticism: his principal concern is to rank the editors discussed according to how nearly they approximate what

[16] Randall McLeod (as 'Random Clod'), 'Information on Information', *Text*, 5 (1991), 241–81; D. F. Foxon, *Pope and the Early Eighteenth-Century Book Trade*, rev. and ed. James McLaverty (Oxford, 1991); James McLaverty, 'The Mode of Existence of Literary Works of Art: The Case of the *Dunciad Variorum*', *Studies in Bibliography*, 37 (1984), 82–105.

[17] See, for examples, the exchange between McGann and T. H. Howard-Hill in *Text*, 5 (1991); for a defence of the principles of the New Bibliography, see G. Thomas Tanselle, *Textual Criticism since Greg* and *A Rationale of Textual Criticism* (Philadelphia, 1989).

[18] R. B. McKerrow, 'The Treatment of Shakespeare's Text by his Earlier Editors (1709–1768), in Peter Alexander, ed., *Studies in Shakespeare: British Academy Lectures* (London, 1964), 103–31.

is taken as correct procedure. Peter Seary's recent monograph on the editorial work of Lewis Theobald is in many respects a model of the detailed reconstruction of editorial practice that can be provided by this kind of study: it is a work interested in the relatively autonomous history of textual criticism as an emergent discipline, not in using editions of Shakespeare as a malleable index of the taste of the age.[19] In this it is certainly preferable to such an attempt as Wolfgang Kowalk's study of Pope's edition, in which the 1723–5 text is read off against Pope's copy-text, Rowe's 1714 edition, to provide statistical information of a somewhat etiolated kind about Pope's aesthetic preferences.[20]

But Seary's study and others like it start with a number of disadvantages, disadvantages which have closer analogies with the development of the history of science than with the development of literary history. When history of science is written as a history of inspired and objective scientists emerging miraculously from benighted and pre-scientific cultures neither our understanding of the scientists nor of the cultures in question is furthered. The merit of a book such as Thomas Kuhn's *The Structure of Scientific Revolutions* was that it enabled historians of science to begin understanding the history of science as a history of scientific discourses without therefore relegating the particular concepts or discoveries of those discourses to a contingent or accidental status.[21] The analogy is a useful one, not because Kuhn's work could provide us with a methodology for all history of philology, but because an approach akin to that of pre-Kuhn history of science has generally held sway amongst historians of textual criticism. Those textual critics selected for commendation will be taken as enlightened pioneers, ahead of the unenlightened culture of textual criticism within which they worked. The history of textual criticism becomes a Whig history of progressive scholars overcoming obstinate backwardness to reach our present scientific understanding. Any approach which sets out as if from a scientific understanding to chart the pioneering efforts by which that understanding was won may find the ground moving beneath its feet, not only because there is as yet no such standpoint, but because the attempt to write the history of textual criticism as if there were is so often obliged, misleadingly, to measure earlier textual-critical theory and practice by its own (sometimes incommensurable) standards.

[19] Seary, *Theobald*.
[20] Wolfgang Kowalk, *Popes Shakespeare-Ausgabe als Spiegel seiner Kunstauffassung* (Berne, 1975).
[21] Thomas S. Kuhn, *The Structure of Scientific Revolutions*, 2nd edn. (Chicago, 1970).

This difficulty is not mended, on the other hand, by lurching towards its contrary: by reading the history of the theory and practice of textual criticism as a set of merely superstructural or epiphenomenal symptoms of the political rhetorics contemporary with it. Jonathan Bate's *Shakespearean Constitutions* has offered a timely reminder that no body of texts, not even Shakespeare's, is infinitely malleable to any political purpose;[22] conversely, much of the recent work on the 'appropriation' of Shakespeare fails to take any interest in the means by which a philological culture which became precisely *disapproving* of such appropriation grew up. Why, for example, do eighteenth-century editions of Shakespeare emend and adapt so little when compared with theatrical reworkings from the same period?[23] To ask this question is not to suggest that eighteenth-century editorial culture could have entirely avoided appropriating Shakespeare for its own ends, but to insist that any inquiry into the history of Shakespearian textual criticism needs first of all to grasp its relative autonomy from the other miscellaneous kinds of 'appropriation' with which it is often lumped; yet, at the same time, to seek to understand the rise of the relative autonomy of scholarship, rather than regarding such autonomy as in no need of explanation. The contributions of a book such as Gary Taylor's *Reinventing Shakespeare* (1989) to the history of Shakespearian textual criticism show what can happen when unreflective political categories are read directly into that history. For Taylor, Rowe's edition of 1709 is 'Whig', whilst Pope's of 1723–5 is 'Tory'.[24] If we were to follow such a logic through, Theobald's 1733 edition would be another 'Whig' text, given that Walpole's name appeared on Theobald's list of subscribers.[25] The gulf in editorial method between Rowe and Theobald would disappear into the all-swallowing box labelled 'Whig'. At a later stage in Taylor's work, attitudes towards Shakespeare's text are identified with attitudes towards the British constitution: thus 'Capell's control of the text had to be total, for only a dictatorship could enforce revolutionary change',[26] whilst 'Ritson was less afraid [than Malone] of change, more willing to see and attack "corruption" in the most venerable texts or institutions'.[27] Here 'change' in the first instance means a return to the Quartos and First Folio for copy-text, in the second a willingness to abandon them. The easy equivalence implied by the phrase 'texts or institutions' collapses once this has been noticed.

---

[22] Bate, *Shakespearean Constitutions*, 210–11.

[23] For theatrical adaptations of Shakespeare see C. B. Hogan, *Shakespeare in the Theatre 1701–1800* (2 vols., Oxford, 1952); G. C. Branam, *Eighteenth Century Adaptations of Shakespearean Tragedy* (Berkeley, Calif., 1956); and, now, Dobson, *National Poet*.

[24] Taylor, *Reinventing Shakespeare*, 81.   [25] *1733*, i, p. [lxxxv].

[26] Taylor, *Reinventing Shakespeare*, 143.   [27] Ibid. 147.

Nevertheless, we should be wary of any account of the history of Shakespearian textual criticism which would have the effect of sealing the practice off from the culture and society which it served. Margreta de Grazia has convincingly argued in her *Shakespeare Verbatim* (1991) that a history of textual criticism as a gradual progress towards New Bibliographical enlightenment in fact makes it impossible fully to grasp those moments at which a decisive epistemological break occurs. Yet at the same time she shows that the theory and practice of Shakespearian editors cannot be directly mapped on to the political rhetorics contemporary with them. *Shakespeare Verbatim*, instead, uses a single edition, that of Edmond Malone, to argue illuminatingly for the sudden appearance in the 1790s of what de Grazia regards as the central features of an 'Enlightenment' historical scholarship. She suggests that these are substantially those of contemporary positivist Shakespearian scholarship: the use of systematic bibliographical evaluation to decide on the appropriate copy-text for each play, instead of the use of the previous edition or 'received' text to provide copy-text for the next; the construction of Shakespeare as an autonomous authorial subject; the periodization of the history of English language and culture. Many of the aims of such a project are diametrically opposed to those of a work like Seary's: where Seary wishes to celebrate Theobald as a pioneer, de Grazia's book is implicitly critical of the supposedly 'Enlightenment' historical scholarship which she sees as first appearing (in the systematic form she describes) with Malone. But de Grazia's anxiety to avoid what she calls, following Foucault, a 'genealogical' account of changes in the theory and practice of textual criticism in the vernacular, according to which Malone's work would be the culmination of a long series of developments in such theory and practice throughout the century, leads to a theoretical difficulty not in fact unlike that faced by Seary: the departure represented by Malone's work appears as a kind of inexplicable historical fault-line opening up in the 1790s, whilst, conversely, the complex variety of theories and practices of English textual criticism predating Malone is presented as a pre-enlightened consensus. In such circumstances it must, for example, be more than a merely contingent difficulty with de Grazia's account that Edward Capell not only abandoned the use of the received text for copy years before Malone, but published a volume of edited early texts with the explicit intention of demonstrating his new editorial method.[28]

---

[28] Edward Capell, *Prolusions: or, select Pieces of antient Poetry,—compil'd with great Care from their several Originals, and offer'd to the Publick as Specimens of the Integrity that should be found in the Editions of worthy Authors* (London, 1760).

3

Where Taylor's account, unsustainably, reads party-political categories directly into the practice of eighteenth-century textual criticism, both Seary's and de Grazia's tend to insulate the activity of the chosen critics from the intellectual (and ultimately also from the political) cultures to which they belong. For a model of how the historian of textual criticism can attend to the relative autonomy of the practice of textual criticism without therefore separating it entirely from its surrounding culture, we might turn instead to work in recent decades on the history of classical philology. Anthony Grafton's work, first in a monograph on Scaliger, and subsequently in a variety of essays on individual figures in the history of humanist and enlightenment classical and scriptural philology, has been able both to do justice to the complex individual circumstances of each of his chosen philologists, and to show how their work relates, whether antagonistically or consensually, to the intellectual cultures and practices from which it emerges.[29] Especially influenced by an Italian tradition in the history of humanism represented by such scholars as Giorgio Pasquali and Sebastiano Timpanaro, Grafton has been able to show how complex are the links between public attitudes to scholarship, the ways in which scholars imagine themselves and their work, and the organization of their philological practice.[30] He has worked with especial subtlety at the exchanges between humanism and the rationalist enlightenment, exchanges for whose investigation eighteenth-century textual criticism is a crucial field. *Defenders of the Text: The Traditions of Scholarship in an Age of Science* (1991) has shown that between Bacon's definitive gesture of natural-scientific hostility to philology ('Down with everything philological') and Isaac Casaubon's lament at experimental natural philosophy's philistine contempt for humanism, lies an unpredictable series of interdependences and negotiations.[31] The value of such an approach for the historian of eighteenth-century vernacular textual criticism is that it can help us see how philology was neither conceived of as having a natural or obvious place as an independent discipline within a framework of divided intellectual labour, nor as a malleable vehicle for external political

---

[29] Anthony Grafton, *Joseph Scaliger: A Study in the History of Classical Scholarship* (Oxford, 1983); many of his essays are collected in *Defenders of the Text: The Traditions of Scholarship in an Age of Science* (London, 1991).

[30] For Grafton's Italian antecedents, see Sebastiano Timpanaro, *La genesi del metodo del Lachmann* (Florence, 1963); Giorgio Pasquali, *Storia della tradizione e critica del testo*, 2nd edn. (Florence, 1952).

[31] Grafton, *Defenders*, 2.

and cultural programmes. Instead, both the right of textual criticism to exist as an independent field of inquiry, and the best procedures for such a field of inquiry, were contested throughout the century, but especially in its first half. Any account of Shakespeare's editors and textual critics in the eighteenth century needs to be able to discuss both these aspects together without collapsing them into each other.

It will be essential, then, to consider simultaneously two often discontinuous strands in the history of eighteenth-century textual criticism. On the one hand, we shall need to answer a whole series of questions about the textual-critical practice of Shakespearian scholars in the eighteenth century. What were their practices in determining which text to use for copy? To what extent does their work show evidence of any bibliographical evaluation of the early Quartos and Folios? By what bibliographical, linguistic, or aesthetic canons was emendatory practice sanctioned? We shall evidently need to be aware of the frequency with which editorial practice is at odds with stated theories or principles of textual criticism in the eighteenth century: Grafton has pointed out that the history of classical scholarship has too often been carried out simply as a survey of prefatory theories about editing, without looking at the practice of the scholars who deploy them.[32] Yet it would be equally mistaken to regard such ideas as a mere collection of rhetorical formulas. That the relationship between theory and practice in eighteenth-century editing is rarely one of perfect correspondence does not allow us to regard its theory as irrelevant to its practice. Instead we can find, not only in prefaces and pamphlets about editing, but also in the very broad range of other work drawing—whether satirically or in good faith—on the culture of textual criticism, evidence of attitudes towards the scholar and scholarship which are intimately, if complicatedly, related to the practice of textual criticism in the eighteenth century.

In what follows I shall in effect be tracing the impact of two divergent strains in the adaptation of classical humanism to vernacular culture. On the one hand, Shakespeare editing in the period is closely linked to eighteenth-century aspirations to refine and settle the English language: without settled texts of a canon of classic authors there could be no authoritative basis on which to render the English language as pure and stable as the classical languages were considered to be. Editors of Shakespeare were conscious that in fixing and purifying the text of Shakespeare they were also fixing and purifying the English language, and they im-

---

[32] Anthony Grafton, 'The Origins of Scholarship', *American Scholar*, 48 (1979), 236–61 (p. 260).

agined this task as analogous to that which had been performed by classical humanists for stylistic standards in Greek and Latin. It was this
awareness which made the debate as to who was fit to criticize Shakespeare's text such a pointed one: if the texts of authors which were to form
the basis of a pure and stable language were to fall into the hands of those
unfit to judge of such matters, the language might be contaminated with
impurities and instabilities. For many critics in early eighteenth-century
England, this was precisely the threat posed by the second current of
classical humanism, an increasingly historicist philology which seemed to
its opponents to be the fiefdom of impolite pedants less interested in
restoring or polishing the canon of admired classical texts than in scepti-
cally disintegrating it.[33] The conflicting humanisms of a Temple and a
Bentley which had been so publicly set against one another in the Phalaris
controversy were to clash repeatedly in the eighteenth-century development of vernacular philology.

The 'scholars' and 'gentlemen' of this study's title are not to be taken as
mutually exclusive groups. Both categories were ambiguous throughout
the century and are in continual need of contextualization if their force in
particular passages is to be understood; Marilyn Butler has pointed out,
for example, the ambiguous significance of the category of the 'gentleman'
referred to in the title of the *Gentleman's Magazine* even when the magazine started in 1731.[34] Scholarly self-representations habitually oscillated
between the poles, as Francis Atterbury put it, of the 'professed Pedant'
and the 'Gentleman of Letters';[35] editors were in some cases happier to be
identified as the specialist scholar, in others as the gentleman of letters. I
shall argue that the impact of these contrasting representations of scholarly inquiry can be traced not merely in eighteenth-century editors' statements about editing, but also in their editorial practice. Those editors who
regard professed scholars as low and interested intruders upon a public
cultural domain are more likely vigorously to defend the use of a *textus
receptus* for copy-text and to argue more liberally that obsolete or disliked
syntax and vocabulary represent textual corruption. Those editors who

---

[33] For the pedigree of these two currents within humanism, see Grafton, *Defenders*, 27; on
the split between them in England, see John F. Tinkler, 'The Splitting of Humanism:
Bentley, Swift, and the English Battle of the Books', *Journal of the History of Ideas*, 49 (1988),
453–72, and Joseph M. Levine, *The Battle of the Books: History and Literature in the Augustan
Age* (London, 1991).

[34] Marilyn Butler, 'Oxford's Eighteenth-Century Versions', *Studies in the Eighteenth
Century*, 12 (1988), 128–36 (p. 131).

[35] *A Short Review of the Controversy between Mr. Boyle and Dr. Bentley, With Suitable
Reflections upon it* (London, 1701), 20.

wish to argue that the specialist knowledge of the professed scholar is an indispensable prerequisite for editing show a stronger interest in biblio-graphical research and collation and in preserving characteristically Eliza-bethan or Shakespearian syntax, vocabulary, and metre.

No editor in the period in question is prepared to classify himself unambiguously under either of these headings; rather, they represent poles of editorial theory and practice between which each of the editors, in varying ways and with varying results, anxiously negotiates in an attempt to appear neither the minute pedant nor the ignorant dilettante. The case of the anti-philological wits that excessively minute scholarship was low, interested, and intellectually partially sighted was countered by advocates of a world of learning conceived as the sum of minute parts of exact knowledge; and it can be shown by looking at such a controversy as that over the text of the New Testament how these attitudes affected dis-cussion of the use or abandonment of a received text. Pope's history of Shakespeare's text and his idea of editorial procedure were decisively influenced by a notion of just taste in language and style as disinterested and gentlemanly; but Pope's own contingent position as a paid editor led to contradictions in his account of editing which are reflected in the contradictions of his editorial practice. The hostile reponses to Pope's edition were critically motivated by dissent from the idea that editors or writers should be disinterested or gentlemanly, and by an insistence, instead, that they should be informed or qualified specialists. This dissent was linked both to a newly historicist approach to the idea of linguistic correctness and to an insistence on the importance of detailed biblio-graphical evaluation. Such criticism was in part what prompted Pope, with the help of William Warburton, to modify his account of minute scholarship in a way which allowed that amateur vanity could threaten Shakespeare's text as much as professional interestedness.

All later editors had to negotiate this double bind of Pope's. Despite his unprecedented interest in an historical understanding of Shakespeare's English and in bibliographical research, Lewis Theobald was not able to make a systematic break with the use of a received text for copy or with the idea of using an edition of Shakespeare as a means to refine the language; Warburton responded to the *Dunciad*'s view of textual criticism by invok-ing an idea of the fit editor of Shakespeare as simultaneously comprehen-sive of view and minute of attention, and attempted to use his own textual-critical practice as a forum for the display of such qualities. Johnson no less than Warburton was preoccupied with the elusive middle ground between vanity and interest. Yet his explicit writerly professionalism led him largely to renounce any idea of using the *Dictionary* or its many Shakespearian illustrative quotations as a way of fixing or purifying the language. Johnson faced Warburton's dilemma by invoking a compromise between the idea of textual criticism as a special branch of the division of intellectual labour, on the one hand, and an idea of editing as the candid accumulation of the divided labours of previous editors, on the other. If we consider theory and practice together in this way, we can begin to see that the notorious inconsistencies of early eighteenth-century editorial practice are no casual effect of their editors' indolence or stupidity. They are directly related to the conflicting representations of minute scholarship (and of literary labour in general) within which each of the editors constructed his own anxious and inconsistent notion of the editor's task.

The scope of the present study has been determined by a number of considerations. It would not have been practicable to give an account of editorial work on Shakespeare throughout the century which adequately addressed both its theory and its practice, because time-consuming collations of eighteenth-century editions with their copy-texts are the indispensable condition of any assessment of certain aspects of their editors' practice. The editors of the first half of the century form a relatively cohesive unit because of their practical decisions in each case to take the text of an earlier eighteenth-century editor to provide copy for their own text (although two of them are clearly in doubt about the validity of this procedure). The work of these editors therefore forms the natural source-material for the present account, in that it displays the continual tensions between notions of gentlemanly editing and their associated procedures of linguistic and stylistic correction and bibliographical eclecticism, on the one hand, and nascent scholarly professionalism with its associated linguistic and stylistic historicism and bibliographical anti-eclecticism, on the other. For this reason the study ends with the last editor to use the work of a predecessor to provide the copy-text, Samuel Johnson, and stops short of the first editor to abandon the tradition of the received text, Edward Capell. Nevertheless some caveats are offered in the conclusion about taking even Capell's or Malone's work as either a pioneering breakthrough or a Foucaultian epistemological break. Because I am concerned here above all with the negotiations made by editors between textual-critical theory and editorial practice, little discussion has been devoted to editions like Rowe's or Hanmer's which lack prefatory methodological comment and detailed annotation alike.

Wilson's scorn for those who would know whether Twain wrote 'ssst' or 'sssst' and for whom it matters that Howells spelt 'millionaire' 'millionnaire' echoes Pope's for anyone enquiring whether 'To sound in Cicero or *C* or *K*': conspicuously, in the 1720s and 1730s, such as the dunce-editor Lewis Theobald. But what is at stake here is more than a trifling argument about trifles. The antagonism between minute scholars and general critics persists, not simply as some kind of natural feature of literary culture, but in close association with a ramifying division of intellectual production which is increasingly unable to conceptualize the public cultural sphere as more than the opaque sum of its mutually unintelligible parts. If this book will often focus upon the political motives for scorn of pedantry in the classic era of such scorn, it nevertheless in no way wishes to see the subsequent victories of historicist approaches to language and anti-eclectic editorial procedures as unalloyed triumphs. Alarm at interested minuteness is not simply ideological. Such alarm is, indeed, in part a conservative reflex at the thought of vulgar access to a public sphere misrepresented as a stable, disinterested, and organic whole. But it also registers, especially in such a powerful and lucid text as Book IV of *The Dunciad*, a justifiable anxiety at the impending commodification of all culture.

This book, then, does not propose to narrate the triumph of sound scholarship over what foolishly resists it. At its origin, rather, has been a wish to exhibit the rhetoric of disinterested universality and the rhetoric of minute specificity as torn halves of a public culture, to which, however, they could by no means add up;[36] to exhibit these, not merely as rhetorics but as a set of presuppositions informing the minutest details of practical philological procedure in the period. In the course of this exposition it will be suggested that the aporias of vernacular textual-critical theory have, from the start, been more than methodological: they are intimately bound up with divisions of intellectual labour and with representations of such divisions. 'Theory' of editing has often not, properly speaking, been *theory* at all, since it has frequently accepted the framework for its argument as simply given from outside, by the market sectors: how is the editor to prepare a faithful text for 'the' general reader, or 'the' student reader, or 'the' scholarly reader? These are not epistemological questions; nor, for so long as they take historically produced and mutable readership

---

[36] Cf. T. W. Adorno, 'On the Fetish Character in Music and the Regression of Listening', in J. M. Bernstein, ed., *The Culture Industry: Selected Essays on Mass Culture* (London, 1991), 26–52, 30–1.

categories as givens, are they even properly ethical questions either. The work of a scholar such as Randall McLeod has demonstrated what can be lost when assumptions about what is too minute or accidental for 'general' readers to care about are used to cut short theoretical reflection. McLeod illuminates, for example, the significance of the use of two different founts for the 'w' in the word 'we' in an Elizabethan text of Harrington's translation of Ariosto:

English printers often acquired their types from more advanced publishing cultures, among whom the Italians and French had little use for the letter w. As a result, the w's in English Renaissance books often mix founts. This visual incongruity between the two settings of 'we' in this volume is thus a small-scale reminder of the marginality of contemporary English culture—which fact is writ large as the Englished Italian of the whole book.[37]

When general readers are taken to be those for whom such historically and materially specific typographical features of a text are dispensable, a theoretically unexamined division of intellectual labour between specialist and general reader is taken as a given. The recent work of textual critics such as McLeod and McGann suggests, conversely, that any division of labour between literary critics and general readers, on one hand, and editors, on the other, is open to question. Textual criticism is not identical with editing, and reflection on textual criticism need not place itself at the service of demands for a canon of editorial practice. This study proceeds not from the external vantage point of its own set of prescriptions for such practice, but immanently, from within the theories and practices of the editors considered. Its implications are therefore not prescriptive. Yet it can indicate the difficulties consequent upon too quickly detaching apparently epistemological issues in editorial procedure from their contexts in cultural production. Such a warning remains relevant not only to the history of editing and textual criticism but also to all attempts prescriptively to determine their future methodologies.

---

[37] Randall McLeod (as 'Random Clod'), 'Information on Information', *Text*, 5 (1991), 241–82, (p. 246)

I

The Culture of Scholarship in Early Eighteenth-Century England

THE RELATIONSHIP between eighteenth-century Shakespearian textual criticism and its classical and scriptural relatives has sometimes been approached from a rather misleading angle. Some attention has been paid to the derivation of early Shakespearian editorial procedures from classical scholarship (although there has been almost no recognition of the relationship between scriptural and Shakespearian textual criticism).[1] But scholars have more often wished to lament the influence of classical scholarship on what is taken as the fundamentally different discipline of Shakespearian textual criticism. This is particularly true of accounts deriving from a New Bibliographical perspective.[2] The distinction between the editing of printed books and the editing of codices was an essential one for Greg and McKerrow: because any stemma of printed books was likely to be unilinear, rather than (as so often occurred with classical manuscripts) branched, an entirely different series of editorial procedures were considered applicable to manuscript textual criticism than to that of printed texts.[3] McKerrow's article on Shakespeare's text in the early eighteenth century emphasized the responsibility of classical textual criticism for the bibliographical eclecticism of editors from Rowe to Johnson, rather than the fact that, without classical textual criticism, there would have been no attempt to re-edit, rather than reprint, the text of Shakespeare at all, or that procedures of eighteenth-century classical textual criticism were not in fact undifferentiatedly eclectic.[4] Conversely, where the aim

[1] See, in particular, R. F. Jones, *Lewis Theobald, his Contribution to Scholarship* (New York, 1919), 71–92.
[2] See, for an example, S. K. Sen, *Capell and Malone, and Modern Critical Bibliography* (Calcutta, 1960), 7.
[3] See F. P. Wilson, *Shakespeare and the New Bibliography*, rev. and ed. Helen Gardner (Oxford, 1970), 97–8.
[4] R. B. McKerrow, 'The Treatment of Shakespeare's Text by his Earlier Editors (1709–1768)', in P. Alexander, ed., *Studies in Shakespeare: British Academy Lectures* (Oxford, 1964), 103–31.

is to present an eighteenth-century editor as an early pioneer of the New Bibliography, coincidence in method and opinion between such an editor and the twentieth-century scholars is given more weight than the influence of classical and scriptural philological attitudes and techniques.[5]

The need to understand attitudes towards the re-editing of vernacular texts in the context of attitudes towards classical and scriptural editing is clear, if only because scholars working on English texts so often compared Shakespearian textual criticism to its classical and scriptural counterparts. Lewis Theobald expressed the hope that the editing of English texts might render the same service to the English language that classical textual criticism had performed for standards of Greek and Latin, and declared his intention of modelling his edition of Shakespeare on Richard Bentley's Amsterdam edition of Horace.[6] Matthew Concanen introduced a letter of Theobald's in *The London Journal* with the remark that 'We are the only people in Europe who have had good Poets among them, and yet suffer their reputation to moulder, and their memory as it were to rust, for want of a little of that *Critical* care, which is as truly due to their merit as to that of the antient Greek and Roman Writers.'[7] Johnson referred to a guide to the textual criticism and interpretation of classical texts as a precedent for his own procedure in editing Shakespeare.[8] Alexander Cruden, best known for his biblical concordance, was able in 1741 to regard it as a primary purpose of his *Verbal Index to Milton's Paradise Lost* to provide what he regarded as the only scholarly item lacking to Milton studies, a complete concordance:

MILTON has been for some Years past so far treated as a Classic, that the most learned Persons have writ *Dissertations* and *Notes* upon this Work; and there is, as I am inform'd, an Edition of it ready for the Press, with an *Interpretation* in Prose, in the Margin, for the Use of Foreigners and Young People amongst us: So that

---

[5] Peter Seary, *Lewis Theobald and the Editing of Shakespeare* (Oxford, 1990).

[6] Theobald, *1733*, i, p. lxii; John Nichols, *Illustrations of the Literary History of the Eighteenth Century* (8 vols., London, 1817–58; repr. New York, 1966), ii. 621.

[7] Quoted in Jones, *Theobald*, 97–8.

[8] The guide, as Arthur Sherbo notes, was Pierre Daniel Huet's *De Interpretatione* (1661). See Samuel Johnson, *Johnson on Shakespeare*, ed. Arthur Sherbo (2 vols., New Haven, Conn., 1968), i. 106: 'nor would Huetius himself condemn me, as refusing the trouble of research, for the ambition of alteration'. See also *1765*, i. 110, where Johnson refers to Scaliger's procedure in transposing some lines of Virgil as a precedent for a transposition of some lines of Shakespeare's text.

there is nothing wanting of all that properly belongs to a classic Author, but what is here offer'd to the Public.[9]

As for scriptural textual criticism, Theobald's remarks in his *Shakespeare Restored* demonstrate his familiarity with debates about the text of the New Testament;[10] Warburton was still adding to *The Divine Legation of Moses Demonstrated*, and to its digressions on the text of scripture, when his edition of Shakespeare appeared in 1747;[11] whilst Johnson could be found in the middle of Scotland in 1773 discussing with Boswell the importance of Benjamin Kennicott's work on the Hebrew text of the Old Testament.[12]

There is an obvious prima facie case, then, for the influence of classical and scriptural philology on eighteenth-century vernacular textual criticism. Yet this hardly simplifies the task of a reconsideration of the criticism of English texts in the period. As Anthony Grafton has pointed out, the history of classical and scriptural philology is itself rather richer in sweeping surveys of its terrain, often based on prefatory statements about editing, than in detailed individual monographs.[13] The history of classical and scriptural textual criticism in the early eighteenth century is not entirely uncharted water, but no account exists which would allow us to take it as a unified tradition.[14] It follows that it cannot be the hope of the present chapter to provide a full account of classical and scriptural textual criticism at the beginning of the century. None the less, an examination of debates and quarrels in these disciplines can provide both an understanding of what was at stake in the spectrum of available representations of the textual critic—whether of classical, scriptural, or vernacular texts—at the close of the seventeenth century and in the early part of the eighteenth, and an understanding of how these representations related to central issues in editorial practice: the bibliographical evaluation of variants, the literal proximity of emendations to existing attested readings, and the

[9] Alexander Cruden, *A Verbal Index to Milton's Paradise Lost. Adapted to every Edition but the First* (London, 1741), p. iii.

[10] Theobald, *Shakespeare Restored* (London, 1726; repr. 1971), p. iv.

[11] See, for examples, Warburton, *The Divine Legation of Moses Demonstrated*, 4th edn. (London, 1765), iv. 46, 94–5.

[12] James Boswell, *The Journal of a Tour to the Hebrides, with Samuel Johnson, LL.D.*, ed. R. W. Chapman (Oxford, 1924), 185–6.

[13] Anthony Grafton, 'The Origins of Scholarship', *American Scholar*, 48 (1979), 236–61 (p. 260).

[14] See, for examples, Sebastiano Timpanaro, *La genesi del metodo del Lachmann* (Florence, 1963), 14–25; Adam Fox, *John Mill and Richard Bentley: A Study of the Textual Criticism of the New Testament 1675–1729* (Oxford, 1954).

use of the most recent printed edition or *textus receptus* to provide copy for
the next.

I

The question of the importance or otherwise of textual criticism to the late
seventeenth- and early eighteenth-century world of letters is a puzzling
one. We do not have to go far to find insistences that the whole activity
was a trifling waste of time: this was a principal burden of many of the
polemical attacks of the Christ Church wits on Bentley in the controversy
over the Epistles of Phalaris, of much of the response to Bentley's edition
of Horace in 1712, and of the assault by Pope and his allies on Bentley and
Theobald from 1728 to the mid-1740s. Writers as different as Chesterfield
and Samuel Richardson could concur on the question of the value of
editorial work: in the early 1730s Richardson voiced the opinion that 'Mr.
Pope . . . undervalued his Genius in stooping to the Drudgery of being an
Editor',[15] whilst in 1750–1 Chesterfield thought it necessary to advise his
son to 'take care not to understand editions and title-pages too well. It
always smells of pedantry, and not always of learning.'[16] Such characterizations present textual criticism not merely as a trifling activity, but also
as socially and intellectually degrading.

But there is also plenty of evidence to show that in particular contexts
or on particular occasions textual criticism could command the interest of
a sizeable public. Richard Bentley was in his lifetime an incomparably
more important public intellectual than any classical scholar could hope to
be today. Although Bentley is now by some distance the least well-known
of the club which he gathered together—whose other members were
Locke, Newton, Wren, and Evelyn—he would not have appeared a less
significant figure to many of his contemporaries.[17] Equally significantly,
textual criticism could command the serious attention of many who were
leading figures in other fields. John Locke's recurrent interest in textual-
critical matters, to offer one example, is apparent from his correspondence. Throughout the last years of the century his letters testify to his
interest in the unsettling new critical work on the texts of the Old and

---

[15]   Richardson is quoted in John Barnard, ed., *Pope: The Critical Heritage* (London, 1973),
236.
[16]   Philip Dormer Stanhope, 4th earl of Chesterfield, *Letters*, ed. Bonamy Dobree (6 vols.,
London, 1932), iv. 1517.
[17]   For Bentley's club see James Henry Monk, *The Life of Richard Bentley, D.D.*, 2nd edn.
(2 vols., London, 1833), i. 96.

New Testaments produced by the French scholar Richard Simon.[18] Clearly, more was at stake in textual criticism of the Bible than in secular editing, but defenders of minute scholarship were able to argue that good work in the former was furthered by advances in the latter.[19]

The idea that excessively minute textual criticism was not only a trifling, but also an intellectually and socially belittling, activity could be seen most forcefully presented in the reactions of many sections of the world of letters to the textual criticism and other minute philology of Richard Bentley. There were often extra-literary reasons for attacking Bentley, not least his significant role in the conversion of Cambridge University into a Whig stronghold.[20] But Bentley was attacked not only because of personal and party-political hostility towards him, but also because he was the foremost representative of the new minute philology: a philology which took a historicist approach, rather than a rhetorical one, to classical Greek and Latin texts.[21] Whereas Temple, working like his supporters with a notion that the Greek language in its classical epoch was essentially a fixed and stable entity, had presented the suppositious letters of Phalaris as both the most ancient and the finest examples of Greek prose, Bentley's long *Dissertation upon the Epistles of Phalaris* argued, often from an unprecedentedly detailed understanding of the continuous historical development of Greek, that the letters were a much later fabrication by a sophist. It is true that the Christ Church wits who wrote Boyle's *Dr. Bentley's Dissertations on the Epistles of Phalaris, and the Fables of Æsop, Examin'd* for him in 1699 could not between them muster anything approaching Bentley's learning.[22] But the chosen weapons of this group of wits also indicate their distaste for minute criticism as such and their sense that its aims and procedures represented the threat of an increasingly specialized and even professionalized philology to what they took to be their own disinterested and gentlemanly humanism. The same

[18] *The Correspondence of John Locke*, ed. E. S. De Beer (8 vols., Oxford, 1976–89), iii. 491, 516–17; viii. 126.

[19] See, for such an argument, Francis Hare, *The Clergyman's Thanks to Phileleutherus for his Remarks on The Late Discourse of Free-Thinking* (London, 1713), 36–7.

[20] For an account of this process see John Gascoigne, *Cambridge in the Age of the Enlightenment* (Cambridge, 1989), ch. 4, 'The Creation and Consolidation of Whig Cambridge'.

[21] Naturally, neither historicist philology, nor an opposition between minute and general criticism, originated in the 1690s; for some aspects of the growth of the former, see Anthony Grafton, *Joseph Scaliger: A Study in the History of Classical Scholarship* (Oxford, 1983); for an early instance of the latter see Grafton, *Defenders*, ch. 1, 'Renaissance Readers and Ancient Texts'.

[22] The authors are identified in Joseph Levine, *The Battle of the Books: History and Literature in the Augustan Age* (London, 1991), 59, as Atterbury, Smalridge, Alsop, John and Robert Freind, and William King.

concerns are evident in much of the response to Bentley's 1711 text of Horace. Here too there were contingent reasons for the abuse directed at Bentley: the edition had appeared with an encomiastic dedication to Harley which marked a change of party on Bentley's part.[23] But both the bulk of the hostile response to Bentley's work on Phalaris and on Horace, and its persistent return to the topics of the lowness, vulgarity, and interestedness of pedantic or excessively minute textual criticism, indicate that a broader cultural case was being made: a case against the depredations of the low and interested specialist upon a cultural heritage which should be in disinterested and gentlemanly hands.

At the crudest level, this case is manifested in the jibe that Bentley himself is of low birth: *The Life and Conversation of Richard Bentley* thought it worth pointing out that Bentley was 'descended from as mean a Stock as ever Heart cou'd wish, and of a Family, for these many Ages last past, most eminently obscure'.[24] But criticism of Bentley's vulgarity was more often concentrated on the way in which his English and Latin style alike were thought to reflect his mean origins. 'Boyle' complains that 'It can hardly be imagin'd, how one, that lives within the Air of a Court, shou'd prevail with himself to deal in such dirty Language: the Chairmen at St. *James*'s, I dare say, manage their Disputes with more decency.'[25] Bentley was the King's library-keeper at the time of the controversy. What is objectionable in the lowness of his style and character is less his vulgarity than his social presumption: the impoliteness of his language persists despite his living 'within the Air of a Court'. 'Boyle' is quick to seize on Bentley's reference to the royal manuscript requested by Boyle as 'our Manuscript'[26] as an expression of just such ill-bred presumption: '*Our MS*! that is, His Majesty's and Mine . . . An Expression as much too familiar for a Library-keeper, as *Ego & Rex Meus* was for a Cardinal.'[27] Later the examination goes on to present such a mistaking of appropriate social levels not merely as a feature of Bentley's personality but as a defining characteristic of pedantry as such: 'The first and surest mark of a *Pedant* is, to write without observing the receiv'd Rules of Civility, and Common Decency: and without distinguishing the Characters of Those

[23] Monk, *Life of Bentley*, i. 305–7.

[24] *The Life and Conversation of Richard Bentley, Delivered in his own Words, for the most part from his own Writings* (London, 1712), 6.

[25] *Dr. Bentley's Dissertations on the Epistles of Phalaris, and the Fables of Æsop, Examin'd*, 3rd edn. (London, 1699), 11–12.

[26] Richard Bentley, *A Dissertation upon the Epistles of Phalaris, Themistocles, Socrates, Euripides and Others; And the Fables of Æsop* (London, 1697), 67.

[27] *Dr. Bentley's Dissertations . . . Examin'd*, 21.

he writes to, or against: For Pedantry in the Pen, is what Clownishness is in Conversation; it is *Written Ill-breeding*.'[28]

Pedantry, for the authors of *Dr. Bentley's Dissertations . . . Examin'd*, is not merely socially inept but also presumptuously levelling in its refusal to distinguish exalted from mean opponents. It was just this levelling tendency to which the anonymous author of *A Short Account of Dr. Bentley's Humanity and Justice* also objected, protesting that it was unacceptable for Bentley 'to treat a Person of his [Dean Aldrich of Christ Church's] Dignity, Worth and Station in the Church, the Head of one of the best Colleges in *Europe* . . . as if he had been upon his own Level'.[29] As Atterbury's *Short Review of the Controversy* (also published anonymously) later put the point: 'Men of ingenuous Education, should not be handled coarsely, even when there's reason to use them severely',[30] although ''tis allowed to use Men of a lower rank more coarsely'.[31] Such dislike for Bentley's supposed vulgar inability to observe canons of social and stylistic decorum later found expression in anti-Bentleian burlesque. In 1712–13 a translation of Bentley's text and notes of Horace was issued in 24 parts. There Bentley was made by the English version of his notes comically to present exalted topics in low language: he refers, for example, to '*Homer* and *Virgil*, whose Heroes were great Driv'lers, and much addicted to Whining and Sniv'ling . . .'.[32] Elsewhere Bentley is made to refer to the celebrated Dutch scholar Heinsius as 'that very bright Fellow, *Nick Heinsius*'[33] and to introduce variant readings from manuscripts with the words 'In the mean time, we have some old Parchments that help us out here at a dead lift.'[34]

In part such ridicule of Bentley's vulgar diction reflected the commonplace opinion that scholars necessarily lacked the social polish of the man of the world: as the *Vindication of An Essay concerning Critical and Curious Learning* (1698) remarked, 'There is a vast difference betwixt the Qualifications, which may make a Man appear advantagiously enough in an University, and those which will render him acceptable and Eminent in

[28] Ibid. 93.

[29] *A Short Account of Dr. Bentley's Humanity and Justice, To those Authors who have written before him* (London, 1699), 5.

[30] *A Short Review of the Controversy between Mr. Boyle and Dr. Bentley, With Suitable Reflections upon it* (London, 1701), 62.

[31] Ibid. 61.

[32] *The Odes, Epodes and Carmen Seculare of Horace, in Latin and English; With a Translation of Dr. Ben-ley's Notes. To which are added Notes upon Notes* (24 parts, London, 1712–13), part 1, p. 29. The tr. and additional notes are variously attributed to William Oldisworth or to William King; see Jones, *Theobald*, 'Appendix A', pp. 256–7.

[33] Ibid., part 2, p. 19.   [34] Ibid., part 2, p. 7.

the World.'[35] The contrast between the public and polished man of the world and the retired and contracted scholar was set out at length in such classical primers for gentlemen as Henry Dodwell's 'Invitation to Gentlemen, to acquaint themselves with Ancient History', prefixed to late seventeenth- and early eighteenth-century reprints of Degory Wheare's *The Method and Order of Reading both Civil and Ecclesiastical Histories*, and Henry Felton's *Dissertation on Reading the Classicks and Forming a Just Stile* (1715). Dodwell insisted that 'The peculiar Employment of a *Gentleman*, who would be eminently serviceable to his Country in that Station, should be to accomplish himself in *Politicks*, and the Art of *War*: but both of them are very alien from the Profession of him who aims at *Learning* in *general*'.[36] Bentley's opponents took the Phalaris controversy as an exemplary instance of the contrast between scholars contracted both in spirit and in the extent of their social experience and gentlemen who were taken to be correspondingly capacious in both respects. For Temple, the contrast between the antagonists in the Phalaris controversy was one between a gentleman 'brought up and long conversant with Persons of the greatest Quality at home and abroad' and 'a young Scholar that confesses He owes all the Comforts of his Life to his Patron's Bounty, that knows no more of Men and Manners than he has learnt in his Study'.[37] Tom Brown, similarly, remarked that 'all the *Polite Judges* in *Europe* were pleased to see an *Arrogant Pedant*, that had been crouding his Head twenty Years together with the Spoils of *Lexicons* and *Dictionaries*, worsted and foiled by a *Young Gentleman*'.[38]

The harsher insistence of Bentley's opponents in the Phalaris controversy, upon the excessively minute critic's ill-breeding and vulgarity, was linked to a presentation of such a critic—the 'professed Pedant', in Atterbury's words—as intruding professionally and interestedly upon a culture which ought to be the domain of the disinterested 'Gentleman of Letters'.[39] When Bentley criticized Barnes as 'a learned *Greek* Professor' who 'gratuitously undertakes to apologize' for the Epistles of Phalaris[40] the authors of *Dr. Bentley's Dissertations . . . Examin'd* saw the opportunity to gloss Bentley's remark so as to illustrate the interestedness of the

---

[35]   *A Vindication of An Essay concerning Critical and Curious Learning* (London, 1698), 3.
[36]   Degory Wheare, *The Method and Order of Reading both Civil and Ecclesiastical Histories . . . The Third Edition, with Amendments. With Mr. Dodwell's Invitation to Gentlemen, to acquaint themselves with Ancient History* (London, 1710), sig. A4ʳ.
[37]   Quoted in Levine, *Battle of the Books*, 38.
[38]   'Original Letters Lately Written by Mr. Brown', in *The Works of Monsieur Voiture* (2 vols., London, 1705), i. 65–140 (pp. 133–4); quoted in Levine, *Battle of the Books*, 65.
[39]   *Short Review*, 20.   [40]   Bentley, *Dissertation upon Phalaris*, 43–4.

professed pedant: 'that is, (for I can make no other sense of it) by defending the Authority of the Epistles, *without having any thing for his Pains*.
This looks as if the Dr thought Learned Men were to set a Price upon
their Civilities, and never part with a Favour till they had their Fee.'[41]
Atterbury's *Short Review*, likewise, regarded criticism in Bentley's hands
as a 'trade' and made a direct comparison between the interestedness of
the critic and that of the bookseller: '*Criticks* and Booksellers suffer their
good dispositions to be over-rul'd by their Trade as often as any
men . . .'.[42] Atterbury concluded, after examining relations between Bentley and his bookseller, that 'a Critick commonly acts with less sincerity in
the concerns of his own Trade than the Book-seller does in his'.[43]

Bentley's alleged refusal to hand over the library's manuscript of
Phalaris for use in the preparation of Boyle's edition is taken as a strat-
agem to protect his professional interests and those of a cartel of pedants:

> By Dr *Bentley*'s way of treating Sir *William Temple*, Sir *Edward Sherburn*, and my
> self, one would imagine, that he had vow'd hostility to all Gentlemen pretending
> to Letters; that he thought they broke in upon a Trade, which none but those of
> the Body corporate of Profess'd Scholars ought to deal in; and so, looking upon
> 'em as the *East-India* Company does upon Interlopers, was resolv'd to use 'em
> accordingly.[44]

The comparison of the textual critic to an interested tradesman can be
seen in similarly full-blown form in one of the pamphlets attacking Bentley after the publication of his edition of Horace in 1711. *Five Extraordinary Letters, Suppos'd to be Writ to Dr. Bentley, upon his Edition of Horace*
includes a letter which, playing on the improvements to the metrical 'feet'
of Horace which Bentley regarded as one of the achievements of his
edition, satirizes emendators of classical texts as a professional association
of foot-surgeons or '*Corn-Cutters*'.[45] The comparison of textual critics to
chiropodists mocks a metaphor which textual critics often used approv-
ingly to describe their own labours: comparing themselves to surgeons,
restoring ancient authors lying sick in a corrupt text to full health.[46] But
the pamphleteer's humble petition on behalf of the textual critics '*and
others their poor distressed Brethren the* Corn-cutters *of* Frogland' introduces the further representation of textual critics as forming an organized
trading interest. The echo of such a depiction of textual critics as low

---

[41] *Dr. Bentley's Dissertations . . . Examin'd*, 40.   [42] *Short Review*, 12.
[43] Ibid. 15.   [44] *Dr. Bentley's Dissertations . . . Examin'd*, 17.   [45] Ibid. 11.
[46] In the 18th cent. the metaphor was used repeatedly by Lewis Theobald, amongst
others; see, *The Censor*, i, 2nd edn. (London, 1717), 30–1, and *Shakespeare Restored* (London, 1726; repr. 1971), p. iv.

literary tradesmen can be found in Pope's Declaration, prefixed to the 1735 text of the *Dunciad*, describing verbal critics as 'Haberdashers of points and particles'.[47]

These charges are not merely a way of belittling the importance of textual critics and their activities, but have significant consequences for the way in which textual critics are taken to carry out their tasks and how they are believed by their opponents to view their chosen texts. Whereas the gentlemanly reader treats Greek and Latin texts as living wholes, the excessively minute textual critic will regard them as mere objects, as raw materials for his trade. As 'Boyle' later sarcastically noted, 'an Ill Critic, who sets up the Trade without a Stock to manage it, must be perpetually upon the Plunder'.[48] In William King's *Dialogues of the Dead* (1699), 'Democritus' is made to remark on the way in which textual corruption can raise the value of an ancient inscription:

You are much besides the Mark old Friend, if you would have a Stone legible. A huge Marble would *sell for nothing*, if it had above a dozen Letters on it, *That's the Stone for Money* that requires Spectacles, and an Iron-Feskew to make Letters where a Man can't find 'em. It is not a Criticks business to read Marbles, but out of *Broken pieces* to guess at 'em, and then positively to restore 'em.[49]

The fashion for textual criticism is here ironically taken to have artificially raised the price of mere fragments of ancient marbles. The professional interest of the textual critic has come to replace the real usefulness or beauty of such objects as a means of deciding upon their value, so that the business of minute criticism turns the transmission of classical heritage into an inflated market. It is accordingly no surprise that the rocketing price of South Sea stock could later be co-opted as a metaphor for the schemes of textual critics: in 1721 Conyers Middleton referred to Bentley's plan for a new edition of the Greek text of the New Testament as '*Bentley*'s Bubble'.[50]

King's satire introduces a second main head of objections to the way in which textual critics use texts: they delight by profession in what is broken or fragmentary, and consequently their attention is given to minute parts of works considered (so the wits complain) in isolation. Textual critics are taken as expert index-combers and consulters of dictionaries, as the ac-

[47] Alexander Pope, *The Dunciad*, ed. James Sutherland (London, 1963), 237.

[48] *Dr. Bentley's Dissertations . . . Examin'd*, 226.

[49] William King, *Dialogues of the Dead: Relating to the Present Controversy Concerning the Epistles of Phalaris* (London, 1699), 46.

[50] Conyers Middleton, *Remarks, Paragraph by Paragraph, upon Proposals Lately publish'd for a New Edition of a Greek and Latin Testament, by Richard Bentley* (London, 1721), 18.

cumulators of immense stores of disparate learning which they are then incompetent to assemble into meaningful wholes. One of Bentley's earliest editorial projects (never in the event completed) was for a parallel edition of three of the most important classical lexicons, to be modelled in its format upon Brian Walton's 1657 London Polyglot edition of the Bible;[51] the wits repeatedly made use of the opportunity afforded by this known project of Bentley's to represent him as a quarrier of indexes and lexicons. The preface to Alsop's 1698 edition of Aesop describes Bentley as 'in volvendis lexicis satis diligentem' (diligent enough in turning over dictionaries);[52] *Dr. Bentley's Dissertations . . . Examin'd* describes Bentley as one who has been enabled to 'set up for a Critic' not by native genius but 'by the help of Leisure and Lexicons'.[53] In King's *Dialogues*, 'Hesychius', one of the lexicographers whose text Bentley had planned to edit, is presented in conversation, responding indignantly to his interlocutor's insistence that although 'all Wit, Arts, Genteel and Mannerly Conversation, are contain'd in Dictionaries . . . the joyning them is the Art our Dictionaries will never teach a Man': 'So then, you would have a Man put words together, properly to make sence of 'em! Very fine! How then could I, or my Friend *Bentivoglio* [Bentley] be Authors?'[54] King satirizes the near-sightedness of what Pope was later to call 'the Critic Eye' as incapable either of seeing the texts it examines as a whole, or of putting coherent whole texts of its own together.[55] The pedant's partial social perspective, that is, is accompanied by a partial epistemological perspective.

Such views meant that just those aspects of the editor's task which Bentley and many of his fellow scholars regarded as the necessary condition of sound textual work came in for particularly severe criticism. The full-scale collations of a wide variety of manuscript sources which Bentley so often carried out or had carried out for him,[56] for example, were part of

[51] *The Correspondence of Richard Bentley*, ed. Christopher Wordsworth (London, 1842), i. 10.

[52] Quoted in Levine, *Battle of the Books*, 102.

[53] *Dr. Bentley's Dissertations . . . Examin'd*, sig. π3^r.

[54] *Dialogues of the Dead*, 27. For a later survival of this trope, see Samuel Johnson, *Prefaces, Biographical and Critical, to the Works of the English Poets* (10 vols., London, 1779–81), vii. 231, 'Life of Pope': 'When an objection raised against his [Pope's] inscription for Shakspeare was defended by the authority of *Patrick*, he replied,—*horresco referens*—that he would allow the publisher of a Dictionary to know the meaning of a single word, but not of two words put together.'

[55] Pope, *Dunciad*, ed. Sutherland, 366.

[56] John Walker, e.g., spent a full year in Paris collating MSS in preparation for Bentley's planned edn. of the Greek New Testament: Monk, *Life of Bentley*, ii. 122.

the long process by which classical textual criticism developed from a merely eclectic use of manuscript variants to the systematic stemmatics of Lachmann: such conscientious collation opened the way for evaluation of the relative authority of manuscript sources to be undertaken before they were quarried for various readings.[57] To 'Boyle', however, such collation was precisely the least significant part of textual criticism:

I have follow'd our Dissertator thro' a long Scene of Impertinence; and am come at last to That Part, where he Places his greatest Strength: that is indeed, the most Trivial Part of all, the MSS. I told the Reader in my Preface, that I only made use of such different Readings in the MSS, as conduc'd to the better understanding the Text; for I always thought it a Ridiculous piece of Pedantry, to load a Book with various Lections to no purpose: but this I find Dr *Bentley* calls *Skill in using MSS*.[58]

For the authors of *Dr. Bentley's Dissertations . . . Examin'd* the only ration-ale for the collecting of variants would necessarily be an entirely eclectic one: only those variants which might in themselves improve or elucidate the text are to be recorded, rather than those variants which might help to determine the relative authority of manuscripts. Joseph Addison, for one, agreed with 'Boyle': a various reading would be useful whenever it 'gives us a different Sense, or a new Elegance in an Author', but not when an editor 'only entertains us with the several ways of Spelling the same Word, and gathers together the various Blunders and Mistakes of twenty or thirty different Transcribers'.[59] The palaeographical assessment of codices through the collation of variants could not, for Addison, be a worthwhile topic for a printed text. Henry Felton, advising a young nobleman upon a course of studies, reinforced this point, warning against 'the Infection of the less, and lower Critics, who are capable of nothing but collating Manuscripts . . . various Readings will be only troublesome, where the Sense and Language are complete without them'.[60]

Similarly, the 'literal' criticism of which Bentley was an especially noted exponent—insisting that emendations should wherever possible

---

[57] Bentley's own practice, of course, still remained in many respects eclectic. See Sebastiano Timpanaro, *La genesi del metodo del Lachmann* (Florence, 1963), 16–17.

[58] *Dr. Bentley's Dissertations . . . Examin'd*, 217.

[59] *The Spectator*, ed. Donald F. Bond (5 vols., Oxford, 1965), no. 470, iv. 162.

[60] Henry Felton, *A Dissertation upon Reading the Classicks and Forming a Just Stile* (London, 1713; repr. Menston, 1971), 48; for a response to Felton, and to Swift's description of antiquaries in his *Proposal for Correcting, Improving and Ascertaining the English Tongue* (London, 1712; repr. Menston, 1969), 40, as 'laborious Men of low Genius', see Elizabeth Elstob, *An Apology for the Study of Northern Antiquities* (London, 1715; repr. New York, 1956), pp. xxix–xxxv.

deviate from the existing reading of an authoritative copy by no more than a single letter—is taken by his opponents as an exemplary feature of the minute critic's narrowness of vision. The burlesque translator and anno-tator of Bentley's text of Horace regarded the idea that 'the Fate and Fortune of the greatest Authors' might depend upon the emendation of a single letter, or even upon a collection of such alterations, as a laughable fiction of the interested critic.[61] Literal alterations are taken as a self-evidently trivial matter, controversy over which results only from the desire for self-display of the interested critic. This is also a central point of one of the later (and wittier) contributions to the corpus of anti-Bentleiana, a Gulliverian *Account of the State of Learning in the Empire of Lilliput, Together with the History and Character of Bullum the Emperor's Library-Keeper*, printed in 1728 and possibly written by Arbuthnot.[62] 'Bullum' (Bentley) is an expert in the ancient Blefuscudian language, but, as 'Gulliver' remarks with mock-surprise, this has done little for his own politeness:

> It might have been expected, that from so long an Acquaintance with those admirable Writers, he should have grown more Polite and Humane; but his Manner was never to regard the Sence or Subject of the Author, but only the Shape of the Letters, in which he arrived to such Perfection, that, as I have been assured, he could tell, very near, in what Year of the *Blefuscudian* Commonwealth any Book was written; and to this, and to restoring the old Characters that were effaced, all his Labour was confined.[63]

Once more the minute critic's narrowness of vision is taken to reduce what should be a living whole to inert and partially viewed material. What makes this account especially telling is that Bentley's literal criticism is here directly linked to his interest in chronology and in a historical ap-proach to the language and authorship of classical texts; it is his expertise in the external shape of letters which allows him an exact knowledge of Blefuscudian linguistic chronology.

This dislike of Bentley's historicism is an important thrust of the wits' attack on Bentley's literal minuteness. It was a central principle of Bent-ley's *Dissertation upon the Epistles of Phalaris* to argue from the historical mutability of the Greek language that particular passages of the suppositious epistles could not have been written until a date well after Phalaris's

---

[61] *The Odes, Epodes, and Carmen Seculare of Horace, in Latin and English*, part 3, p. 11.

[62] The pamphlet's authorship is discussed in *Gulliveriana V: Shorter Imitations of Gulliver's Travels*, ed. Jeanne K. Welcher and George E. Bush (New York, 1974), 'Introduc-tion', p. xxviii.

[63] Ibid. 206–7.

death.[64] For the authors of *Dr. Bentley's Dissertations . . . Examin'd*, however, Greek was to be thought of as essentially invariant. Although there might have been some small changes over centuries, these did not alter the essential character of the language: Greek was 'incomparably the most fix'd and enduring [language] of any that we are generally acquainted with',[65] and certainly not to be compared in its history with English, 'the most Fickle and Fleeting of any'.[66] Clearly, were Bentley's radically historical view of the classical languages to be accepted, any project of using those supposedly stable languages as an example by which to fix and purify the unstable English language would be in severe difficulties.[67]

The excessively minute and historicist criticism of Greek and Latin texts, then, was for a wide range of influential writers a potentially damaging assault on the stability of the Greek and Latin languages and of their literary canons, carried out by scholars who were too often low, interested, and of narrow or partial intellectual vision. Even where the wits could imagine a worthwhile function for textual criticism, it was the most philologically advanced aspects of textual criticism—the beginnings of a systematic evaluation of codices, the insistence that conjectural emendations should be close to existing attested readings, the understanding of the classical languages as historically variable—to which they took strongest exception.

2

The influence of the wits' representation of excessively minute and historicist textual criticism as low, interested, and partial is indicated by the extent to which those who wished, to varying degrees and in varying ways, to defend minute criticism, felt obliged to concede ground to the wits' attacks on excessive minuteness. *An Essay Concerning Critical and Curious Learning* (1698), for example, insisted that textual criticism had been indispensable to the revival of learning at the Reformation and consequently to the present (supposedly flourishing) condition of the universities.[68] Despite his advocacy of the uses of textual criticism,

---

[64] Bentley, *Dissertations upon Phalaris*, 51–3. Bentley expanded these arguments in later edns.: see the edn. by Wilhelm Wagner (Berlin, 1874), 391–419.

[65] *Dr. Bentley's Dissertations . . . Examin'd*, 70.   [66] Ibid. 72.

[67] For the interest of Bentley's opponents in such a project, see *Dr. Bentley's Dissertations . . . Examin'd*, 69.

[68] 'T.R.', *An Essay Concerning Critical and Curious Learning* (London, 1698; repr. Los Angeles, 1965), 4–5.

'T.R.'[69] believes that an historical understanding of the Greek language (which he, like the Gulliverian satirist in 1728, also associates with a minute attention to literal detail) can be ranked amongst the 'little insignificant things' concerning which some scholars have taken 'wonderful Pains',[70] and is of no value in the elucidation of classic canonical texts.[71] To be 'nicely'—minutely—skilled in the historical development of the Greek language can only obstruct, rather than illuminate, our view of the timeless virtues of its best authors.[72] Others who wished to defend the value of minute philology found it necessary to insist upon the genius necessary to the great textual critic in order to combat the argument that textual criticism involved only a kind of mechanical drudgery requiring the meanest intellectual powers. When William Wotton argued that post-Reformation philology (or, as Wotton put it, 'grammar') was amongst the glories of the moderns, he expected to face objections to any idea that minute scholarship could be regarded as an authentic branch of learning at all:

But here I expect it should be objected, That this is not to be esteemed as a Part of Real Learning. To pore upon old MSS. to compare various Readings; to turn over *Glossaries*, and old *Scholia* upon Ancient Historians, Orators, and Poets; to be minutely critical in all the little Fashions of the Ancient *Greeks* and *Romans*, the Memory whereof was, in a manner, lost within L or a C Years after they had been in use; may be good Arguments of a Man's Industry, and Willingness to drudge; but seem to signifie little to denominate him a great Genius, or one who was able to do considerable Things himself.[73]

In the objections anticipated here, an excessively minute focus is once more associated with an interest in knowledge of merely transient aspects of Greek and Roman culture, and with merely mechanical labour, 'Willingness to drudge'. Accordingly, although Wotton adds parenthetically that the discovery of good copies and a perfect command of the edited author's language often 'require great Sagacity, as well as great Industry',[74] the main burden of his defence of textual criticism rests upon the genius and taste required properly to emend a corrupt text: 'There are Thousands of Corrections and Censures upon Authors to be found in the Annotations of Modern Critics, which required more Fineness of

---

[69] As Curt A. Zimansky points out on p. iv of his 'Introduction' to the 1965 repr., the usual ascription to Thomas Rymer is based only on Thomas Hearne's MS guess of 1704.
[70] *Essay*, 8.   [71] Ibid. 9.   [72] Ibid. 17.
[73] William Wotton, *Reflections upon Ancient and Modern Learning*, 3rd edn. (London, 1705), 358.
[74] Ibid. 359.

Thought, and Happiness of Invention, than, perhaps, Twenty such Volumes as those were, upon which these very Criticisms were made.'[75] Wotton finds himself obliged to make the principal value of minute criticism reside neither in the provision of accurate texts nor in a historical understanding of Greek and Latin language and culture, but in a kind of emendatory display which was frequently to surface in Shakespearian textual criticism in the course of the eighteenth century. It was in such a spirit that Francis Hare was able to regard it as an addition to the glory of Bentley's Horace that Bentley had lacked access to many of the best manuscripts.[76] For Hare, far from being grounds for complaint, the supposed paucity of Bentley's materials only adds to his praise.

Nevertheless, Hare was amongst the writers (aside from Bentley himself) prepared to insist upon the indispensability of the minuter and more mechanically laborious elements of textual criticism. As with the wits' attacks on textual criticism, there were other motives for Hare's defence alongside the cultural and scholarly issues at stake: Hare was a supporter of Bentley's stance against free-thinking.[77] But Hare's defence of Bentley's textual criticism cannot be reduced to its occasion. In his effusive pamphlet, *The Clergyman's Thanks to Phileleutherus for his Remarks on the late Discourse of Freethinking* (London, 1713), Hare attacks the notion of the relation between whole and parts in scholarship so frequently invoked by critics believing that 'all you have done is nothing more than a Dispute about a *Comma*, or a single *Letter*':[78] such critics 'consider not, that great things consist of little ones, and those of lesser still; and that if the least things are neglected, that neglect will of consequence necessarily affect the whole; in which there can be no Beauty or Exactness, but what arises from the Beauty or Exactness of the Parts'.[79] Here we are presented with a set of presuppositions about the nature of literary labour and its potential advancement which contrast markedly with those of the gentlemen of letters. In Hare's view scholarship is necessarily syncretic: what it therefore requires is not that each scholar should be capable of surveying the whole (however much Bentley may in Hare's view be possessed of just such comprehensive capacities) but that an accumulation of partial and minute labours will together add up to the edifice of exact knowledge. On other occasions Bentley could be presented as himself uniting the minute

---

[75] William Wotton, *Reflections upon Ancient and Modern Learning*, 3rd edn. (London, 1705), 359. [76] *Clergyman's Thanks*, 7.
[77] Monk, i. 349. Bentley and Hare later fell out over Hare's edn. of Terence: Monk, *Life of Bentley*, ii. 223.
[78] Hare, *Clergyman's Thanks*, 41. [79] Ibid. 41–2.

labour necessary to accurate learning with the genius insisted upon by Wotton. Thomas Rud chose the terms of his flattery carefully when he wrote to Bentley in 1716 that Bentley most unusually combined just those qualities which were essential to good textual criticism and yet were rarely found together:

> Men of excellent parts are seldom willing to give themselves so much trouble as must be undergone in collecting and collating so many MSS. and seeking from other Writers whatever may be of use to give light to their own. And persons of great industry often want that ἀγχίνοια κριτική [critical acuteness] without which they will not be able to make a right use of the helps they have.[80]

Such a vision of the ideal textual critic as both minute and inspired, both diligent and tasteful, was to resurface in Shakespearian editors' self-representations later in the century.

3

It is hardly surprising that the arguments rehearsed above could take on especially acute significance in the realm of the textual criticism of the Old and New Testaments and of other religious documents. The fear that secular classical texts might be mutilated by low, interested, and minute textual critics was paralleled, in the field of sacred criticism, by the fear that sacred texts would be altered by textual critics with sectarian interests at heart. The history of the printed Greek and Hebrew texts of the New and Old Testaments respectively shows that, by the beginning of the eighteenth century, some such fear had been at work for a century and a half: in each case a particular printed text (the sixteenth-century text edited by Stephanus for the New Testament, and the text given in the 1522 Complutensian Polyglot for the Old Testament) had become the received text or *textus receptus* and had subsequently acquired an authority of its own, despite the evidence of subsequent scholarship that the received text was based on rather poor manuscripts.[81] Those printing texts of the Greek New Testament or of the Hebrew Old Testament were obliged to follow the received text and to print 'variations' from other manuscripts (including many readings now regarded as more authoritative) only in the margins. Anxieties about the possible sectarian misuse

---

[80] Thomas Rud to Richard Bentley, 22 July 1716, *Correspondence of Richard Bentley*, ii. 514–15.
[81] See Bruce M. Metzger, *The Text of the New Testament: Its Transmission, Corruption and Restoration* (Oxford, 1964), 95–118.

of scriptural textual criticism became especially acute at the end of the seventeenth and beginning of the eighteenth centuries because of the rise of the newly critical methods of investigating the texts of the Old and New Testaments whose principal exponent was the French Oratorian Richard Simon. Simon argued that what he took to be his demonstration of the corruption of the extant Hebrew text was characteristically Catholic, because it showed the limitations of the Protestant principle of *sola scriptura*: if the sacred text was itself uncertain, humanly mediated rather than unproblematically inspired, readers would necessarily be thrown back upon ecclesiastical tradition for guidance as to its true readings.[82] The French ecclesiastical authorities, however, generally took a different view of the matter.[83] The reception of Simon's work in England, and of the whole idea that the scriptural text might be uncertain and in need of editing, was complex. Leading clerics evolved a response to the difficulties raised by Simon which insisted that, although the text as it was now received might have suffered some small corruptions in transmission, such corruptions would never affect central articles of faith or morality because we could be certain that God's providence would have ensured that these remained unaffected by textual corruption.[84] This was the line taken by Bishop Burnet, in the section of his *Exposition of the Thirty-Nine Articles of the Church of England* dealing with the text of scripture:

In general we may safely rely upon the Care and providence of God, and the Industry of Men, who are naturally apt to preserve things of that kind entire, which are highly valued among them. And therefore we conclude, That the Books of the Old Testament are preserved pure down to us, as to all those things for which they were written; that is, in every thing that is either an Object of Faith, or a Rule of Life: And as to lesser Matters which visibly have no Relation to either of these, there is no reason to think that every Copier was so divinely guided, that no small Error might surprize him.[85]

Burnet's position is typical in its concession to a secular moment in the consideration of the sacred text: for Burnet there is no need to insist upon a 'perpetual Miracle' permanently protecting sacred texts from all possible sources of corruption.[86]

---

[82] See e.g. Richard Simon, *Histoire Critique du Vieux Testament* (Rotterdam, 1685), 405; quoted in William McKane, *Selected Christian Hebraists* (Cambridge, 1989), 148.

[83] See McKane, *Christian Hebraists*, 112.

[84] See Gerard Reedy, SJ, *The Bible and Reason* (Philadelphia, 1985), 107–13.

[85] Gilbert Burnet, bishop of Salisbury, *An Exposition of the Thirty-Nine Articles of the Church of England*, 3rd edn. (London, 1705), 85.

[86] The phrase is Bentley's, from his *Remarks upon a late Discourse of Free-thinking*, 5th edn. (London, 1716), 76.

From such a perspective, scriptural textual criticism could still be taken as, at best trifling and at worst dangerous, meddling with a text which in all its essentials remained divinely protected. But Burnet's representative view could also be regarded as a limitation within which textual criticism could safely be carried out. Richard Bentley, for example, agreed with Burnet and others that the sacred text was 'competently exact indeed, even in the worst MS now extant; nor is One Article of Faith of Moral Precept either perverted or lost in them'.[87] Nevertheless, Bentley insisted that automatic defenders of 'the' text, such as Daniel Whitby, 'did not reflect at all what that Word really means'. 'The' text referred to by writers like Whitby was the *receptus* derived from Stephanus's sixteenth-century edition: 'Now this specific *Text* in your Doctor's Notion seems taken for the Sacred Original in every Word and Syllable: and, if the Conceit is but spread and propagated, within a few Years that *Printer*'s Infallibility will be as zealously maintain'd as an *Evangelist*'s or *Apostle*'s.'[88] Francis Hare, as so often, put the case for the applicability of Bentleian textual criticism most forcefully by arguing that it was a typically Protestant form of intellectual activity:

'tis certain that the Advancement Learning made in the last Age, was owing to the Advances that were made in *Critick*, a nice and scrupulous *Critick*, that extended its Care and Skill to the minutest things: And when they come once to be neglected, a Neglect of the greater will soon follow; . . . we shall become an easy Prey to the wicked Patrons of *Papal Superstition*, or to the more wicked Advocates of *Atheism*, and for want of sufficient Learning to maintain our Ground against those dangerous Extremes, shall either foolishly receive as *true*, the ridiculous *Legends* and impious *Forgeries* of *Rome*, in the place of the most authentick Histories; or more foolishly give up to *Atheists*, as Fictions and Impostures, not only those, but the *Oracles* of God himself.[89]

For Hare textual criticism is one of the characteristic legacies of the Reformation, and a willingness critically (and minutely) to examine the sacred text differentiates Protestant reason both from papist superstition and from atheist scepticism. A Protestant approach to the text is, for Hare, necessarily a 'nice and scrupulous' one: any disdain for minute inquiry will result either in Roman credulity or in free-thinking.

Yet many remained far from convinced by Bentley's and Hare's case, and the terms of the attack on their application of minute textual criticism to the scriptures echoed those of the attacks on minute criticism of secular classical texts. The debate can be seen at its sharpest in the controversies

---

[87] Ibid. 69.   [88] Ibid. 68.   [89] Hare, *Clergyman's Thanks*, 44–5.

of the 1720s over the text of the Greek New Testament. John Mill's 1707 text of the New Testament retains the *receptus* derived from Stephanus and consigns its unprecedentedly copious collection of manuscript variants to the margins. Bentley's *Proposals for Printing a New Edition of the Greek Testament* (1721) points out not only that the received text was based on 'Manuscripts of no great Antiquity' and of no greater authority[90] but also that the apparatus of variants was eclectic to the point of inutility: the marginal readings were 'all put upon equal Credit'[91] despite the greatly varying authority of the sources from which they were taken. The tenacity with which the *receptus* was defended in many quarters can be seen from the concessions which Bentley is prepared to make to this text, despite believing it to be based on unauthoritative manuscripts: 'to leave the free Choice to every Reader, he places under each Column the smallest Variations of this Edition, either in Words or Order, from the receiv'd *Greek* of *Stephanus*, and the *Latin* of the two Popes *Sixtus* V and *Clemens* VIII'.[92] Bentley was determined to forestall any interpretation of his motives for re-editing the text as sectarian ones. Even before the proposals had been published, one correspondent who had heard of their impending appearance had already written to Bentley anxiously, to make sure that he was not intending to leave out a disputed verse in John's Gospel which the correspondent regarded as essential to the defeat of Arianism.[93] Bentley acknowledged that there could be no place for conjectural emendation in the editing of sacred texts[94] and assured readers of his *Proposals* that the prospective editor 'draws no Consequences in his Notes, makes no oblique Glances upon any disputed Points, old or new'.[95]

Despite Bentley's caution (he had gone so far as to seek the prior approval of the archbishop of Canterbury for his project),[96] there were many who found his proposals deeply repugnant. John Locke had already remarked on the prejudices in favour even of the typographical layout of the received text, which were still prevalent at the beginning of the century and were evident in some of the responses to Bentley.[97] Despite

[90] Richard Bentley, *Dr. Bentley's Proposals for Printing a New Edition of the Greek Testament, and St. Hierom's Latin Version* (London, 1721), 3.

[91] Ibid. 4.   [92] Ibid.

[93] *The Correspondence of Richard Bentley, D.D.*, ed. Christopher Wordsworth (2 vols., London, 1842), ii. 529–32.

[94] Ibid.   [95] Ibid.   [96] Bentley, *Correspondence*, ii. 502–7.

[97] Locke, *An Essay for the Understanding of St. Paul's Epistles: By Consulting St. Paul himself* (London, 1707), p. viii: 'if a Bible was printed as it should be, and the several Parts of it were writ, in continued Discourses where the Argument is continued, I doubt not but the several Parties would complain of it, as an Innovation, and a dangerous Change in the publishing those holy Books.' Quoted in D. F. McKenzie, *Bibliography and the Sociology of Texts* (London, 1986), 46.

his concessions to the *receptus* Bentley nevertheless proposes to relegate it, on occasion, to the footnotes. Worse, he is to 'leave the free Choice to every Reader' as to which reading to accept. Conyers Middleton, in his *Remarks* on Bentley's proposals, seizes upon Bentley's attempt to preclude accusations of sectarianism as an arbitrary encroachment upon authority of papist proportions: it indicates 'an Insolence more than *Popish*, and . . . so far from becoming any *private Regulator* of the Text, that it is more than any *National Church* could justifie to its Members'.[98] Middleton's hostility to what he took to be Bentley's excessively minute scrutiny of the text drew on the line established by the Anglican scholars of the late seventeenth century: Bentley's '*curious* and *nice* Observations' could be of no service to 'the *Christian* Reader' since the received text was in all points, even of the least importance, adequate.[99] Whereas for Bentley the argument that all extant versions of the Greek New Testament preserved all important articles of faith and morals intact meant that work could safely proceed towards the establishment of the most authoritative text, for Middleton an observation that the received text preserved all essentials meant that it should on no account be tampered with.

A number of the other contributions to this debate show the complexity of the climate of thought about the New Testament text contemporary with Bentley's proposals. The author of *A Letter to the Reverend Master of Trinity-College in Cambridge* (1721), significantly, objected not to Bentley's plan to supplant the received text but to the eclecticism of the basis on which he proposed to do so:

I have nothing to object against it, if in this you exactly follow the uniform Plan of any one of your Manuscripts. But if upon your own bare Decision and the mixt Authority of various Manuscripts and Writers you patch up together this new Text; I leave it to the determination of the pious, learned and judicious Readers, whether it were not more adviseable, at least less assuming, to keep untouched the Text hitherto received by the whole Christian Church.[100]

The author of the *Letter* concedes the validity of Bentley's criticism of the *receptus*, but believes it more important to remove the possibility of a critic's private judgement corrupting a text than to arrive at the best

[98] Conyers Middleton, *Remarks, Paragraph by Paragraph, upon the Proposals Lately published by Richard Bentley, for a New Edition of the Greek Testament and Latin Version* (London, 1721), 18.
[99] Conyers Middleton, *Some Farther Remarks, Paragraph by Paragraph, upon Proposals Lately publish'd for a New Edition of a Greek and Latin Testament, by Richard Bentley* (London, 1721), 10.
[100] *A Letter to the Reverend Master of Trinity-College in Cambridge, Editor of a New Greek and Latin Testament* (London, 1721), 5.

possible reading in all cases. A similar line was taken by Leonard Twells, in his objections to the Greek Testament and new English version published anonymously by Daniel Mace in 1729.[101] Mace prefaced his new text and translation with a radical Protestant defence of the importance of scriptural textual criticism. To continue critical work on the text was, for Mace, to defend the intellectual and social advances which were the legacy of the Reformation, during which 'no sooner were the sacred records expos'd to popular view, than Religion began to recover something of her ancient lustre; public liberty reviv'd, and science rais'd her head'.[102] Mace had abandoned the received text in many instances, generally on the basis of the collations available in Mill's 1707 text.[103] But Twells's objections (unlike those of several continental biblical scholars)[104] centred less on Mace's abandonment of the received text than on the lack of a single manuscript as the basis of the new text, and of any set of explicit critical principles by which the most authoritative readings could be established. Twells pointed out that, although 'no single Authority weighs so much with our Author, as that of the *Alexandrian* Manuscript', even this copy was not made the basis for Mace's text.[105] Once again, it is the eclecticism of Mace's procedure which is the principal cause for reproach (although Twells's own procedure in particular cases is scarcely less eclectic, consisting as it often does of a series of rough estimates of the net bulk of authorities on either side of a question).[106]

Opponents of what was taken as 'innovation' in sacred texts, then, did not always find the thorough *receptus*-conservatism of a Whitby or a Middleton easy to sustain. They were consequently drawn to conduct the debate on grounds which increasingly conceded the insufficiency of the received text. This is not to say that the debate had been won by critics of the *receptus*. As late as 1753 the first stages of Benjamin Kennicott's landmark work on the text of the Old Testament could give rise to alarm on the grounds that the authority of scripture as a whole could only be

---

[101] *The New Testament in Greek and English. Containing the Original Text Corrected from the Authority of the most Authentic Manuscripts: And a New Version Form'd agreeably to the Illustrations of the most Learned Commentators and Critics*, ed. Daniel Mace (2 vols., London, 1729).

[102] Ibid. i, p. iv.

[103] For Mace's textual work, see H. McLachlan, 'An Almost Forgotten Pioneer in New Testament Criticism', *Hibbert Journal*, 37 (1938–9), 617–25.

[104] Ibid. 619.

[105] Leonard Twells, *A Critical Examination of the late New Text and Version of the New Testament* (London, 1731), 4.

[106] For examples of such rough estimates of amassed authorities, see ibid. 9 (on Mace's omission of the doxology from the end of the Lord's Prayer) and 31 (on Matt. 17: 12).

weakened by any criticism of its text: Fowler Comings saw Kennicott's work as a pernicious charter which would make each reader his own textual critic.[107] But the frequency with which texts appeared which were prepared to depart from the *receptus* in particular instances (although still taking it as their copy-text) suggests that the description of all such figures as lonely 'pioneers' needs some modification: the text which Edward Wells produced between 1709 and 1719,[108] Bentley's specimen in his *Proposals*, Mace's edition, and later William Bowyer's work[109] were each prepared to make many departures from the received text. Rather, we should recognize the existence of a whole current of work in New Testament textual criticism which believed with Bentley and Hare (and partially persuaded some opponents of textual-critical innovation) that an engagement with the minutiae of the sacred text was not a dangerous incursion of the private individual into ecclesiastical territory, but necessary to the defence of Protestant learning. Kennicott was able to point to the advances made along these lines in New Testament criticism as a precedent for his own work on the Old Testament.[110]

An instructive analogy in this respect to the controversies over the text of scripture is provided by that over the text of the Thirty-nine Articles which took place in the early years of the century. Burnet's *Exposition* of the Articles (which was to remain a standard work of reference for over a century) admitted that some early texts and manuscripts of the Articles did not contain a clause in the twentieth article asserting the Church's authority in controversies of faith, and which had appeared in all texts of the Articles since the early years of the seventeenth century.[111] Burnet's somewhat cursory solution to the problem did not satisfy those (such as the deist Anthony Collins) with an interest in demonstrating that the Church's authority in such matters was usurped, and in his *Priestcraft in Perfection* Collins challenged defenders of the clause to produce any English text of the Articles printed in or before 1571 containing the

---

[107] Fowler Comings, *The Printed Hebrew Text of the Old Testament Vindicated* (Oxford, 1753), 4.

[108] See, for an example, Edward Wells, *A Specimen of An Help for the More Easy Understanding of the Holy Scriptures* (Oxford, 1709).

[109] William Bowyer, *Critical Conjectures and Observations on the New Testament*, 3rd edn. (London, 1782). See Bruce M. Metzger, *Chapters in the History of New Testament Textual Criticism* (Leiden, 1963), 'Appendix: William Bowyer's Contribution to New Testament Textual Criticism'.

[110] Benjamin Kennicott, *The State of the Printed Text of the Old Testament Considered* (2 vols., Oxford, 1753–9), i. 10.

[111] Burnet, *Exposition*, 16.

clause.[112] Collins insisted that they could not; he concluded that doubt was thereby thrown on all printed books entrusted to clerics, and that religion in consequence should rest, in exemplary deist fashion, 'on those Reasons which must of course occur to every body, without the assistance of Forgery from the Priests'[113] (although Collins went on, strangely, to present scripture itself as invulnerable to such tampering).[114] In response Thomas Bennet not only produced texts printed in 1571 containing the controverted clause[115] but presented a 141-page collation of the minutest variations of the entire texts 'of 18 the most Ancient and Authentic Copies'[116] of the Articles, with the aim of showing that the disputed clause was the work of the 1571 Convocation at the latest. In the course of his argument Bennet examined typographical detail to prove that the copies which he referred to as C, D, and E were not only of the same edition but of the same impression:

... when a Book is reprinted, tho' the Compositor follows a printed Copy, and sets Page for Page, yet constant Experience proves, that he will sometimes drive out, and at other times get in, a Word or a Syllable in a Line, or perhaps a Line in a Page. He will also very frequently, perhaps several times in a Line, in spight of all his Care, set wider or closer than the Copy he follows. None that knows any thing of Printing, can doubt of these Matters. Now in the Copies C, D, E, the Distance between Words is exactly the same throughout; nor is there one letter driven out or got in, in any one Line of either the Title or the Body of any one Article from the first to the last.[117]

Bennet went on to remark that, even were all these features to be by some miracle reset identically, it would tax belief to think that the compositor 'can also fix the same blind or battered Letters, form the very same Crookednesses in Lines or Words, make the very same Letters lean or stand disorderly'.[118]

Bennet's work offers a startling instance of the way in which Protestant (in this case specifically Anglican) apologists could be driven by pointed opposition such as Collins's to take a deep interest in the textual minutiae

---

[112] Anthony Collins, *Priestcraft in Perfection: or, a Detection of the Fraud of Inserting and Continuing this Clause (The Church hath Power to Decree Rites and Ceremonies, and Authority in Controversys of Faith) In the Twentieth Article of the Church of England* (London, 1710), 21.

[113] Ibid. 47.

[114] Ibid.: 'How great a value we Protestants ought to set upon the Holy Scriptures, those inestimable Treasures of Wisdom and Knowledg, since there is nothing but uncertainty to be met with every where else . . .'.

[115] Thomas Bennet, *An Essay on the Thirty Nine Articles of Religion, Agreed on in 1562 and Revised in 1571* (London, 1715), 9, 79.

[116] Ibid., title-page.   [117] Ibid. 317–18.   [118] Ibid. 318.

of sacred or liturgical texts. Whereas Burnet's *Exposition* had been confident that such matters could be left to divine providence, Bennet undertakes a textual study whose interest in typographical detail as a means of identifying different impressions of the same edition was unprecedented in any field of textual criticism. Bennet was prepared to work minutely despite the censure he anticipated, as the defensive remarks of his preface show.[119] Equally significantly, Bennet was prepared to make a central argument about the authority of a critical clause in an ecclesiastical document turn on the professional knowledge of printers: claiming that he has established that the impression of copies C, D, and E was the first published in 1571, Bennet declares 'I challenge any Printer in *England* (and my Argument being built upon some Skill in their Trade, Printers are certainly the most competent Judges of it) to disprove what I have said, or even to render it doubtful.'[120] Bennet was on the board of curators of Cambridge University Press; at the beginning of the century the curators were involved in making the most minute decisions about the physical make-up of the books to be published.[121] From the perspective of the well-established academic specialism of analytical bibliography it might seem obvious that an investigation of the printed texts of the Thirty-nine Articles would want to deploy the expertise of professional printers; in 1715 such a procedure was anything but obvious, not merely because nothing like an academic discipline of 'bibliography' existed, but because any such method would grant the expertise of distrusted professionals a degree of authority over the text of a liturgical document. Bennet came to know Richard Bentley through his work for the Press;[122] like Bentley's work and Hare's apologies for it, Bennet's extraordinary *Essay* insists that the defence of liturgical texts cannot be left to providence, but depends precisely on specialist accuracy in matters of the minutest detail.

It is clear that some features of the various debates over the texts of scriptural and ecclesiastical documents were peculiar to *critica sacra*. But, as we shall see, the absence of any tradition of vernacular textual criticism meant that arguments first adumbrated in controversies over both classical and scriptural textual criticism were often appealed to both by those who wished to restrict, and by those who wished to promote, textual criticism. We have seen, in particular, how frequently disputes about textual criticism's usefulness and legitimacy, and about particular aspects

[119] Ibid., p. xxiv.   [120] Ibid. 344.
[121] See William L. Williamson, 'Thomas Bennet and the Origins of Analytical Bibliography', *Journal of Library History*, 16 (1981), 177–86 (pp. 181–2).
[122] Ibid. 181.

of its methodology, moved between two contrasting sets of attitudes. From the perspective of wits and those whom Atterbury called 'Gentlemen of Letters' and from that of defenders of scriptural orthodoxy alike, textual criticism could be represented as the disintegrating incursion of low, interested, and excessively minute specialists and professionals upon a textual heritage which required disinterested curation rather than historical criticism. From the perspective of advocates for textual criticism— those whom Atterbury regarded as the 'professed Pedants'—the whole of learning was the sum of the minute parts scorned by the wits, and only the patient labour of specialist scholarship could be adequate to the investigation of these parts. These sets of attitudes should be thought of as opposing rhetorics rather than as permanently irreconcilable creeds: few of those who undertook or wrote about textual criticism in the century did not have feet in both camps at some point in their careers. Nevertheless, the arguments about textual criticism's nature and function raise, in an especially acute way, disagreements about what the world of learning was, and who was best fitted to take charge of it. The most forceful advocates of the minute labour of qualified specialists saw their work as offering the possibility of an enlightened historical understanding of language and culture. For the most thoroughgoing opponents of minute criticism, as we shall see later, the enthusiasm of specialist scholars for a learning imagined as the sum of its parts raised the spectre of a culture no longer conceivable as a living whole, but converted into a collection of materials or products—a culture rendered unintelligible to any individual reader or writer by its multiple divisions of intellectual labour. The impact of these deep disagreements about the world of learning and its participants was to make itself felt in the theory and in the practice of Shakespearian textual criticism for most of the rest of the century.

2

The Idea of a Settled Language and the Instability of Gentlemanly Editing

I

THE CONTROVERSIES over the criticism of classical and scriptural texts bore witness to anxieties at the possible depredations of low and interested specialists upon a public cultural inheritance. But at the beginning of the century the minute criticism of vernacular texts lacked sufficient examples to seem worrying in any parallel way. It was certainly the case that edited texts of works in the vernacular had appeared prior to 1700. Shaaber and Black have demonstrated that the Second, Third and Fourth Shakespeare Folios can scarcely be regarded as mere reprints but must be thought of as edited texts;[1] the extent of Jacob Tonson's labours on the 1688 text of *Paradise Lost* indicates that he must be thought of as the editor, rather than merely as the publisher, of that volume.[2] But these publications lacked named editors and, equally significantly, lacked the obtrusive evidence of editorial labour which so offended the wits in edited classical and scriptural texts of the period. Late seventeenth- and early eighteenth-century edited and annotated texts of earlier vernacular works appeared for a wide variety of reasons, yet the desire to restore sick or damaged texts to health or wholeness, so often appealed to by the classical scholars, was rarely emphasized.

On occasion the publication of an edited text could be prompted by quite openly political motives. The edition of Drummond of Hawthornden which appeared in Edinburgh in 1711 wore its Jacobitism on its sleeve: 'Our Author was a true TORY, and seriously concerned about the

---

[1] Matthew W. Black and Matthias A. Shaaber, *Shakespeare's Seventeenth-Century Editors, 1632–85* (New York, 1937).
[2] Stuart Bennett, 'Jacob Tonson an Early Editor of *Paradise Lost*?', *The Library*, 6th ser. 8 (1986), 156–9.

HEREDITARY RIGHT and MONARCHY'.[3] Conversely, John Fortescue-Aland's text of his ancestor Sir John Fortescue's *The Difference between an Absolute and Limited Monarchy* offered support to the 1688 settlement.[4] Such motives, of course, did not preclude philological work: the partisan editor or editors of Drummond could nevertheless imagine a reader sufficiently curious to 'give himself the Pains to compare this with the former Editions' and thus to discover that 'we have corrected a great many Errors, and supplied a great many Defects'.[5] Fortescue-Aland's scholarly interests are more prominently displayed, despite his apologetic tone: 'I could not forbear making some Remarks on the Language; which I the rather have done, to rescue our Author from the Ignorance of some, and Malice of others, who are apt to take these old Ideoms, for the Mistakes of the Author . . .'.[6] Nevertheless both these edited texts indicate their political purposes quite clearly: neither claims to be principally valuable as providing an accurate text or as a contribution to the advancement of learning.

Those overseeing the republication of vernacular texts, even of more celebrated authors than Drummond and Fortescue, often found it unnecessary to discuss textual matters at all. This could apply even where those responsible were named: although Nicholas Tate drew attention to his own part in the 1714 text of Sir John Davies's *The Original, Nature and Immortality of the Soul* by pointing out to its dedicatee that 'I have here got a useful Poem reprinted . . .',[7] Tate's preface concerns itself largely with Davies's efficacy as an antidote to Lucretian and Hobbesian scepticism,[8] and makes no mention of textual questions. The same is true of the 1729 Waller of which Elijah Fenton was named as the 'publisher'.[9] Somewhat later, even a *Collection of Old Ballads* advertising itself on its title-page as 'Corrected from the best and most Ancient COPIES Extant' could content itself with simply repeating, rather than explaining, this claim in its preface.[10] A 1718 edition of Daniel was devoid of any discussion of the text whatsoever.[11] Even as late as 1748 an edition of Drayton

---

[3] *The Works of William Drummond, of Hawthornden* (Edinburgh, 1711), [i].

[4] Sir John Fortescue, *The Difference Between an Absolute and Limited Monarchy*, ed. John Fortescue-Aland (London, 1714).

[5] *Works of Drummond*, p. [i].   [6] Fortescue, *Absolute and Limited Monarchy*, p. xli.

[7] Sir John Davies, *The Original, Nature, and Immortality of the Soul* (London, 1714), 'Dedication'.

[8] Ibid., p. [v].

[9] *The Works of Edmund Waller Esq'. in Verse and Prose Published by Mr. Fenton* (London, 1728).

[10] *A Collection of Old Ballads: Corrected from the best and most Ancient Copies Extant* (London, 1727), p. viii.

[11] *The Poetical Works of Samuel Daniel* (London, 1718).

could appear without any information as to how the text had been prepared.[12]

Indeed, the idea of an application of the techniques of minute philology to vernacular texts was often taken, at the beginning of the century, as a transparently comic one. Several commentators ridiculed the excessive minuteness of classical textual critics by a burlesque application of their techniques to low or insignificant vernacular texts. Joseph Addison, although he made the usefulness of numismatics to classical textual criticism a recurrent theme of his *Dialogues upon the Usefulness of Ancient Medals*,[13] satirized in *Spectator*, no. 470, the excessive accumulation of various readings by overwhelming a slight English love-lyric with variants of a ludicrously minute kind quarried from supposed manuscripts, printed copies, and edited texts of the lyric: 'The *and* in some manuscripts is written thus, &, but that in the *Cotton* Library writes it in three distinct Letters.'[14] Richard Johnson used a similar device in his *Aristarchus Anti-Bentleianus* (1717) to ridicule Bentley's textual criticism by providing mock conjectural emendations for an old English ballad, 'Tom Bostock';[15] whilst the burlesque translation of Bentley's Horace argued for the absurdity of Bentley's readiness to take verbal echoes of one poet's work in another as evidence of direct influence by pointing out how easily (and, by implication, absurdly) the technique could be applied to English texts: 'Suppose one were to Criticize upon the *English* Poets after the same manner, and should find in one of them—*Oh ye Gods!*—and then justifie the Passage by Authorities, what a Noise might he make with our *Miltons, Drydens, Lees, Otwayes, Congreves, Addisons* and the rest?'[16] For this writer, the very idea of applying minute verbal attention to vernacular texts was self-evidently absurd. Facing such potential ridicule, editors sometimes preferred to cast themselves less as their authors' scholarly restorers, comparable to classical scholars, than as their gentlemanly executors. John Hughes declared in introducing his 1715 text of Spenser

---

[12] *The Works of Michael Drayton, Esq; A Celebrated Poet in the Reigns of Queen Elizabeth, King James I and Charles I* (London, 1748).

[13] Joseph Addison, *Dialogues upon the Usefulness of Ancient Medals* (London, 1726; repr. New York, 1976), 27: 'A reverse often clears up the passage of an old poet, as the poet often serves to unriddle a reverse'; 33: 'when I was at *Rome*, I took occasion to buy up many Imperial Medals that have any affinity with passages of the ancient Poets. So that I have by me a sort of poetical Cash, which I fancy I could count over to you in *Latin* and *Greek* verse.'

[14] *The Spectator*, ed. Bond, no. 470, iv. 163.

[15] Richard Johnson, *Aristarchus Anti-Bentleianus* (London, 1717), 109–12; J. H. Monk, *The Life of Richard Bentley, D.D.*, 2nd edn. (2 vols., London, 1833).

[16] William Oldisworth, ed. *The Odes, Epodes and Carmen Seculare of Horace in Latin and English: With a translation of Dr. Bentley's Notes. To which are added, Notes upon Notes* (24 parts, London, 1712), part 3, p. 22.

that 'AN Editor of the Works of a dead Author ought to consider himself as a kind of Executor of his Will; which he should endeavour to perform with the same Care, and, in every Circumstance, after the same manner he believes the Author himself would have done, if living.'[17] Although the Daily Courant had claimed that Hughes's edition was 'carefully corrected by a collation of all' former texts of Spenser,[18] and although, as Jewel Wurtsbaugh notes, Hughes can be shown to have consulted a copy of the First Quarto of The Faerie Queene and either the 1609 Folio of that poem or the 1611 First Folio of the Works,[19] Hughes makes no mention of any such labour himself.

One notable omission from the list given by the annotator of the burlesque Bentley is Chaucer. In the cases of pre-Renaissance English authors, the provision of annotated and edited texts was less likely to appear merely comic, given the obvious difficulty of representing Chaucer's English as in all essentials the same language as early eighteenth-century English. Edited texts of pre-Renaissance English and Scots authors begin earlier than those of Renaissance and seventeenth-century writers to remark explicitly on their own methodology. Ruddiman's 1710 text of Gavin Douglas's Scots translation of the Aeneid—whose title-page loudly advertises its own accuracy—is an interesting case in point. Ruddiman believes it incumbent upon him to satisfy possible enquiries as to how the edition has been prepared: 'the Curious . . . will be desirous to know what Methods have been used, and by what Means we have been assisted in this Performance'.[20] Accordingly, an unusually full account of the criteria for editorial decisions is given: the printed 1553 text has been emended with reference both to a copy of the Latin text of the Aeneid, and to a manuscript of Douglas's translation. Ruddiman's account declares vehemently against conjectural emendation, but also makes quite clear the thoroughly eclectic basis upon which Douglas's text has been edited:

In some places the Printed and MS. Copies have different Readings, both which agree very well with the Sense of the Original; and then we thought ourselves at Liberty to choose which of the two pleas'd us best: And the other may be seen amongst the Various Readings at the End of the Work. It was once design'd to have given a full List of all

---

[17] The Works of Mr. Edmund Spenser . . . Publish'd by Mr. Hughes (London, 1715), pp. [iii–iv].

[18] Daily Courant (22 Aug. 1715); quoted in J. Wurtsbaugh, Two Centuries of Spenserian Scholarship (Baltimore, 1936), 35.

[19] Ibid. 35–6.

[20] Virgil's Aeneis, Translated into Scottish Verse, by the Famous Gavin Douglas, Bishop of Dunkeld. A new Edition. Wherein The many Errors of the Former are corrected, and the Defects supply'd, from an excellent Manuscript (Edinburgh, 1710), [i].

the Errors *of the* Printed Copy: *But that required more Labour than the thing was worth, and wou'd have swell'd the Book above measure.*[21]

Not only is there (unsurprisingly) no thought of determining the relationship between printed text and manuscript before emendation takes place, but the 1553 printing, despite its '*innumerable and gross Errors, through the Incorrectness of the Copy, or Negligence of the Printers, or probably both*'[22] is here put upon an equal footing with the manuscript, with disagreements to be arbitrated, for all the vehemence against conjectural emendation, by editorial judgement alone. As with many contemporary attitudes to classical textual criticism, variants have no palaeographical or bibliographical function: they need only be listed where they might (as judged by comparison with an unspecified Latin text whose resemblance or otherwise to Douglas's source is not enquired into) provide a possible reading. Indeed Ruddiman did not scruple to admit that the manuscript only formed a basis for his printed text after p. 45 of that text, since he had completed work to that point before hearing of the manuscript's existence.[23]

The first edited eighteenth-century text of Chaucer bears further witness to an expectation of readerly inquisitiveness as to editorial procedure. The editor chiefly responsible for the volume, John Urry, died shortly before its publication in 1721, and Timothy Thomas, who took over the task of introducing the volume, felt obliged to alert the public to the licence involved in some of Urry's preferred procedures: he notes that Urry had frequently supplied metrically defective lines with extra syllables but had omitted to execute his 'just, useful and necessary . . . Design' of 'enclosing such words in hooks thus [   ] to distinguish them from what he found justified by the authority of MSS'.[24] The edition displays an awareness of the possibility that not only successive transcriptions, but successive printed texts, were likely to evidence a decline rather than an improvement in textual accuracy. Thomas rebuts the claim of the 1687 publication to have been prepared by collation with 'the best MSS' and points out that it 'has all the defects of the former ones, with many additional errors of its own'.[25] Yet once more, as with the Ruddiman text of Douglas, there is little indication as to how any assessment of what 'the

---

[21] Ibid.   [22] Ibid.
[23] *Virgil's Aeneid translated into Scottish Verse by Gavin Douglas, Bishop of Dunkeld*, ed. David C. F. Coldwell (4 vols., Edinburgh, 1957–64), 103.
[24] Timothy Thomas, 'Preface' to *The Works of Geoffrey Chaucer*, ed. John Urry (London, 1721), sig. K1r.
[25] Ibid., sig. M1r.

best MSS' were might have been carried out: Urry's catalogue of manuscripts consulted pays much attention to their appearance but gives little
evaluation of the authoritativeness of their texts and makes no attempt
either to determine the relationship between individual manuscripts or
that between manuscripts and later printed texts.[26]

2

For post-medieval texts, in any event, the question of the propriety or
otherwise of editorial labours on vernacular texts could not be dissociated
from disagreements about the state of the English language itself, and
about the best procedures for reforming it. The late seventeenth and early
eighteenth centuries saw many suggestions, and some controversy, as to
how the English language might be redeemed from its current barbarity
and converted into a tongue as pure and as stable as the classical languages
were considered to be.[27] One important aspect of such a project would
necessarily be the provision of a canon of English texts which could be
unhesitatingly recommended as models to those who would write a pure
English style. The authors of *Dr. Bentley's Dissertations . . . Examin'd*, for
example, having contrasted the impermanence of standards of usage in
English unfavourably with what they considered to be the fixity of Attic
Greek,[28] commented on the indispensability of such linguistic models to
the reformation of the language: 'we have few things in our Tongue writ
with any tolerable Degree of perfection; and They therefore who would
write or speak well, have no Patterns to look up to, no sure Rule, but
the present Mode of the Age, to guide themselves by'.[29] The need for a
canon of appropriate models was evident not only in its own right but
because the possibility of providing any authoritative dictionary had come

---

[26]   Timothy Thomas, 'Preface' to *The Works of Geoffrey Chaucer*, ed. John Urry (London,
1721), sigs. K1ʳ–K2ʳ.

[27]   See, for examples, Thomas Sprat, *History of the Royal Society*, ed. Jackson I. Cope and
Harold W. Jones (London, 1959), 40–4; Daniel Defoe, *An Essay upon Projects* (London,
1697; repr. Menston, 1969), 227–51; Jonathan Swift, *A Proposal for Correcting, Improving
and Ascertaining the English Tongue* (London, 1712; repr. Menston, 1969); John Oldmixon,
Reflections on Dr. Swift's Letter to the Earl of Oxford (London, 1712; repr. Menston, 1970);
Arthur Maynwaring, *The British Academy* (London, 1712; repr. New York, 1967); Thomas
Stackhouse, *Reflections on the Nature and Property of Languages* (London, 1731; repr.
Menston, 1969).

[28]   *Dr. Bentley's Dissertations on the Epistles of Phalaris, and the Fables of Æsop, Examin'd*,
3rd edn. (London, 1699), 70, 72.

[29]   Ibid. 69.

increasingly to seem to depend upon the availability of illustrative quotations from literary authorities to support the words and senses of words listed. The success of the Italian Accademia della Crusca and of the Académie française in collectively producing dictionaries according to this plan led those contemplating the likely nature of any English dictionary to think illustrative quotations centrally important to any such plan; when Joseph Addison was seriously contemplating the need for such a dictionary in the early years of the century, one of his preparatory steps was to make a collection of illustrative quotations from the works of Tillotson.[30]

At a time when, as we have seen, the intellectual and social value of the textual criticism even of classical texts was widely questioned, and when the very idea of publishing critical editions of vernacular texts was seen as merely laughable by some commentators, the growing demand for language reform furnished an obvious public justification for the labours of Shakespearian editors. If dictionaries, for example, were to rely for their illustrative quotations upon corrupt texts of the English classics which would be needed to provide the patterns of linguistic purity, how could the corruption of the language itself be avoided? Early eighteenth-century editors were, accordingly, almost unanimous in presenting their labours as a public, and specifically as a national, service. This had less to do with Shakespeare's status as the greatest of English authors (which in any case was only fully established by the end of the century, and by a process of which these editions themselves formed part) than with the way in which the editing of his work raised important issues about how correct taste in language and letters might be defined. Pope regarded a thorough criticism of Shakespeare's work as offering 'the best occasion that any just Writer could take, to form the judgment and taste of our nation' not because he thought Shakespeare certainly the greatest English writer but because Shakespeare provided the most conspicuous examples of beauties and faults.[31]

Others emphasized the analogy between the services which humanism had performed for the classical languages and those which a similar attention to texts in the vernacular could accomplish for English. George Sewell's preface to the volume containing Shakespeare's poems, published as a supplement to Pope's text in 1726, suggested that

[30] See Mary Segar, 'Dictionary-Making in the Early Eighteenth Century', *Review of English Studies*, 7 (1931), 210–13.
[31] *The Prose Works of Alexander Pope*, ed. Norman Ault and Rosemary Cowler (2 vols., Oxford, 1936–86), ii. 13.

What then has been done by the really Learned to the dead Languages, by treading backwards into the Paths of Antiquity, and reviving and correcting good old Authors, we in Justice owe to our own great Writers, both in Prose and Poetry. They are in some degree our *Classics*; on their Foundation we must build, as the Formers and Refiners of our Language.[32]

Lewis Theobald remarked, only half ironically, that Shakespeare's text was sufficiently corrupt for him to stand 'in the Nature of a Classic Writer',[33] and, like Sewell, hoped that what classical textual critics had done for contemporary standards in Greek and Latin might be done by editors of Shakespeare for English.[34] William Warburton's preface to his text of the dramatist insisted most explicitly of all that nothing could be done towards the settling of the language without the prior labours of textual critics.[35]

John Barrell's account of eighteenth-century grammars and dictionaries has argued that their authors and editors relied on an idea of a community of polite speakers and writers of the language which was closely modelled on the community of the electorally enfranchised, and whose ideal member was a gentleman able to take a disinterested view of public affairs from a position of propertied independence.[36] Many of those who were to argue for this conception of the language, however, were themselves not propertied gentlemen but professional writers or scholars; and the same applied to editors of Shakespeare. Pope's view of Shakespeare, and of the state of Shakespeare's text, is decisively influenced by an idea of just taste and language as disinterestedly gentlemanly. But Pope resists both in theory and in practice the wholesale recasting of Shakespeare towards which such a view might seem to lead him, out of a loyalty to established procedures of textual criticism which are more characteristic of one strand within the culture of scholarship than of the gentleman of letters. The conflicting attitudes towards textual criticism evident in Pope's preface to his edition of Shakespeare, and in his text and annotations, are hence intimately connected with a wider paradox in Pope's position as a professional writer whose literary career none the less depended in part upon his self-construction as a disinterested gentleman.

---

[32] *The Works of Mr. William Shakespear. The Seventh Volume*, ed. George Sewell (London, 1726), p. vii.

[33] Lewis Theobald, *Shakespeare Restored* (London, 1726; repr. 1971), p. v.

[34] *1733*, i, p. lxii.   [35] *1747*, i, p. xxv–xxvi.

[36] John Barrell, *English Literature in History, 1730–1780: An Equal, Wide Survey* (London, 1983), 110–75.

3

Unlike Warburton, Pope does not explicitly claim lexicographical significance for his edition of Shakespeare, although when he talked to Spence
in 1744 about the best sources of illustrative quotations for any English
dictionary, Shakespeare was on the list.[37] Nor does he make such a clear
comparison as Theobald between classical textual criticism and the establishment of an English text. But the textual history given in his preface
indicates the extent to which both aspirations to contribute towards a
polite national taste and language, and the specialist methods of classical
and scriptural philology, have formed Pope's idea of the Shakespearian
editor's task. What kind of public institution Shakespeare's text should
be, and what kind of editors and critics should be entrusted with forming
it, are questions which Pope's preface canvasses both in his general criticism of Shakespeare's beauties and faults and in his history of the text. His
opening account of Shakespeare's 'characteristic Excellencies' culminates
with a curiously paradoxical suggestion. Pope praises Shakespeare's
ability to focus both on the most important part in an argument and on the
most important point in the motivation of a character; and he remarks on
how surprising this ability is:

This is perfectly amazing, from a man of no education or experience in those great
and publick scenes of life which are usually the subject of his thoughts: So that he
seems to have known the world by Intuition, to have look'd thro' humane nature
at one glance, and to be the only Author that gives ground for a very new opinion,
That the Philosopher and even the Man of the world, may be *Born*, as well as the
Poet.[38]

Shakespeare's ability convincingly to delineate thoughts and sentiments
from a sphere of life of which he has no personal knowledge (since he is,
as Pope later remarks, a theatrical professional rather than a 'Man of the
world') is a phenomenon so difficult to explain that it must be expressed
as paradox. Shakespeare becomes an honorary intuitive participant in the
'publick scenes of life' from which his trade excludes him. Such a position, however, only presents Pope with further difficulties once he comes
to discuss Shakespeare's faults. Once Shakespeare's genius has been established as not merely poetical but also philosophical and political, his
faults become still harder to explain: 'But I think I can in some measure

---

[37] Joseph Spence, *Observations, Anecdotes and Characters of Books and Men*, ed. James M.
Osborn (2 vols., Oxford, 1966), i. 171.
[38] Pope, *Prose Works*, ii. 14.

account for these defects, from several causes and accidents; without which it is hard to imagine that so large and so enlighten'd a mind could ever have been susceptible of them.'[39] Shakespeare's mind has already been granted the gentlemanly attributes of being 'large and enlighten'd': any lapses from such a standard into what is implicitly narrow and unenlightened must be explained as 'accidents' or 'Contingencies'.[40] Whilst Shakespeare's knowledge of the world (which in most writers might be expected to be acquired rather than innate) is in him a quality he is born with, his lapses from such knowledge are inessential and accidental.

The superfluity of possible explanations which Pope goes on to offer for Shakespeare's accidental moments of lowness indicates his eagerness to demonstrate the prior gentlemanliness of his subject. The first explanation given is that Shakespeare's initial purpose in writing was a purely professional one and was hence more liable to influence from the taste of his audience.[41] Since his audiences, initially, were 'generally composed of the meaner sort of people'[42] it followed that 'therefore the Images of Life were to be drawn from those of their own rank: accordingly we find, that not our Author's only but almost all the old Comedies have their Scene amongst *Tradesmen* and *Mechanicks*'.[43] Such explanations give us a clearer idea of where Pope believes Shakespeare's defects to lie: Pope objects not merely to the 'mean buffoonry, vile ribaldry and unmannerly jests of fools and clowns',[44] which he goes on to represent as pleasing the meaner sort, but to the 'Images of Life' being drawn from, and the scene set among, such people. Conversely, once 'the encouragement of the Court had succeeded to that of the Town; the works of his riper years are manifestly raised above those of his former'.[45] Nevertheless, Pope's second explanation for Shakespeare's lapses from large enlightenment confirms the suspicion, already aroused by his acknowledgement that Shakespeare initially wrote simply for subsistence, that Shakespeare may, in any case, be rather 'of the meaner sort' than 'of the better sort'[46] himself: 'Another Cause (and no less strong than the former) may be deduced from our Author's being a *Player*, and forming himself first upon the judgments of that body of men whereof he was a member.'[47] Players habitually cater for 'the Majority',[48] and hence not only their own productions but also their judgements will be formed upon mercenary considerations: 'Players are just such judges of what is *right*, as Taylors are of what is *graceful*.'[49]

[39] Pope, *Prose Works*, ii. 14–15.   [40] Ibid.   [41] Ibid. 15.   [42] Ibid.
[43] Ibid.   [44] Ibid.   [45] Ibid. 16.   [46] Ibid. 15.   [47] Ibid. 16.
[48] Ibid.   [49] Ibid.

Whereas the emphasis of the first explanation is that any playwright writing for the meaner sort would be obliged to adopt subjects familiar, and spectacles pleasing, to them, the emphasis of the second is rather that mercenariness as such disables judgement. Tailors supply clothes to gentlemen: it is not the low social provenance of their clients, but their necessarily professional approach to taste as such, which renders them unfit to judge. This second explanation, then, supplies a deficiency in the first, in that it may be used to account for the presence of low or otherwise faulty passages in plays thought to have been written for a gentle audience.

The most flexible weapon in Pope's exegetical armoury, however, is the notion of editorial and theatrical corruption. Since the editors were also men of the theatre, such corruption can be shown to 'have risen from one source, the ignorance of the Players, both as his actors, and as his editors'.[50] Defects which Pope believes too gross to be admitted into the text may thus be charged to 'the first Publishers' or to the actors, and removed from the text. In the question of Shakespeare's want (or other- wise) of learning, for example, readings which would seem to demonstrate such a want conclusively can be regarded as almost certainly editorial. 'Nothing is more likely than that those palpable blunders of *Hector*'s quoting *Aristotle*, with others of that gross kind, sprung from the same root [editorial ignorance] . . .'[51] Accordingly (although the relationship between Pope's theory and practice is not always such a simple one) in Pope's text of *Troilus and Cressida* Hector does not mention Aristotle but merely refers generally to 'graver sages'.[52] The deficiencies which render Shakespeare potentially unsuitable as a model for style and language in Pope's account (not social meanness merely, but also mercenariness) are also those which, in less qualified form, render the players categorically unfit to influence the text either as editors or as actors. Pope emphasizes the meanness of the Elizabethan players when compared with early eight- eenth-century actors:

the Judgment, as well as Condition, of that class of people was then far inferior to what it is in our days . . . the top of the profession were then meer Players, not Gentlemen of the stage: They were led into the Buttery by the Steward, not plac'd at the Lord's table, or Lady's toilette: and consequently were intirely depriv'd of those advantages they now enjoy, in the familiar conversation of our Nobility, and an intimacy (not to say dearness) with people of the first condition.[53]

---

[50] Ibid. 20.   [51] Ibid.
[52] Ibid. The emendation had first appeared in *1709* (iv. 1841); but the remarks quoted here show that Pope was aware of the reading of the Folio and early Quartos.
[53] Pope, *Prose Works*, ii. 23.

The point is not merely that actors were themselves of lower status, but that such lower status deprived them of the conversation of people of the first condition (a conversation whose necessity to Shakespeare's being a 'Man of the world' has earlier been waived) so that not only their respectability, but also their 'judgment' suffers by comparison with that of the early eighteenth-century's 'Gentlemen of the stage'.

The influence of this idea of the defective judgement of the players as actors and as editors can be seen in the account which Pope gives of the relative authority of the individual Quartos available to him and that of the First Folio. The Quartos are better texts in almost every respect, Pope argues, because the players have had a greater influence over the Folio.[54] So that, for example, 'in the old Editions of *Romeo* and *Juliet* there is no hint of a great number of the mean conceits and ribaldries now to be found there'.[55] In other plays 'the low scenes of Mobs, Plebeians and Clowns, are vastly shorter than at present'.[56] Nor does the fact that many passages which appear in the Quartos are absent from the Folio at all embarrass this generalized bibliographical schema, since these passages can be presented by Pope as beauties insensitively cut by those responsible for the insertion of so many faults.[57] It is not that Pope believes the Quartos to have been published with Shakespeare's approval and supervision (although he indicates three possible exceptions):[58] 'every page is so scandalously false spelled, and almost all the learned or unusual words so intolerably mangled, that it's plain there either was no Corrector to the press at all, or one totally illiterate'.[59] It is, rather, simply that further opportunities for theatrical and editorial corruption beyond those taken in the already corrupt Quartos have occurred by the time the Folio comes to be published.

The one respect in which Pope is prepared to commend the editorial work of the First Folio editors reveals as much as those in which he condemns their text. He describes their claim to have presented a text purged of earlier corruptions as 'true as to the literal errors, and no other'.[60] The Folio editors' competence is restricted at widest to correcting mistakes confined to a single letter, and perhaps to the correction of clear misprints alone. Where the players are not 'totally illiterate' their

---

[54] Pope, *Prose Works*, ii. 21.   [55] Ibid.   [56] Ibid.   [57] Ibid. 22.
[58] Ibid. 21. The possible exceptions named are *Henry IV, Parts 1 and 2* and *A Midsummer Night's Dream*. Pope's 'TABLE of the Several Editions of *Shakespear*'s Plays, made use of and compared in this Impression' indicates that the specific texts in question are the 1600 Roberts Quarto of *A Midsummer Night's Dream* (in fact one of the misdated 1619 Pavier Quartos), the 1599 Quarto of *Henry IV, Part 1*, and the 1600 Quarto of *Henry IV, Part 2*. *1723–5*, vi, sigs. 4O1ʳ, 4O1ᵛ.
[59] Pope, *Prose Works*, ii. 20–1.   [60] Ibid. 21.

literacy is restricted to matters of the most minute detail. They lack the large and enlightened views of the author of the plays and are consequently confined to literal, rather than general, criticism. Once again actors are censured not simply for being social inferiors but for being, consequently, partial or interested. Whereas such considerations have been dealt with delicately where Shakespeare himself has seemed liable to such objections, the account of the players is more directly censorious. The Elizabethan stage is at times portrayed as an arena for the war of all against all in which the strong tyrannize over the weak: Pope argues, for example, that speeches are assigned in the text to the wrong character 'sometimes perhaps for no better reason, than that a governing Player, to have the mouthing of some favourite speech himself, would snatch it from the unworthy lips of an Underling'.[61] The clear implication of such arguments is that the fittest guardian of Shakespeare's text, like the ideal canonical poet, will not be a professional of any kind, but a self-sufficient man of the world.

Whilst Pope himself is safe enough from accusations of inferior conversational partners and a consequently impaired judgement, this second argument against the fitness of the players to act as the custodians of Shakespeare's text has the disadvantage that it is equally applicable to Pope himself. Pope was paid £100 for his work on the edition and to this extent became a professional editor;[62] equally importantly, textual criticism as such was an activity which had developed its own specialist methods, methods which were not always helpful to the gentlemanly restoration of Shakespeare's text. Moreover, it was associated with professional scholars such as Richard Bentley, and by virtue of such associations, was less easy to present as the harmless leisure pursuit or the disinterested act of public service of a gentleman. The characterization of the fit editor implicitly presented in Pope's account of editorial corruption, therefore, was at least partially contradicted by the canons and contemporary social status of editing as such.

The difficulty is one which emerges abruptly towards the end of Pope's preface. Pope gives an extended account of the many kinds of deficiency in the text which, in the light of his depiction of the social provenance and mercenary habits of mind of the Elizabethan actors and actor-editors, can now be regarded as the result of editorial and theatrical corruption. This long list culminates in what appears to be a declaration that the opportu-

---

[61] Pope, *Prose Works*, ii. 23.
[62] David Foxon, *Pope and the Early Eighteenth-Century Book Trade*, rev. and ed. James McLaverty (Oxford, 1991), 89.

nities for reform of the text afforded by an understanding of the extent of editorial and theatrical corruption are very substantial indeed:

> If we give in to this opinion, how many low and vicious parts and passages might no longer reflect upon this great Genius, but appear unworthily charged upon him? . . . From one or other of these considerations, I am verily perswaded, that the greatest and grossest part of what are thought his errors would vanish, and leave his character in a light very different from that disadvantageous one, in which it now appears to us.[63]

But immediately afterwards Pope explains that the injuries done Shakespeare by his players are irreversible ones: 'It is impossible to repair the Injuries already done him; too much time has elaps'd, and the materials are too few.'[64] Pope is willing to regard offensive passages as corrupt, we here discover, without being in possession of materials which would in all such cases provide uncorrupted readings. Pope claims to have edited, instead, 'with a religious abhorrence of all Innovation, and without any indulgence to my private sense or conjecture'.[65]

This remark has most often been quoted in order to comment on the apparent disparity between this declaration of editorial conservatism and Pope's editorial practice.[66] But it has been misunderstood. Pope's description of his abhorrence of innovation as 'religious' is when seen in the context of scriptural philology more than a merely metaphorical one. We have already seen how the powerful persistence in scriptural philology of the *textus receptus* was linked to a fear that those with merely private purposes might have greater scope to pursue those purposes were the received text to be abandoned.[67] It is not only Pope's 'religious abhorrence of all Innovation' which indicates the influence of the procedures of scriptural textual criticism upon his account of how Shakespeare's text should be edited but also the claim that he has refused 'any indulgence to [his] private sense or conjecture'. Lewis Theobald's *Shakespeare Restored* immediately recognized Pope's claim religiously to have abhorred innovation as a reference to scriptural textual criticism.[68] Departure from the First Folio and early Quartos in Pope's text, therefore, should not occasion too much surprise: real evidence of a contradiction between Pope's theory and his practice of editing is only to be found where Pope deviates (without authority from earlier copies) from his copy-text, Rowe's third edition of 1714.[69]

---

[63] Pope, *Prose Works*, ii. 24.   [64] Ibid. 24.   [65] Ibid. 24–5.

[66] See e.g. T. R. Lounsbury, *The First Editors of Shakespeare* (London, 1906), 86.

[67] See above, pp. 33–39.   [68] Theobald, *Shakespeare Restored*, p. iv.

[69] Peter Seary, *Lewis Theobald and the Editing of Shakespeare* (Oxford, 1990), 132–3. Rowe's own copy-text was the Fourth Folio of 1685: see R. B. McKerrow, 'The Treatment

4

Pope's textual-critical practice, I shall argue, oscillates between the sub-stantial revisions of Shakespeare which took place in performance texts such as the late seventeenth-century 'Players' Quartos', on the one hand, and a philological insistence, on the other, that emendations should be properly attested by existing copies.[70] In this analysis little attention will be paid either to Pope's degradation of certain passages in the plays to the foot of the page, or, conversely, to the marginal marks of approbation set against certain passages. These highly visible features of Pope's text have been extensively examined elsewhere,[71] and whilst they are undoubtedly of some interest as a (rather unsurprising) index of Pope's taste, they do little to illuminate the central topic of interest here, which is Pope's negotiation between criteria of linguistic and stylistic correctness on the one hand, and his fledgling textual-critical and bibliographical theory on the other. Pope makes it clear, in any case, that the passages degraded to the foot of the page are nevertheless to be considered as having been included in the text: a discussion of one scene in *The Two Gentlemen of Verona* which Pope claims is 'compos'd of the lowest and most trifling conceits' leaves him remarking of such scenes in general: 'I wish I had authority to leave them out, but I have done all I could, set a mark of reprobation upon them.'[72] Although Pope did occasionally omit a disliked phrase or passage entirely,[73] despite the sentiments here expressed, such a note indicates Pope's awareness that the editor's task is not the same as the general critic's or the adaptor's.

The text taken by Pope for copy, Rowe's 1714 text (a reprint of Rowe's own 1709 text) had itself been based upon the previous edition of Shake-speare, the Fourth Folio of 1685. Rowe's approach to his copy-text was in general conservative; long stretches of the 1709 text differ little from that given in the Fourth Folio. Some instances of Rowe's treatment of the text of *Hamlet* demonstrate his use of that Folio to provide copy for his own edition: Rowe's text frequently gives a reading for which there is no other

---

of Shakespeare's Text by his Earlier Editors, 1709–1768', in P. Alexander, ed., *Studies in Shakespeare: British Academy Lectures* (London, 1964), 103–31 (p. 110).

[70] For the 'Players' Quartos', see Hazelton Spencer, '*Hamlet* under the Restoration', *Publications of the Modern Languages Association*, 38 (1923), 770–91.

[71] See, for examples, Wolfgang Kowalk, *Popes Shakespeare-Ausgabe als Spiegel seiner Kunstauffassung* (Berne, 1975), 410–88; John Butt, *Pope's Taste in Shakespeare* (London, 1936), 4–21.

[72] *1723–5*, i. 157.

[73] See, for an example, *1723–5*, vi. 417, where Pope dislikes Hamlet's couplet resolving not to harm the Queen enough to omit it (compare *1714*, vi. 361).

authority than the Fourth Folio. In Rowe's text of 'Lucianus''s speech immediately before murdering 'Gonzago', we read of '*The* natural Magick, and dire property', where all authorities apart from the 1685 Folio give '*Thy* . . .';[74] Hamlet's '*for on* Monday morning 'twas so indeed'[75] and the Ghost's 'With Witchcraft of his Wits, *and* traiterous Gifts'[76] are further instances of readings supported by the Fourth Folio alone. Nevertheless, Rowe did on occasion depart from his copy-text. Rowe's Polonius warns his daughter that 'you'll *tender* me a fool', not 'render' as in the Fourth Folio;[77] Ophelia herself remarks 'You are naught, you are naught, I'll *mark* the Play' in Rowe's text, not 'make' as in the second, third and fourth Folios;[78] later she sings of 'True-love *showers*' in Rowe's text, not of 'flowers' as she does in the Third and Fourth Folios.[79] There is no evidence that Rowe consulted any earlier Folio; none of the departures from his copy-text listed above is supported by an earlier Folio alone. But he did add Quarto material, to *Hamlet* at least; McKerrow calculates that about 131 of the 231 Quarto lines omitted in the First Folio text of that play are supplied to the text by Rowe.[80] As McKerrow indicates, Rowe supplied such material from one of the Players' Quartos which were published in 1676, 1683, 1695, 1703 (the Players' Quartos were themselves published one from the other and differ so little as to make identification of Rowe's source for his Quarto material impossible, given the small size of the sample).[81] Proofs of Rowe's use of Quarto copies in the editing of other plays are uncertain.[82]

A page-by-page collation of Pope's text of *Hamlet* with that given in Rowe's third edition shows the extent to which Pope's practice bears out the contention of his generalized bibliographical theory that the early Quartos generally provide better texts than the First Folio because the First Folio has undergone corruption by illiterates or near-illiterates twice over. In the overwhelming majority of cases where Pope departs from the 1714 text with support from earlier copies, that support comes from the Quartos rather than from the First Folio; Pope frequently deviates from Rowe's text to insert a reading from one or all of the Quartos even where Rowe's reading is the same as that of the First Folio. At the same time it is clearly the case that nothing like a stemmatic understanding of the relationship between the Quartos themselves is at work here. In those

---

[74] *1709* 2419; Furness 258.   [75] *1709* 2403; Furness 171.
[76] *1709* 2385; Furness 100.   [77] *1709* 2381; Furness 72.
[78] *1709* 2416; Furness 244.   [79] *1709* 2437; Furness 331.
[80] McKerrow, 'Treatment', 108. McKerrow's remains the best available account of Rowe's text.
[81] Ibid.   [82] Ibid. 109.

cases where not all the Quartos support the departure from Rowe's text, Pope is as likely to follow the Third and Fourth Quartos as the Second.[83]

But the implication of Pope's preface, that he religiously abhors departures (other than those *ex fide codicum*) from the received text, rather than from an Elizabethan or Jacobean copy-text, is confirmed by his practice when appending variants to his text. The point here is not so much that there are very few such variants appended, in proportion to the number of departures from Rowe's text, but that when Pope does append such variants, his primary concern is to give the reading of the received text, even if this means leaving out the reading of the First Folio or early Quartos. Pope gives a line from *King Lear* as 'Ten masts attacht make not the altitude'; but notes '*at least*' as the variant at the foot of the page. This, however, is the reading only of Rowe's edition; meanwhile, the reading of both Quarto and Folio, 'at each', goes entirely unrecorded.[84] Because such scruples as Pope has in his textual-critical practice concern departures from the received text rather than any earlier text, he is also free to leave Rowe's reading in place in those cases where he prefers it to an available Quarto variant. An analysis of a passage from Pope's text of Gertrude's description of the death of Ophelia will give an example of his typical practice in this respect:

> There on the pendant boughs, her coronet weeds
> Clambring to hang, an envious sliver broke;
> When down *her* weedy trophies and her self
> Fell in the weeping brook; her cloaths spread wide,
> And mermaid-like, a while they *bore* her up;
> Which time she chaunted snatches of old tunes,
> As one incapable of her own distress,
> Or like a creature native, and *indewed*
> Unto that element: . . .[85]

The italicized words represent departures from Rowe's 1714 edition. Rowe's '*the* weedy trophies' is supported by the First Folio (and also by the Second, Third, and Fourth Folios); Pope, instead, reads 'her weedy trophies' with the Quartos. Rowe's '*bear* her up' is taken over from the Fourth Folio; Pope replaces it with 'bore', following the first three Folios and the Quartos. Rowe's 'deduced | Unto that element' is the reading of the Second, Third, and Fourth Folios only; Pope replaces it with the

---

[83] For some instances in which Pope follows the later Quartos alone, see *1723–5*, vi. 348 ('And carriage of the articles design'd'), 399 ('And for my part, *Ophelia*'), and 466 ('The cannons to the heav'ns').

[84] *1723–5*, iii. 85.   [85] *1723–5*, vi. 449; compare *1714*, vi. 386–7.

reading of the First Folio and the Quartos. The factor common to all these departures from Rowe's text is support from the Quartos for Pope's reading; his practice here would seem to bear out his prefatory assessment of the Folio as in general less reliable than the Quartos. But if we consider the passage more closely it becomes clear that Pope's use of the Quartos is selective. The Quartos all read 'snatches of old *lauds*' for 'tunes': Pope presumably dislikes the more obsolete word and so does not insert it. Similarly the Second and Third Quartos read 'her *cronet* weeds' for the Folios' and the received text's 'coronet'; Pope ignores this variant. Such practice is typical of Pope's eclectic use of Quarto variants: he frequently ignores them even in cases where it is not immediately evident why he might object to them.[86]

Nevertheless, despite the flexibility given to Pope by his use of a received text which can be selectively deviated from where promising variants present themselves, he is also prepared to make outright alterations where he thinks the defects in the received text sufficiently serious. The collation of Pope's text of *Hamlet* with his copy-text indicates the extent of his silent emendations made upon grammatical or other linguistic grounds. Two double negatives, for example, are removed by Pope: 'Nor do not saw the Air too much' becomes 'And do not saw the air too much',[87] whilst a little later 'nor 'tis not strange' becomes likewise 'and 'tis not strange'.[88] Pope also emends 'on the view and *know of* these contents' to 'knowing', evidently disliking the use of 'know' as a substantive.[89] A whole series of expressions which Pope finds obsolete or obscure are simply replaced: 'In hugger-mugger' becomes, notoriously, 'In private';[90] 'Sallets' are simplified to 'salts';[91] 'each particular hair' will, in Pope's text, 'stand on end' rather than 'stand an end';[92] 'Implorators' become 'implorers'.[93] Such a pattern of linguistic emendation can also be seen at work in Pope's editing of other plays in the canon. Accusative cases are added to the relevant personal pronouns, so that, for example, '*Who* I my self struck down' in *Macbeth* becomes 'Whom I my self . . .',[94] whilst, later in the same play, the line '*Who* may I rather challenge for Unkindness' becomes

---

[86] Failures to depart from Rowe's text are, of course, not recorded in the table of collations; but see, for a few of very many examples in which Pope follows *1714* rather than an available Quarto variant, *1723–5*, vi. 379, 'And since so neighbour'd to his youth and humour' (Q₂ haviour, Q₃ hav r [*sic*], Q₄ havour); 421, 'That it is proof and bulwark against sense' (Qq be). Furness 131, 287.

[87] *1723–5*, vi. 404; *1714*, vi. 350.
[88] *1723–5*, vi. 411; *1714*, vi. 356.
[89] *1723–5*, vi. 461; *1714*, vi. 396.
[90] *1723–5*, vi. 437; *1714*, vi. 377.
[91] *1723–5*, vi. 392; *1714*, vi. 341.
[92] *1723–5*, vi. 369; *1714*, vi. 321.
[93] *1723–5*, vi. 364; *1714*, vi. 318.
[94] *1723–5*, v. 553; *1714*, vi. 264.

'Whom may I rather challenge . . .'.[95] Elsewhere Pope emends to bring the number of subject and verb into conformity, so that in *Love's Labour's Lost* 'to study, three years are but short' (replacing 'is but short').[96] Double comparatives and superlatives in the texts of *Measure for Measure* and *Julius Caesar* are replaced by a variety of manœuvres.[97]

On other occasions, indeed, Pope's editing approaches the condition of adaptation. Malcolm Goldstein pointed out in *Pope and the Augustan Stage* that several of Pope's emendations to the text of *Julius Caesar* in his edition were drawn from adaptations by Sheffield of that play into two separate pieces (*The Tragedy of Julius Caesar* and *The Tragedy of Marcus Brutus*) which Pope had seen through the press in 1721.[98] Certainly Pope's emendatory practice in *Hamlet* bears witness to the influence of the tradition of theatrical revision. In many cases emendations are made not (as far as can be seen) because the English is thought to be incorrect, obsolete, or unintelligible, but in order to make stylistic improvements. Most notably, '*To grunt and sweat* under a weary life' stands, in Pope's text, 'To groan and sweat':[99] the only conceivable authority, if such it be, for the reading is the 'Players' Quarto' of 1676.[100] Similarly Pope is prepared to tidy up Shakespeare's metre by the simple expedient of finding longer or shorter synonyms to replace words in metrically defective or hypermetrical lines respectively: Hamlet's dying request to Horatio 'To tell my Story' is condensed in Pope's text to read 'To tell my tale',[101] just as at the beginning of the play 'Dar'd to the combat' has become 'Dar'd to the fight'.[102]

Pope's editorial practices, then, are extremely various and in some ways self-contradictory: a generalized bibliographical theory as to the superior value of the Quartos appears to have been followed, but followed selectively and with exceptions made where Pope considers the available attested readings, for a variety of reasons, unacceptable. Yet this does not mean that his practice cannot be interpreted. Many commentators have remarked on the gaps between Pope's theory of editing and his practice—such as his failure to record emendatory departures from the received text in the margin—without noticing the important analogies between the contradictions in Pope's editorial theory and those of his editorial prac-

[95] *1723–5*, v. 559; *1714*, vi. 268.   [96] *1723–5*, ii. 99; *1714*, ii. 12.
[97] *1723–5*, v. 259: 'With the most bold, and the best hearts of *Rome*'; i. 344: 'To some more fitting place'.
[98] Malcolm Goldstein, *Pope and the Augustan Stage* (Stanford, Calif., 1958), 39–41.
[99] *1723–5*, vi. 401; *1714*, vi. 347.   [100] *1676*, 39.
[101] *1723–5*, vi. 469; *1714*, vi. 404.   [102] *1723–5*, vi. 348; *1714*, vi. 306.

tice. Pope's prefatory account of editing argues, aprioristically, that most of the linguistic and stylistic infelicities of the text as we now have it cannot be Shakespeare's but must be the result of the corruption of his texts by near-illiterates, yet admits that contemporary editors are rarely in possession of the materials necessary to remedy this situation; Pope's practice often seizes the opportunity to correct Shakespeare's English, yet also shows evidence of a clear insistence that critical editing cannot be collapsed into wholesale revision. These parallel complexities are not the result merely of Pope's indolence or incompetence, as is sometimes claimed: John A. Hart has demonstrated, and the collations given in Appendix 2 show, the extent of Pope's provision of new readings by means of collation.[103] Rather they reflect a real contradiction in the conditions of the text's production: the 1723–5 text was produced by an editor deeply suspicious of the motives for and likely results of textual criticism, who at the same time was a paid editor aware that textual criticism had become an increasingly specialized activity with preferred procedures clearly distinct from those of adaptation or revision. The responses to Pope's edition were to show that those who wished to dissent from Pope's account of fit editing and the fit editor were aware of the contradictions in his theory and practice of textual criticism and were prepared to exploit them. In the process both the history of the text given by Pope and the validity of his editorial procedures were to be brought into question.

[103] John A. Hart, 'Pope as Scholar-Editor', *Studies in Bibliography*, 23 (1970), 45–9.

3

The Venal and the Vain:
The Attack on Gentlemanly Editing

EVER SINCE Johnson, many critics have taken Pope's hostility to textual criticism as a simple result of his own discomfiture in the field.[1] As we have seen, however, Pope's distrust of minute criticism predated his own edition and was evident even in its preface. His satirical attacks on it need to be seen not merely as the result of hurt pride,[2] but in the context of the Scriblerian distrust of 'the new "professional" scholars' upon which Brean Hammond has remarked.[3] The principal textual-critical responses to Pope's editorial work were prompted by a desire to contest the view that the disinterested gentleman of letters was the best custodian of Shakespeare's text. This disagreement with the presuppositions of Pope's work had important consequences for the project of using critical editing to help polish and refine the English language. It also prompted in part the *Dunciad*'s new and more complex representation of minute criticism. In Pope's later satire on excessively minute criticism both the interested specialist and the leisured dilettante are taken as potential corruptors of the text. Moreover, excessively minute scholarship is taken, both in the *Dunciad* and in a number of other works of the 1730s, not only as low and interested, but as complicit with, and akin to, arbitrary government. The result is a shift of emphasis in Pope's view of textual criticism which has an important influence on the self-representation and editorial practice of Pope's successors.

I

Lewis Theobald, for one, was unimpressed by Pope's claim to have edited with 'a religious abhorrence of all innovation', not merely because he

---

[1] Samuel Johnson, *Prefaces, Biographical and Critical, to the Works of the English Poets* (10 vols., London, 1779–81), vii. 117.

[2] Felicity Rosslyn has recently made a similar point: *Alexander Pope* (London, 1990), 82.

[3] Brean Hammond, 'Scriblerian Self-Fashioning', *Yearbook of English Studies*, 18 (1988), 108–24 (p. 110).

believed that Pope had not kept his promise, but because of what he took to be the comparison both between Shakespeare's text and scripture, and between Shakespearian and scriptural textual criticism, implicit in such a claim:

> I cannot help thinking this Gentleman's *Modesty* in this Point too *nice* and *blame-able*; and that what he is pleased to call a *religious Abhorrence* of *Innovation*, is downright *Superstition*: Neither can I be of Opinion, that the Writings of *SHAKESPEARE* are so *venerable*, as that we should be excommunicated from good Sense, for daring to *innovate properly*; or that we ought to be as cautious of altering *their* Text, as we would That of the *sacred Writings*.[4]

Theobald, indeed, goes on to claim that even in the case of scripture there are many thousands of various readings, and that, had Bentley's edition of the New Testament been completed, it would have shown that there were a great many more such variants than had been thought.[5] There is more than a simple sneer at Pope's Catholicism at stake in the description of his abhorrence of innovation as superstitious: it echoes that tradition of advocacy for scriptural textual criticism as the legacy of the Reformation which we saw exemplified earlier in Francis Hare's defence of Bentley's works.[6] Equally significantly, Theobald regards Pope's reluctance to intrude his conjectures into the text as an evasion of the professional task upon which he has embarked: 'FOR my own part, I don't know whether I am mistaken in Judgment, but I have always thought, that whenever a *Gentleman* and a *Scholar* turns *Editor* of any Book, he at the same Time commences *Critick* upon his *Author*'.[7] An editor is consequently bound to employ all possible helps to restoring the text to sense in a way which Pope, the gentleman of letters turned occasional minute critic, may consider pedantic or unnecessary.

Theobald wishes to argue that it is not the disinterested gentleman alone, but any qualified person, who may edit Shakespeare. He emphasizes the similarities between Shakespearian and classical scholarship: 'As *SHAKESPEARE* stands, or at least ought to stand, in the Nature of a Classic Writer, and indeed, he is corrupt enough to pass for one of the oldest Stamp, every one, who has a Talent and Ability this Way, is at liberty to make his Comments and Emendations upon him.'[8] Shakespeare's ambiguously canonical status prompts conclusions strik-

---

[4] Lewis Theobald, *Shakespeare Restored* (London, 1726; repr. 1971), p. iv.
[5] Ibid.   [6] See above, Ch. 1, s. 3.
[7] Theobald, *Shakespeare Restored*, p. v.   [8] Ibid.

ingly different from Pope's as to who should be entrusted with the super-vision of his text. Theobald's challenge to Pope's notion of the fit editor, however, is one which operates within the limits of a consensus. An analogy which Theobald draws with the medical profession indicates as much:

CERTAINLY, that Physician would be reckon'd a very unserviceable Member in the Republick, as well as a bad Friend to himself, who would not venture to prescribe to a Patient, because not absolutely sure to cure his Distemper: As, on the other hand, he would be accounted a Man of very indifferent Morals, if he rashly tamper'd with the Health and Constitution of his Fellow-Creature, and was bold to try Conclusions only for private Information.[9]

Theobald's point is not that professional expertise, proceeding according to interested ends, could never threaten the nation's citizens: clearly professional knowledge can be abused in the pursuit of private gain. But his willingness to regard the analogy as a fair one indicates that he does not regard this professional status as a disqualification in itself. Indeed, the analogy carries the further implication that professionalism is a necessary quality of the textual critic: it is a rash patient who submits him or herself to the prescriptions of an amateur doctor.

Whilst Theobald's 'Introduction' to *Shakespeare Restored* shows him determined to question Pope's animus against professionals, he does not explicitly challenge Pope's characterization of the players as the particular professionals responsible for the corruption of Shakespeare's text. Much of Theobald's introduction and book, after all, is concerned to widen, rather than restrict, the area on which 'good Sense' may be licensed to comment, and his reluctance voluntarily to remove possible explanations for textual corruption is therefore hardly surprising. But he does give some important (if implicit) indications that he is reluctant to join Pope in identifying what is purely theatrical with what is low or corrupt. *Shakespeare Restored* is dedicated to John Rich, with whom Theobald had collaborated on many pantomimes.[10] Theobald also draws attention to Rich's intention of erecting a monument to Shakespeare.[11] More signifi-cantly, he is occasionally prepared to adduce early eighteenth-century stage practice in support of a criticism of Pope's text. Apparently on metrical grounds, Pope omits the words 'lost, lost' from the lines

[9] Ibid., p. iv.   [10] See R. F. Jones, *Lewis Theobald* (New York, 1919), 24–30.
[11] Theobald, *Shakespeare Restored*, 'Dedication'. For Rich's intention to erect a monu-ment, and the subsequent history of the project, see Morris Brownell, *Alexander Pope and the Arts of Georgian England* (Oxford, 1978), 354–6.

> . . . your Father lost a Father,
> That Father lost, lost his . . .[12]

Theobald objects not only that 'all the editions that I have met with, old and modern' include the words omitted by Pope, but also that 'so, I know, the Players to this Day constantly repeat it'.[13] The words 'to this Day' suggest that the players' delivery of the line may bear witness to Elizabethan stage practice and may carry authority for this reason.

Theobald's examination of the text displays fidelity to the techniques developed over more than two centuries of humanist textual criticism of the classics and most famously deployed, in early eighteenth-century England, by Richard Bentley. Where Pope is reluctant to draw attention to the arguments by which he arrives at his readings, Theobald is delighted to do so. One of Pope's most startling emendations in his text of *Hamlet* is to the passage in which Hamlet compares a cloud to three entirely different beasts and secures Polonius's assent to all three comparisons. Pope's copy-text, Rowe's third edition of 1714, reads thus (following the Folio tradition):

> *Ham*. Methinks it is like a *Wezel*.
> *Pol*. It is back'd like a *Wezel*.[14]

Pope emends this to:

> *Ham*. Methinks it is like an *Ouzle*.
> *Pol*. It is black like an *Ouzle*.

He appends the note: 'An *Ouzle* or *Blackbird*: it has been printed by mistake a *Weesel*, which is not black.'[15] Here are concealed several stages of reasoning which Pope finds it superfluous to explain to the reader. Firstly, the reading 'back'd' which appears in all the Folios, and also in the oldest Quarto then available (as 'backt'), has been emended to read 'black'. The only copies reading thus are the later Quartos printed in 1611, 1622, and 1637, and the substantially adapted 'Players' Quartos', the first of which was printed in 1676.[16] Nor does Pope in any way indicate that the copies are at variance over the word, despite the protestations of his preface. Presumably Pope dislikes the conversion of the noun 'back' into a verb, and hence opts for the alternative 'black'. This, however, produces

---

[12] Quoted from Pope's copy-text, *1714*, vi. 310; Pope's alteration can be found in *1723–5*, vi. 354.

[13] *Shakespeare Restored*, 13.   [14] *1714*, vi. 360.   [15] *1723–5*, vi. 416.

[16] Hinman, p. 777, l. 2251; Allen and Muir 640; Furness 272; *1637*, sig. H2ʳ; *1676*, 49; *The Tragedy of Hamlet, Prince of Denmark* (London, 1703; repr. 1969), 46; *Hamlet, Prince of Denmark: A Tragedy* (London, 1718; repr. 1969), 62.

a phantasmal black weasel, which must immediately be regularized into a blackbird, on the authority of no copies whatever. Here lies a further stage of silent reasoning: 'Wezel' is similar enough to 'Ouzle' to have been a mistake for it, and so the emendation is one which may justifiably be made.

Each of these steps is in 1725 familiar from classical philology. What is ungrammatical (here the substantive verb) must be corrected, if possible by finding an alternative reading in the available codices; if no satisfactory reading can be found in the copies, an emendation for which the reading in the copies could plausibly have been a mistake is preferable to one bearing no literal relation to any attested reading. Pope's preface explains his method of placing commas and stars against passages and scenes of which he approves as a device to avoid critical ostentation: 'This seems to me a shorter and less ostentatious method of performing the better half of Criticism (namely the pointing out an Author's excellencies) than to fill a whole paper with citations of fine passages'.[17] Evidently Pope's scruples attach equally to ostentation in general criticism's less distinguished 'minute' or 'verbal' counterpart. Pope's aesthetic of annotation is clearly akin, perhaps directly indebted, to Addisonian and anti-Bentleian objections to the accretion of information useless to the general reader.[18] We might compare this aesthetic of annotation with Pope's praise of Shakespeare's power over our passions: 'Yet all along, there is seen no labour, no pains to raise them; no preparation to guide our guess to the effect, or be perceiv'd to lead toward it'.[19] The intrusion of the professional labour of the textual critic on to the page would constitute, Pope's silence about his arguments for emendation implies, as great an obstacle to our passion or pleasure as the poetical labourings of a playwright. Theobald's discussion of the same passage is by no means one of his most extensive criticisms of Pope's text; it none the less indicates how different is his idea of the interest of the textual critic's reasonings to the reader:

I am afraid his Reasoning, that *it has been printed by* Mistake *a* Weesel, *because a* Weesel *is not* black,—will not be altogether so incontestible; when we come to see that the Second Edition in *Folio*, and several other of the Copies have a *various Reading*, in which there is not the least Intimation of *Blackness*.[20]

The point here is not that Pope concealed dubious reasonings in order to arrive at a text more satisfactory to himself but that Pope concealed what

[17] Alexander Pope, *The Prose Works*, ed. Norman Ault and Rosemary Cowler (2 vols., Oxford, 1936–86), ii. 25.
[18] See above, Ch. 1. [19] Pope, *Prose Works*, ii. 14.
[20] *Shakespeare Restored*, 97.

were, in the context of contemporary scholarship, a perfectly acceptable set of reasonings because of his dislike of the ostentatious display of specialist or minute critical labour.[21] Theobald, by contrast, is eager to display his own bibliographical work.[22]

Whereas Pope, in his evaluation of the relative authority of the Quartos and of the First Folio, had characterized literal criticism as the province of those incompetent to adjudicate more general matters, Theobald is prepared to dwell at length upon literal questions and upon the literal proximity of such conjectures as he ventures to already attested readings. His discussion of the following passage from Pope's text offers an example:

> . . . So loving to my Mother,
> That he permitted not the winds of Heav'n
> Visit her face too roughly . . .[23]

Here Theobald recognizes that the reading 'permitted not' derives from the 'Modern' acting editions.[24] He replaces it with 'let e'en', a reading whose advantage over Pope's, as he is at pains to point out, is its closeness to the incomprehensible First and Second Folio reading 'beteene': 'I am verily perswaded, our Author's Words were so very like it, that it is only a Corruption from the Mistake of a single Letter, and two Words getting too close together. See, how easy a Change restores you the Poet's own Words and Meaning.'[25] Theobald offers, not only a reading close to the attested one, but also a conjectural history of error for the reading of the first two Folios. Similarly, when he finds a main verb wanting in Pope's text of Hamlet's long warning to Horatio and Marcellus not to intimate that they know the reason for his 'antick disposition', and proposes to supply one by altering 'To note' to 'denote', he emphasizes the literal proximity of the new reading to the old: 'This small Change of two Letters not only gives us a *Verb* that makes the whole Tenour of the Speech clear and intelligible; but a *Verb* too, that carries the very Force and Sense which we before wanted in this Place.'[26]

Other passages in Theobald's book are even more open in their display of diligence: no less than eighteen parallel passages are adduced to a passage in Pope's Act 1, scene 2, to demonstrate Shakespeare's linguistic habit of turning nouns into verbs.[27] This instance of editorial labour is

[21] Indeed, Theobald's own text of *Hamlet* subsequently reverted to Pope's reading: *1733*, vii. 305.

[22] Theobald refers to the Second Folio because, as Peter Seary has demonstrated, he did not have access to a copy of the First Folio until May 1729: Seary, *Lewis Theobald and the Editing of Shakespeare* (Oxford, 1990), 234.

[23] Ibid. 19.   [24] Ibid.   [25] Ibid.   [26] Ibid. 59.   [27] Ibid. 8–11.

especially significant: it indicates to what extent a thorough application of the canons of contemporary classical philology must further obstruct the prospect, already perforce qualified in Pope's edition, of regarding Shakespeare's failures to meet early eighteenth-century standards of correct grammar, lexicon, and taste as instances of removable corruption. The stricture on Shakespeare's habit of turning nouns into verbs as being, simply, ungrammatical, which is implicit in Pope's substitution of 'black' for 'back'd', is replaced by an explicit argument of Theobald's which is to have important implications for the future of both textual criticism and lexicography. 'It is a Licence in our Poet, of his own Authority, to coin new *Verbs* both out of *Substantives* and *Adjectives*'.[28] The method of adducing parallel passages from an author's work as evidence of that author's linguistic habits, first developed by the classical scholar J. C. Scaliger,[29] supports the positive claim that a given author makes his or her own standards of linguistic correctness and that these cannot subsequently be imposed. Theobald here rejects linguistic obsolescence as a sufficient ground for emendation. He notes that, in the passage discussed, the lines 'Giving to you no further personal power | To business with the king . . .' have been emended to read 'Giving to you no further personal power | OF TREATY with the king . . .'. 'This is a Reading adopted, and of a modern Stamp, as I take it; either from Want of Understanding the Poet's genuine Words, or on a Supposition of their being too stiff and obsolete.'[30] Theobald goes on to explain that apparent obsolescence is of no account if it can be shown to be an habitual feature of a writer's language. Just as Scaliger's work was instrumental in the growth of a detailed awareness of how the classical languages had developed historically, so Theobald's work represents one of the first steps towards an understanding that the criteria of correctness by which English syntax and lexicon are to be judged may be historically variable.[31]

We saw earlier that Theobald's challenge to Pope's idea of the fit textual critic took place within the framework of a consensus that professional interests, too narrowly pursued, might represent a threat to the public weal. Theobald's own aspirations to assist in the improvement of the language (quoted at the beginning of this chapter) are, accordingly, only

---

[28] Ibid. 8.

[29] See, for an example, Anthony Grafton, *Joseph Scaliger: A Study in the History of Classical Scholarship* (Oxford, 1983), 193.

[30] Theobald, *Shakespeare Restored*, 7.

[31] Most commentators, however, now gloss 'To business' as 'For business' rather than as an infinitive: see *Hamlet*, ed. Harold Jenkins (London, 1982), 181, and *Hamlet*, ed. G. R. Hibbard (Oxford, 1987), 156.

qualified, not entirely blocked, by his interest in the procedures of classical philology. His ability to employ such procedures selectively emerges in his discussion of the following passage, quoted here from Pope's first edition:

> . . . What may this mean?
> That thou dead coarse again in compleat steel
> Revisit'st thus the glimpses of the moon,
> Making night hideous? and we fools of nature,
> So horridly to shake our disposition . . .[32]

Theobald here objects to (amongst other things) the reading 'we', on the grounds that the pronoun should be in the accusative case: as it stands, the text 'is not *English*'. Given Theobald's attack in his 'Introduction' upon an unreflective submission to textual authority, it is not startling to find him arguing that 'the Countenance of all the printed Copies' is to be overridden here.[33] What is more surprising is his readiness to override the evidence of parallel instances from Shakespeare's work in which the nominative appears where contemporary taste would require an accusative, evidence to which Theobald himself draws attention: 'I must not, however, dissemble, that there are a few Passages more in our Poet, where I have observ'd the *Nominative* of *Pronouns* is used, tho' Grammar requires the *Accusative*.'[34] Theobald goes on to deal with the difficulty by arguing that, in each of the instances which he cites, the pronoun should be emended so as to become an accusative.

The contrast between Theobald's procedure here, and that which he follows in the case of substantive verbs, is striking. But it should not be taken simply as evidence of methodological inconsistency on Theobald's part. After quoting the four parallel passages, Theobald implicitly indicates his awareness of this contrast by explaining why the earlier argument that Shakespeare may issue his own linguistic license should not apply in this case:

It may be alledged from these Instances, and some few more that might be gather'd, that this was a Liberty which *SHAKESPEARE* purposely gave himself, and that therefore it is not an Error of the Copies. Be this, as it will; if *Grammar* and the *Idiom* of the Tongue be directly against it, we have sufficient Warrant to make him *now*, at least, speak true *English*.[35]

---

[32] *1723–5*, vi. 366.   [33] Theobald, *Shakespeare Restored*, 39, 40.
[34] Ibid. 40.   [35] Ibid. 41.

Theobald regards himself as obliged to present such evidence as he knows of even where it does not support his case. Despite his failure to follow his procedure to a conclusion consistent with his earlier use of it, his sense of philological responsibility nevertheless has important consequences here: it forces Theobald to admit that in this case what he is doing cannot be regarded as a restoration of the text from corruption, but must rather be thought of as a direct improvement of it. Theobald's professional canons of scholarly conduct, where they do not entirely prevent the polite improvement of Shakespeare's language, nevertheless present such improvement for what it is, rather than as the rescue, from corruption by illiterates, of an originally correct poet.

The project of settling English by using the classical languages as a model, and of guaranteeing it by an appeal to canonical texts was, then, necessarily compromised precisely by the application of methods developed in the study of Greek and Latin texts to the study of English ones. Pope has his place in the growth of a historical understanding of the language from this compromise (it is after all an implicit recognition of the mutability of a language and its texts to attempt to prepare a critical edition of an English author at all). But the significance of Theobald's explicit discussion of such matters is that it renders the compromise tenable only with difficulty and makes for a clear distinction between historical study of the language and gentlemanly improvements of it. The development of such an English philology is too easily thought of as an organic or inevitable process. Pope's subsequent presentation of Theobald as the first hero of the *Dunciad*, and thus not merely as a vulgar writer, but as the enemy of legitimate culture in general, shows it to have been more akin to a struggle, and one in which wider issues than mere personal pride were at stake.

2

Although *Shakespeare Restored* is by far the best known attack upon the account of Shakespeare's text and of the best ways of editing it given in the preface to Pope's edition, it was not the only substantial contemporary response. In 1729 there appeared *An Answer to Mr. Pope's Preface to Shakespear. In a Letter to a Friend. Being a Vindication of the Old Actors who were the Publishers and performers of that Author's Plays.* The pamphlet is signed on the title-page 'By a stroling PLAYER', and, at the end, 'Anti-

Scriblerus Histrionicus'. It has been almost entirely overlooked by historians of Shakespeare's text.[36] Like *Shakespeare Restored*, *An Answer* wishes to dispute the implication of Pope's preface that only the disinterested gentleman is a fit editor of Shakespeare's text; and like Theobald's book it dissents from Pope only within the limits of a consensus. The 'stroling Player' does not deny that Shakespeare's text is extremely corrupt, but questions Pope's history of that corruption. *An Answer* is prepared to concede that low illiterates may have been responsible for the apparent faults in Shakespeare's English, but not that the Elizabethan actors were such illiterates, nor that their professional interestedness as actors disqualified them as guardians of Shakespeare's text. Where a polemic against the underlying assumptions of Pope's theory of editing led *Shakespeare Restored* to a more fully historical understanding of the idea of linguistic correctness, the parallel polemic by the 'stroling Player' in defence of the competence of professional Elizabethan players as actors and editors of Shakespeare's plays leads him to give an historical account of the conditions under which Shakespeare's texts were produced.

The 'stroling Player' begins by summarizing Pope's arguments so as to emphasize their common basis in Pope's hostility to theatrical influences upon Shakespeare's text:

thus they ['Blunders'] lie on *Shakespear's Judgment* as a Player, who was *the Poet*; on *Hemings* and *Condell's Ignorance* as Players, who were the old *Publishers*; and on the *Illiteracy* of all *his* and *their* contemporary Brethren, who were only the *Actors* and *Performers*; and every one else (even *Prompters* and *Partwriters*, &c,) that had any the least Concern *in the Playhouse*.[37]

An Answer attempts to show that the Elizabethan and Jacobean actors were by no means classically unlearned, let alone the barely literate creatures for whom Pope takes them. Much of the pamphlet is given over to an 'Alphabetical List' of celebrated actors of Shakespeare's time, together with testimonies as to their social and moral respectability: Jacobean plaudits for the philanthropy of the well-to-do Edward Alleyn are quoted,[38] the works of several actor-playwrights are listed,[39] and William Kemp is referred to as 'the only celebrated *Comedian* of those Days, who

---

[36] The exception is Brian Vickers, who reprints substantial selections in *Shakespeare: The Critical Heritage* (London, 1974), ii. 449–57, and draws attention to the importance of the work for the history of Shakespearian textual criticism. For a discussion of the authorship of *An Answer*, see App. 1.

[37] *An Answer to Mr. Pope's Preface to Shakespear . . . By a stroling Player* (London, 1729), 4.

[38] Ibid. 16–18.   [39] Ibid. 22 (Field); 26 (Heywood).

is certainly known to be without the Advantage of a liberal Education'.[40] Such evidence is adduced in order to undermine Pope's contention that Elizabethan and Jacobean actors are not to be compared with their supposedly politer successors. The remark that, whereas eighteenth-century actors sit at the Lord's table, their predecessors 'were led into the Buttery by the Steward' is ironically recapitulated and extended: 'They had no Comfort of polite Conversation! Nor had they any further *Taste of Life or Letters*, than what they cou'd pick up over a Pot of Beer, with their unthinking *Brethren*, in the *Inns*, where they play'd, or in taking a sparing Bottle of my Lord's Wine, *in the Buttery, with his* very learned *Steward*.'[41]

But the 'stroling Player' does not limit himself to arguing that the players were in fact more socially respectable than had been allowed by Pope. *An Answer* attacks the notion of disinterestedness itself which shapes Pope's account. Taking up Pope's own sartorial simile, he insists that the playwright is no more likely to be disinterested than the actor:

the Difference of Judgment between the Poet and the Player, is no more than betwixt one Taylor who cuts out the Cloth according to Rule and Measure, and t'other that makes it up, and fits it to the Body, according to that cutting out. So that both here can be reckon'd no more than Taylors in Judgment as to what is Graceful; and if this were to stand for an Argument, the Poets wou'd be deem'd, of their own Works, no better Judges than the Players. But I see no Necessity for decrying either of their Judgments in this Case; and therefore think it as utterly unreasonable to call *Shakespear*'s Judgment in Question as an Author, because he was an Actor, as to degrade Mr. *Pope*'s Capacity as a Poet because he is *Pope* the Editor.[42]

The 'Player' first collapses the attempt to distinguish between the disinterested dramatist and the professional player: both writers and players sought and seek to content their audience and are therefore equally interested. For the 'Player', there is no need for playwrights to be disinterested, and just as tailors can be relied upon to supply satisfactory clothing, so poets and players will provide satisfactory plays. His final point neatly exploits the complexities of Pope's position as a paid literary labourer who nevertheless implies that responsible writing (and editing) must be disinterested. Pope's attitude towards the actors is later, accordingly, regarded not as the expression of a disinterested distaste for the interested but merely as the result of inter-professional rivalry, 'a general Emulation of Professions, and the Envy of clashing Functions'.[43] The

---

[40] Ibid. 34.   [41] Ibid. 12.   [42] Ibid. 5–6.   [43] Ibid. 44.

'stroling Player' proceeds to give an account of the players' impact on the text which contrasts strongly with Pope's. Whereas Pope cites Hamlet's instructions to the player not to speak more than is set down for him as evidence of the prevalence of interpolation in Elizabethan playhouses, and argues that many such interpolations appear in the First Folio, the 'Player' uses it to argue that when actors did interpolate non-authorial material ''twas utterly condemn'd and exploded'.[44] The 'Player' concedes that interpolations may occasionally have taken place, but argues that they would not have found their way into print. Similarly, he dissents from Pope's related argument that the players were also responsible for the omission of those passages which appeared in Quarto texts but not in the First Folio: ''tis reasonable to think, that what ever Scenes are lopp'd off, and neglected, even to this Day, in the Representation, were then, and are now serv'd so, from some traditional Foundation and Authority from *Shakespear*'.[45]

Given that the 'Player' does not wish to dispute that there are many 'Mistakes'[46] in Shakespeare's text, however, it is incumbent upon him to provide an alternative history of its corruption to that given by Pope. The history which he gives is one which relies on a conjectural reconstruction of the economics of Elizabethan theatrical publishing. The 'Player' uses a quotation from Heywood to argue that plays became the property of the company for which they were written rather than remaining that of the author, and, further, that 'it was then thought against the peculiar Profit of the *Houses*, to have the Plays abroad in the World, and a main Point of Policy to preserve them from the Press'.[47] He goes on to argue, more explicitly than Pope, that, consequently, we cannot think of Shakespeare as having 'publish'd any one Play himself, or even corrected it for the Press, or [*sic*] was any one *Edition* printed from his own original Manu-script';[48] instead, he suggests, 'it is rational to think, that the meaner Class of Printers (who were not under such Restraints and Laws against Pyracies of the Press, which are now in Force) did exhibit surreptitious Copies, taken by the Ear, or by other fraudulent Means'.[49] The particular economic circumstances of the Quartos' publication, rather than the ig-norant interestedness of the players, are here taken to be responsible for the defects which (the 'Player' admits) are to be found in the Quarto texts. Moreover, these economic circumstances are taken as historically vari-

---

[44] *An Answer to Mr. Pope's Preface to Shakespear . . . By a stroling Player* (London, 1729), 23.

[45] Ibid. 14–15.   [46] Ibid. 28.   [47] Ibid. 29.

[48] Ibid. 31.   [49] Ibid. 30.

able: publishing before the advent of even the limited protection of copyright brought by the 1709 Act[50] entails a different relationship between author and text in which there is no reason to expect the author to have overseen publication. The 'Player' presses this point home with a striking bibliographical argument against publishers' claims to the contrary: the claim of the 1599 Quarto of *Henry IV Part 1* to have been 'Newly corrected' by Shakespeare, he points out, is simply reprinted on the title-page of each successive Quarto until that of 1622, 'Six Years after his Death'.[51]

The refusal by the 'Player' to allow theatrical interestedness as a source of error also extends to his account of the conditions of production of the Folio text and his defence of the editorial conduct of the actor-editors, Hemings and Condell. His respect for their work has already been implicitly demonstrated by the way in which his account of the Quartos echoes the reference in their address 'To the great Variety of Readers' to 'stolne, and surreptitious copies':[52] his attempt to defend them leads him to give what was to remain for many years the most detailed account of the likely varieties of copy for that volume. Four categories of copy are distinguished: 'TRUE MANUSCRIPTS', 'FALSE TRANSCRIPTS', 'INCORRECT FIRST COPIES', and 'SOME PRINTED PLAYS'.[53] None of these categories of copy, the 'Player' argues, would be entirely reliable. The term 'true manuscripts' is used not to refer to a pre-theatrical document accurately representing final authorial intentions, but to describe a company prompt-book in which Shakespeare's own corrections would from time to time have been inserted and whose margins would have carried additional theatrical information as to entries of characters and preparation of properties: 'all which were troublesome to the Press, and caused several Absurdities'.[54] The second category, of 'false transcripts' belonging to companies other than Hemings's and Condell's, would have been liable to all these 'Accidents' as well as to errors of the copyists. By 'Incorrect first copies' the 'Player' understands copies 'of some *other* of *his Plays*, that were not in *general Acting*, but only subsisted for the *Run*, and receiv'd not the Success to be the *Stock Plays*';[55] as a result, the 'Player' suggests, what might now be called the 'foul papers' for those plays would only be available in fragmentary form. The 'Player' has already argued that his final category of copy, the already published Quartos, was itself

---

[50] For the limited nature of the protection, see John Feather, 'The Publishers and the Pirates: British Copyright Law in Theory and Practice, 1710–1755', *Publishing History*, 22 (1987), 5–32.

[51] *An Answer*, 30.   [52] Hinman 7.   [53] *An Answer*, 32–3.

[54] Ibid. 32.   [55] Ibid. 33.

subject to still more radical forms of corruption than were the first three categories.

The 'Player' concludes from his examination of the copy for the Quartos and for the First Folio that 'the Trash of these Plays cannot be imputed to them [the players] in gross, for being his Actors; nor can we charge these *two Men* further than as Tradesmen and *Publishers*, and as *Proprietors* only of these *purchas'd Copies*.'[56] Like *Shakespeare Restored, An Answer* challenges the notion of gentlemanly disinterestedness only within the limits of a consensus. The conclusion indicates the limits of this challenge to Pope's history of the text. Although the pamphleteer wishes to refute the argument that the interestedness of the players was responsible for the 'Trash' in Shakespeare's text, he does not wish to dispute that the text contains such trash, nor to admit that any of it may be Shakespeare's responsibility. Indeed, he is willing on occasion to countenance the possibility that the meanness of those producing the text, as well as the difficult circumstances of its production, may be responsible for some of its faults. At the close of *An Answer*, the 'Player' quotes what he describes as the 'notoriously false spelt' epitaph of Shakespeare at Stratford, and treats it as a further instance of the fate of Shakespeare's writings:

in Regard of his own Epitaph above (if that were his Writing, as the Report goes it was) the false Spelling, and irregular Mixture of Characters could not be his, but the Workman's. No more could the *Orthographical* Faults in all his Plays be His, or his *Editors*, but meerly the Blunders of the Mechanics, and the Imperfections of the Press.[57]

Here spelling is seen in a resolutely unhistorical perspective, as though it had always been standardized, and standardized in accordance with eighteenth-century usage. In this passage, the material difference between Pope and the 'Player' lies principally in the variety of illiterate culprits blamed for the corruption of Shakespeare's text: the 'Player' attempts to protect actors and actor-editors by the introduction of 'Mechanics'. Nevertheless his insistence, against Pope, that interestedness is no disqualification for the custodianship of Shakespeare's text has, as in the case of Theobald's *Shakespeare Restored*, important consequences for the development of Shakespearian textual criticism. Whereas Theobald's defence of the fitness of the specialist critic to edit Shakespeare's text had led him to a historicist approach to Shakespeare's language, this parallel assault on Pope's account of the low and interested players produces the beginnings of a systematic bibliographical evaluation, conceived of as a

---

[56] *An Answer*, 34.   [57] Ibid. 47–8.

preliminary to conjectural emendation or the eclectic quarrying of copies for new readings.

3

Although Pope made some small changes to the text of his preface for the second appearance of his edition in 1728 (including a remark that Theobald's *Double Falshood* could not be admitted to the canon)[58] he made no direct response to Theobald's criticisms there; the text itself was changed in some places as a result of the criticisms, but Theobald's part in prompting the change was rarely acknowledged.[59] Pope's reticence is understandable; many of Theobald's points would have been difficult to answer or would have involved admissions of substantial editorial negligence or oversight on Pope's part. Nevertheless, *Shakespeare Restored* formed too lengthy and persuasive an attack on Pope's reputation to be allowed to go unanswered. As James McLaverty has pointed out, the introduction of Theobald as the hero of the *Dunciad* had the advantage of offering an opportunity for a direct assault upon Theobald's supposed pedantry, whilst not exciting any expectation of direct answers to particular criticisms of Pope's text.[60] The publication of *The Dunciad, Variorum* in 1729 offered Pope a flexible armoury not only against Theobald, but against minute criticism in general: the ironic textual and critical notes which first appeared in that text allowed particular verbal-critical techniques to be satirically mimicked without exposing Pope himself to any charge of pedantry.

The *Dunciad*'s attack upon verbal criticism both expanded and modified the arguments of Pope's preface to Shakespeare against narrowly literal criticism. It developed the social argument against literal critics as low and interested, which had first been suggested in the preface, so as to apply these strictures to contemporary textual critics. But it also presented a new and complementary case, that the vanity of the (apparently disinterested) amateur critic could present an equally serious threat to the

[58] Pope, *Prose Works*, ii. 23.

[59] Arthur Sherbo, *The Birth of Shakespeare Studies* (East Lansing, Mich., 1986), 3. For some of the changes, see *1728*, viii. 216 (misnumbered '316': 'canon' for 'cannon'); 269 ('mother's admiration' for 'mother-admiration'); 320 ('Bear Hamlet like a soldier to the stage' for 'off the stage'). There is no record of any response on Pope's part to the pamphlet by the 'stroling Player'.

[60] James McLaverty, 'The Mode of Existence of Literary Works of Art: The Case of the *Dunciad Variorum*', *Studies in Bibliography*, 37 (1984), 82–103 (p. 101).

text of an established author. The progress of textual criticism thus becomes a special instance of the collusion of the low and the high, the venal and the vain, in that destruction of any just or disinterested culture which is the poem's principal action. Textual criticism is represented as antithetical to public virtue: its presumption is taken as akin to, and complicit with, that of 'arbitrary' government. This double-sided social criticism is closely paralleled by a twofold epistemological criticism of the methods of textual critics. On the one hand, they mangle the text by an excessively literal and partial approach to it which fails to keep the whole text sufficiently in mind; on the other, they provide inadequate texts because they are unthinkingly reverent towards textual authority. The *Dunciad*'s social and methodological polemic upon verbal criticism exemplify the complexity of the poem's response to the epistemological and scientific revolutions of the later seventeenth and early eighteenth centuries and towards their cultural and political implications. The *Dunciad* attacks those who would take those revolutions as the occasion for an indiscriminate professionalization, democratization, and secularization of culture. But the poem is not therefore willing simply to recommend a return to earlier patterns of thought. Instead, the notion of Dulness is used to satirize unreflective enlighteners and unreflective opponents of enlightenment alike—and is used, in places, subtly to identify the two. The idea of a consensus amongst the genuinely disinterested who might elude either classification remains for the most part only an ironically and implicitly articulated one.[61]

In the 1735 folio edition of the second volume of Pope's *Works* first appeared a black-letter 'DECLARATION' 'By the AUTHOR'. It launches a general attack on verbal critics as such, characterizing them as

certain *Haberdashers of Points and Particles*, being instigated by the Spirit of *Pride*, and assuming to themselves the name of *Critics* and *Restorers* [who] have taken upon them to adulterate the common and current sense of our *Glorious Ancestors, Poets of this Realm*, by clipping, coining, defacing the images, mixing their own base allay, or otherwise falsifying the same; which they publish, utter, and vend as genuine: The said haberdashers having no right thereto, as neither heirs, executors, administrators, assigns, or *in any sort related* to such Poets, to all or any of them . . .[62]

---

[61] Reference is generally made here to the 4-book version first appearing in 1743. Although Cibber there replaces Theobald as the hero, verbal criticism remains a centrally important target; Pope links his two heroes by bestowing a copy of Theobald's Shakespeare on Cibber (*Dunciad*, ed. Sutherland, p. 279).

[62] *Dunciad*, ed. Sutherland, p. 237.

This goes on to prohibit any future alteration of the text of 'this our *Dunciad*, beginning with the word *Books*, and ending with the words *buries all*'.[63] It is no accident that this mock-proclamation should first have appeared in the 1735 folio, since in the distribution of that volume to booksellers Pope acted for the first time as his own wholesaler, and thereby became effectively his own publisher as well: this (albeit light-hearted) declaration of the author's right to control the details of his text appeared at a time when Pope was exercising an increasingly tight economic control over the production and distribution of his works.[64] The comparison of verbal critics to haberdashers, of course, is reminiscent of the comparison of the players to tailors in Pope's preface to his edition of Shakespeare. But whereas the tailor's wares are staples, the haberdasher is a dealer in luxury or accessory materials. These are no ordinary haberdashers, moreover, for they are animated not by a need to earn a crust, but by 'the spirit of Pride'. This charge introduces into Pope's account of verbal criticism a double bind which is to become critical for future representations of editors and their labours. The characterization of verbal critics as haberdashers who have vainly moved above their professional station has the same force as the suggestion of the prefatory 'Letter to the Publisher' that hack writers should find themselves a proper job: 'I question not but such authors are poor, and heartily wish the objection were removed by any honest livelihood.'[65] If the hacks write for money, they mistakenly confuse writing with a mere employment; if they do not write for money, they must be impelled by vanity. This represents an important modification to the argument of Pope's preface to Shakespeare that players and editors were rendered unfit custodians of Shakespeare's text by their low interestedness. If vanity also disqualifies the verbal critic, the gentleman-amateur may be as unsuitable an editor as the specialist.

This double emphasis is strikingly pursued in *The New Dunciad* (1742), later to become Book IV of the four-book version. Taken together, its attacks on verbal criticism provide a more complex account of the activity than that prefacing Pope's edition of Shakespeare. The portrayal of literal critics, as low, interested, and partially sighted, given in Pope's history of Shakespeare's text is now applied to contemporary textual critics. The oration of Aristarchus (Bentley) to the goddess Dulness offers the most substantial satire of this kind in the text of the poem itself:

[63] Ibid. 238.
[64] See James McLaverty, 'Lawton Gilliver, Pope's Bookseller', *Studies in Bibliography*, 32 (1979), 101–24 (p. 109).
[65] *Dunciad*, ed. Sutherland, p. 15.

> Let Freind affect to speak as Terence spoke,
> And Alsop never but like Horace joke:
> For me, what Virgil, Pliny may deny,
> Manilius or Solinus shall supply:
> For Attic Phrase in Plato let them seek,
> I poach in Suidas for unlicens'd Greek.
> In ancient Sense if any needs will deal,
> Be sure I give them Fragments, not a Meal;
> What Gellius or Stobaeus hash'd before,
> Or chew'd by blind old Scholiasts o'er and o'er.
> The critic Eye, that microscope of Wit,
> Sees hairs and pores, examines bit by bit:
> How parts relate to parts, or they to whole,
> The body's harmony, the beaming soul,
> Are things which Kuster, Burman, Wasse shall see,
> When Man's whole frame is obvious to a *Flea*.[66]

The last six lines of this passage offer an epistemological criticism of the method of verbal critics: their focus on detached minute details makes it impossible for them to comprehend any sense or quality which resides in the relationship between such details. But the passage offers not only an intellectual but also a social criticism of partially sighted pedants. The alleged blindness of 'Slashing Bentley'[67] to literary quality and preference for obscure authors and expressions puts him beyond the pale of gentlemanly learning, beyond a knowledge of those authors, such as Terence and Horace, Pliny and Virgil, an acquaintance with whose works the gentleman of sound taste might reasonably be expected to have. He is a literary poacher whose learning is not his legitimate cultural inheritance but stolen and 'unlicens'd': verbal criticism, as in the latter half of the 'Declaration', is characterized as a depredation upon inheritable cultural property. Thus far, the tenor of this criticism is a familiar one, not only from Pope's preface to his edition (like Hemings and Condell, Bentley and Theobald are too narrow in comprehension to become adequate general critics) but also from David Mallet's *Of Verbal Criticism*, dedicated to Pope and reiterating many of his charges against Theobald and Bentley,[68]

[66] *Dunciad*, ed. Sutherland, pp. 364–6.

[67] The epithet is applied to him both in the 'Epistle to Arbuthnot', l. 164, and in the epistle 'To Augustus', l. 104. Alexander Pope, *Imitations of Horace*, ed. John Butt (London, 1939), 108, 203.

[68] See e.g. David Mallet, *Of Verbal Criticism. An Epistle to Mr. Pope. Occasioned by Theobald's Shakespear, and Bentley's Milton* (London, 1733), 13. Mallet's description of verbal critics as 'To narrow cares in narrow space confin'd' refers neatly both to the verbal critic's marginal position on the printed page and to his cramped garret.

and from Pope's own much earlier discussion of the 'verbal Critick' in the *Essay on Criticism*:

> As Men of Breeding, sometimes Men of Wit,
> T'avoid *great Errors*, must the *less* commit,
> Neglect the Rules each *Verbal Critick* lays,
> For *not* to know some Trifles, is a Praise.
> Most Criticks, fond of some subservient Art,
> Still make the *Whole* depend upon a *Part*,
> They talk of *Principles*, but Notions prize,
> And All to one lov'd Folly Sacrifice.[69]

The partial criticism condemned here, like Bentley's later incursions, is not only 'trifling' but comparable to an offence against 'Breeding'. The way in which a merely partial methodological perspective is accompanied by a merely partial social or political perspective is further emphasized by Warburton, in a note to this passage which appeared in his 1751 edition of Pope's *Works*: 'This general misconduct much recommends that maxim in good Poetry and Politics, *to give a principal attention to the whole*; . . . Ignorance, and the false lights of the Passions, confound and dazzle us; we stop short, and before we get to a *Whole*, take up with some *Part*, which from thence becomes our Favourite.'[70] To dwell upon a part at the expense of the whole is, Warburton suggests, a political as well as literary error which is not an innocent mistake but the consequence of misleading 'Passions'.

The *Dunciad*'s account of scholars in the mass might lead us to think that they are castigated from a position which endorses without qualification the scientific and epistemological revolution of the seventeenth century. The herd of scholars from which Bentley is made to emerge amount to 'A hundred head of Aristotle's friends'; a note makes it clear that a continued adherence to Aristotelian natural philosophy, in the face of Cartesian and Newtonian advances, is here satirized.[71] The scholars are similarly taken to task for attempting to ban Locke's *Essay concerning Human Understanding*.[72] However, the 'critic eye' is a 'microscope of Wit' which fails not by a refusal to examine evidence but by the overly minute and specialized pursuit of it; and Pope's simile of the flea unable to perceive the shape of the human body it sits upon recalls Berkeley's fable upon the limits to the competence of human reason in *The Guardian*, no.

[69] Alexander Pope, *Pastoral Poetry and An Essay on Criticism*, ed. E. Audra and A. Williams (London, 1961), 269–70.
[70] William Warburton, ed., *The Works of Alexander Pope* (9 vols., London, 1751), i. 169.
[71] *Dunciad*, ed. Sutherland, p. 360   [72] Ibid. 361 n.

70.[73] Verbal criticism falls short on the one hand by failing to explain anything, and on the other (as Dulness in general is later said to do) by 'explain[ing] a thing till all men doubt it'.[74] It is both scholastically resistant to enlightenment and unreflectively zealous for it.

Both aspects of this characterization are exemplified in mock textual-critical notes to the poem. Many of the notes show critics mangling the text because their narrowly literal or partial readings fail to take account of qualities of tone which depend upon an understanding of the context for a given passage. Thus 'Bentley' is made to emend Pope's 'Cibberian forehead' to 'Cerberian forehead' on the excessively literal grounds that the hero has been described as 'modest Cibber' and that his poet, therefore, cannot have intended a reference to Cibber's big-headedness.[75] Similarly, 'Theobald' is made to substitute 'glow' for 'burn' by application of his favoured parallel-passage technique and thereby to spoil the intended gibe that Cibber suffered from venereal disease.[76] On the other hand 'Scriblerus' offers his opinion on the momentous question of whether the work's title should be spelt *Dunciad*, *Dunceiad*, or *Dunceiade*, in terms which ridicule a slavish adherence to 'Authority':

One *E* therefore in this case is right, and two *E*'s wrong; yet upon the whole I shall follow the Manuscript, and print it without any *E* at all, mov'd thereto by Authority, at all times with Criticks equal if not superior to Reason. In which method of proceeding, I can never enough praise my very good Friend, the exact Mr. *Tho. Hearne*, who, if any word occur which to him and all mankind is evidently wrong, yet keeps he it in the Text with due reverence, and only remarks in the Margin, *sic M.S.*[77]

This ridicule of laborious and mechanical conservatism in verbal criticism itself follows hard upon an attack on textual innovation. 'Bentley' congratulates those responsible for the inscription on Shakespeare's monument in Westminster Abbey 'for exhibiting on the same Monument the first Specimen of an *Edition* of an author in *Marble*; where (as may be seen on comparing the Tomb with the Book) in the space of five lines, two Words and a whole Verse are changed'. He goes on to advertise the forthcoming '*Total new Shakespear*, at the Clarendon press' (Hanmer's edition).[78] The question to which criticism of the text addresses itself is

---

[73] *The Guardian*, ed. John Calhoun Stephens (Lexington, Mass., 1982), 261–2.
[74] *Dunciad*, ed. Sutherland, p. 369, l. 251.   [75] Ibid. 286 n.
[76] Ibid. 122 n.–123 n.   [77] Ibid. 59 n.
[78] *Dunciad*, ed. Sutherland, p. 267 n. Pope was part of the committee responsible for the erection of the monument but not for the inscription from *The Tempest*, which was only added in 1741. Brownell, *Pope and the Arts*, 356.

here begged in advance: the (unspecified) 'Book' is presumed already to record the authentic text of the passage in question.

The introduction of Hanmer, and the fact that it is 'Bentley' who is made to puff his work, indicates the way in which the double intellectual dullness of textual criticism is matched by the duplicity of its social affiliations. Bentley, the textual critic as professional literary poacher, finds his counterpart in Hanmer, the textual critic as courtly amateur:

> There mov'd Montalto with superior air;
> His stretch'd-out arm display'd a Volume fair;
> Courtiers and Patriots in two ranks divide,
> Thro' both he pass'd, and bow'd from side to side.[79]

Montalto's display of his edition is set up as a royal or aristocratic progress. The gloss on this 'decent Knight' implies that his edition of Shakespeare is a vanity publication: Hanmer is described as 'An eminent person, who was about to publish a very pompous Edition of a great Author, *at his own expence*.'[80] When Pope visited Oxford in October 1743 he reported back to Warburton on Hanmer's edition, then being printed at the Clarendon press: 'all I could see was one Sheet, in the Margins of which were no various readings or marks for any references of any sort, but a fine well-printed Text that covered a multitude of Faults'.[81] The implication of Pope's letter that more attention has been paid to the quality of the printing than to textual accuracy is pursued in the *Dunciad*: Montalto's pride is inspired by the physical size and beauty of his 'volume fair', which is shortly afterwards described as 'pompous' and 'pond'rous', rather than by the quality of the text it contains. Although Warburton, who helped to write the note on Hanmer, had quarrelled with him in 1739 over his plans for the edition, the significance of the passage is not merely biographical.[82] It represents a recognition that not only professional interestedness, but also leisured dilettantism, may produce inadequate editors and verbal critics. Indeed, a league between the venal and the vain is suggested by the description of those whose minions 'lug the pond'rous volume off in state' as 'Apollo's May'r and Aldermen': the Vice-Chancellor and heads of Oxford colleges are taken as the literary equivalents of the mercantile dignitaries of the City of London so often ridiculed in the *Dunciad*.[83]

---

[79] *Dunciad*, pp. 351–2, ll. 105–8.   [80] Ibid. 352 n.

[81] *The Correspondence of Alexander Pope*, ed. George Sherburn (5 vols., Oxford, 1956), iv. 475.

[82] A. W. Evans, *Warburton and the Warburtonians* (London, 1932), ch. 9.

[83] *Dunciad*, ed. Sutherland, p. 353, ll. 117, 116.

This touches on one of the poem's central emphases: the birth of a cultural alliance between courtly ignorance and professional hackery which threatens to eclipse the possibility of disinterested thought altogether. Such an alliance is already referred to in the poem's second line: Theobald (Cibber in the four-book version) is announced as the man who brings 'The Smithfield Muses to the ear of Kings'.[84] The prefatory prose piece 'Martinus Scriblerus of the Poem' makes the establishment of such an alliance the unifying principle of the poem, whose '*one, great* and *remarkable* action' is 'the Removal of the Imperial seat of Dulness from the City to the polite world'.[85] This removal raises the spectre of the mob gone literate and invading the world of polite letters: Martinus notes that our poet 'lived in those days, when (after providence had permitted the Invention of Printing as a scourge for the Sins of the learned) Paper also became so cheap, and printers so numerous, that a deluge of authors cover'd the land'.[86] Such a view of printing instances once more the *Dunciad*'s ambivalence towards mass enlightenment: printing is a salutary scourge to scholasticism, but also threatens indiscriminately to democratize culture.

The notion of an alliance between professional and courtly dullness is further developed in Book IV, where the hypertrophied learning of the pedants finds its counterpart in the intellectual vacuity of the fops by whom they are displaced. In particular, the collapse of any disinterested culture is taken to be the result of the mutual assistance of pedants and arbitrary rulers, the former always disposed to turn learning into a mere matter of words, the latter only too happy to see intellectuals expend their energy on matters so harmless to the government:

> For sure if Dulness sees a grateful Day,
> 'Tis in the shade of Arbitrary Sway.[87]

A long note by Warburton discusses the operation of this alliance in the field of verbal criticism. Commenting upon Dulness's desire for the return of a pedant King (such as James I), he remarks that:

Nothing can be juster than the observation here insinuated, that no branch of Learning thrives well under Arbitrary government but *Verbal*. The reasons are evident. It is unsafe under such Governments to cultivate the study of things of importance. Besides, when men have lost their public virtue, they naturally delight in trifles, if their private morals secure them from being vicious. Hence so great a Cloud of Scholiasts and Grammarians so soon overspread the Learning of Greece and Rome, when once those famous Communities had lost their Liberties.

[84] *Dunciad*, p. 267, l. 2; p. 59, l. 2.   [85] Ibid. 50–1.
[86] Ibid. 49.   [87] Ibid. 359–60.

Another reason is the *encouragement* which arbitrary governments give to the study of *words*, in order to busy and amuse active genius's, who might otherwise prove troublesome and inquisitive. So when Cardinal Richelieu had destroyed the poor remains of his Country's liberties, and made the supreme Court of Parliament merely *ministerial*, he instituted the *French Academy*.[88]

The constituent parts of this attack upon verbal critics are not original to Warburton. The idea that the provision of an academy to regulate language bears the hallmarks of arbitrary government had earlier been put forward by Oldmixon in his response to Swift's proposal for a British Academy; the project for an academy and 'absolute' government were still linked for Johnson towards the end of the century.[89] James I's reputation for pedantry (or for scholarship) was a familiar topic not only for those who ridiculed minute learning but also for those who wished to defend it. In 1720 Pope's archetypal scholarly drudge, Thomas Hearne, had presented what could almost be taken for a mirror image of Warburton's diagnosis: arguing that 'Men of Abilities should joyn together, and large Stipends should be settled upon them, that they may unanimously conspire to carry on the Interest of Learning', Hearne went on to remark that 'It was therefore a glorious and religious work of K. James I who within the space of one year caused Churches to be planted through all Scotland, the Highlands and the Borders, worth 30 l. a year a peece'.[90] But what is striking in Warburton's note is that verbal learning is not merely promoted from above by arbitrary governors, but is also eagerly pursued by citizens who are content to confine themselves to private life. Arbitrary governments encourage philology so as to distract citizens from political questions, but Warburton is also keen to emphasize the point that those who 'have lost their public virtue' in any case need little encouragement to devote themselves to the minutiae of language. Once more verbal criticism is presented as an activity by which private vanity or interest replaces public disinterestedness; now, however, this happens with the encouragement of an arbitrary (or, in the case of Britain, a potentially arbitrary) government.

This conception of the relationship between arbitrary government and verbal criticism, whilst most lucidly put by Pope and Warburton, had

---

[88] Ibid. 358 n.

[89] John Oldmixon, *Reflections on Dr. Swift's Letter to the Earl of Oxford* (London, 1712; repr. Menston, 1969), 6–7. Johnson, *Prefaces, Biographical and Critical*, iv. 'Life of Roscommon', 11–12.

[90] Thomas Hearne, ed., *A Collection of Curious Discourses* (Oxford, 1720), pp. xxvii–xxviii. For a hostile portrayal of James I's as a reign of pedantry, see Robert Dodsley, *A Select Collection of Old Plays* (12 vols., London, 1744), i, p. xix.

already been strikingly implied in other work of the 1730s. A political poem which early in the decade extended Pope's excoriation of dullness from the world of letters to the political sphere, Paul Whitehead's *The State Dunces*, included the lines

> Amidst the *mighty Dull*, behold how great
> An *Appius* swells the *Tibbald* of the State;[91]

Theobald, of course, was associated with Walpole ('Appius') because Walpole had subscribed to Theobald's edition of Shakespeare[92] and because Theobald had dedicated his *Orestes* to Walpole in 1731.[93] Here Theobald's pedantry, taken as firmly established by the *Dunciad*, can be used as a metaphor for Walpole's arbitrary government. A more celebrated analogy to Pope and Warburton's presentation of an alliance between pedantry and arbitrary government is provided by Samuel Johnson's early pamphlet *Marmor Norfolciense* (1739). Johnson's pedant narrator proposes that the interpretation of the prophecy which he has discovered

is not to be expected from any single hand, but from the joint enquiries and united labours of a numerous society of able men, instituted by authority, selected with great discernment and impartiality, and supported at the charge of the nation . . . I humbly propose that thirty of the most distinguish'd genius be chosen for this employment, half from the Inns of Court, and half from the army, and be incorporated into a society for five years, under the name of the *Society of Commentators*.[94]

Once more (as in the early years of the century) the idea of a learned academy is associated with that of a standing army, a perennial target of early eighteenth-century critics of supposedly arbitrary government.[95] The pedant narrator goes on to suggest that such commentators would be of great use in censoring publications and stage-plays: here the link made by the *Dunciad* between minute verbal learning and the methods of a potentially arbitrary government is anticipated.

The implicit and explicit treatment of verbal criticism in the *Dunciad*, and especially in that book of it which Warburton most significantly influenced is, then, intellectually and politically more complex, and often more contradictory, than that in the preface to Pope's edition of

[91] Paul Whitehead, *The State Dunces* (London, 1733), 4.   [92] *1733*, i, p. [lxxxv].
[93] R. F. Jones, *Lewis Theobald* (London, 1919), 148.
[94] Samuel Johnson, *Political Writings*, ed. Donald J. Greene (New Haven, Conn., 1977), 45.
[95] See J. G. A. Pocock, *The Machiavellian Moment* (Princeton, NJ, 1975).

Shakespeare. The central implication of Theobald's attack on the preface, that Pope's approach to textual criticism is a superstitiously pre-enlightened one, is countered by the charge that a merely professional or secular enlightenment is itself mystifying: 'Sworn Foe to Myst'ry, yet divinely dark'.[96] The poem does not deny, however, the servility and unreason implicit in the scholastic tutelage which enlightenment seeks to do away with. Indeed, it seeks to present these apparent sworn foes as intimate friends. By a parallel logic, arbitrary dictation over culture and society combines with private interests to close off the political and cultural space in which the exercise of a disinterested 'public virtue' might be possible. The possibility that verbal criticism might ever have constituted, or might in future constitute, part of such a space, remains in this poem an extremely remote one. But four years after the publication of the fourth book which he had himself so strongly influenced, Warburton himself was to appear before the public as a verbal critic. His edition of Shakespeare and its preface were the occasion for a strenuous attempt to reclaim English philology as a proper sphere for the exercise of public virtue.

[96] *Dunciad*, ed. Sutherland, p. 385, l. 460.

4

Lewis Theobald:
The Specialist Scholar and
his Textual-Critical Practice

DESPITE POPE'S hostility and Johnson's disparagement, Theobald's own edition of Shakespeare has received almost unanimous approval from subsequent, and especially from twentieth-century, historians of the subject. T. R. Lounsbury's lengthy defence of Theobald in *The First Editors of Shakespeare* (1906) was followed by R. F. Jones's *Lewis Theobald* (1919), which first made clear the extent of Theobald's indebtedness to the textual-critical techniques of classical philology; later, more general surveys of the field, such as those of McKerrow and Brian Vickers, have singled out Theobald's criticism for praise; most recently, Peter Seary's full-length book has made an extensive and thoroughly documented case for Theobald's attention to Shakespearian bibliography and (more problematically) for his anticipation of the methods and tenets of the New Bibliographers.[1] What most of these accounts have in common is their tendency to present Theobald's work as an isolated instance of enlightened editing in a largely unenlightened discipline. It is evident that much of Theobald's theory and practice mark a significant break with the previous course of criticism of English texts. But his theory and practice of editing are more closely related to early debates about the fit editor of vernacular texts and the status of textual criticism, and to the editorial procedure of his predecessors, than such characterizations allow. Seary, although he has rightly drawn attention to the influence of polemics against excessive scholarly minuteness upon

---

[1] R. B. McKerrow, 'The Treatment of Shakespeare's Text by his Earlier Editors (1709–1768)', in P. Alexander, ed., *Studies in Shakespeare: British Academy Lectures* (Oxford, 1964), 103–31 (pp. 123–6); Brian Vickers, *Shakespeare: The Critical Heritage, 1692–1733* (London, 1974), 'Introduction', 16–19; Peter Seary, *Lewis Theobald and the Editing of Shakespeare* (Oxford, 1990).

Theobald, regards this influence as having operated on his theory, rather than on his practice, of Shakespearian editing. It is responsible, Seary believes, for the omission from Theobald's preface of more detailed information about the nature of copy for the pre-1623 Quartos and the First Folio.[2]

This judgement overestimates the effect of ridicule on Theobald's statements about textual criticism and underestimates its effect on his practice. As we saw in Chapters 1 and 3, the view of Pope, Mallet, and many others that textual criticism was in itself an excessively narrow activity, whilst prevalent, was not universally shared. Theobald, although anxious about the possibility of being seen as a merely minute, and merely professional, editor, nevertheless continued to defend the idea of the properly qualified and diligent editor argued for in *Shakespeare Restored*; his editorial practice represented a less systematic break with previous editorial practice than has sometimes been argued, and the complex climate of debate about scholarly minuteness is reflected in some of the contradictions of Theobald's editorial practice. It should be possible in the light of the following discussion to understand the persistence in Theobald's work of a received text and of 'corrections' of Shakespeare's syntax and lexicon: not as an accident, but as an indication of the limits to Theobald's ability or willingness to make a systematic break with the culture of textual criticism within which he worked.

I

Theobald's declaration in a letter to Warburton that 'The whole affair of *Prolegomena*, I have determined to soften into *Preface*' certainly suggests a shift from an intention to provide a statement of editorial principles to a less methodological document, and one less likely to appear unnecessarily pedantic to its readers.[3] But Theobald's preface continues to argue for the idea of the qualified specialist editor first adumbrated in *Shakespeare Restored*. Although advertisements of scholarly diligence had become a stock target for Scriblerian satire, Theobald continues to emphasize the extent of his own labours: his assertion that 'I have thought it my Duty, in the first place, by a diligent and laborious Collation to take in the Assistances of all the older Copies' stands at the head of his account of his

---

[2] Seary, *Theobald*, 142.
[3] John Nichols, *Illustrations of the Literary History of the Eighteenth Century* (8 vols., London, 1817–58; repr. New York, 1966), ii. 621.

own editorial conduct.[4] Conversely, the indolence of earlier editors is lamented: Rowe might have been an adequate editor 'had but his Industry been equal to his Talents';[5] an unreflective conservatism in cases where the text cries out for conjectural emendation is regarded as 'an indolent Absurdity'.[6] Theobald's commentary frequently has occasion to rebuke the earlier editors for what he takes to be their laziness generally in failing to collate Elizabethan and Jacobean copies.[7] Theobald is determined enough about the importance of diligence to feel able ('Tho' I should be convicted of Pedantry by some . . .') to append a series of emendations of unrelated Greek texts to the end of his preface.[8] Indeed, the emendations are offered for the explicit purpose of demonstrating that mockers of 'Literal Criticism' such as Mallet have failed to appreciate its real usefulness.[9]

Equally importantly, Theobald's preface insists that textual criticism is a specialist task for which expert qualifications are requisite, a task which is misunderstood by 'Those who cannot form a true Judgment of its Effects, nor can penetrate into its Causes'.[10] Theobald explicitly declares that his conception of this task is modelled on classical philology and that a central claim of his text of Shakespeare to public attention is that he has 'ventur'd on a Labour, that is the first Assay of the kind on any modern Author whatsoever'.[11] A principal part of the edition's value is thus argued to rest in the procedures of its editor. Indeed, Theobald goes so far as to claim that textual criticism is a methodologically consistent 'Art' with its own body of 'Rules'. The short list of rules given are familiar from classical philology: all available copies are to be collated; the author is to be compared with his sources; no emendations are to be made on purely stylistic grounds; emendations allowed into the text are to involve no more than 'the Addition or Alteration of a Letter or two', except where parallel passages from Shakespeare's own work can be brought in evidence.[12]

Theobald's declaration that his text of Shakespeare represents the first real attempt to apply the principles of classical philology to a vernacular text is the more striking in view of the fact that the greatest classical scholar and textual critic of the age had edited *Paradise Lost* shortly before Theobald's Shakespeare appeared. Theobald in fact took pains

---

[4] *1733*, i, p. xlii.   [5] Ibid., p. xxxv.   [6] Ibid., p. xlii.
[7] See, for examples, *1733*, i. 171; vi. 369.   [8] *1733*, i, pp. liii–lxii.
[9] Ibid., p. lii.   [10] Ibid., p. xlii.   [11] Ibid., p. xxxix.
[12] Ibid., p. xli: 'those Errors which have been transmitted down thro' a Series of incorrect Editions'.

inoffensively to distance his own efforts from Richard Bentley's foray into vernacular editing;[13] and the furore over Bentley's Milton is an important context for Theobald's scholarly self-presentation. In Bentley's text, an emendatory imagination which, in his work on Latin and Greek texts, had been restrained by a strong interest in palaeography and historical linguistics, was given startlingly free rein. Bentley's methodological fiction—that an incompetent transcriber-editor had ruined a text which the blind poet had had no opportunity properly to correct—afforded ample opportunities for what in some instances appeared to be wholesale rewriting, based on aesthetic objections to particular passages of Milton's verse. A study of a surviving copy of the 1720 text of Milton with manuscript annotations by Bentley suggests that 'rewriting' is scarcely too strong a term, for the annotations are evidence of a mind in creative ferment. At vi. 239, the word 'Resounded' has been underlined, and in the margin we find:

~~shook~~
~~stood~~ trembling
stood shrank[14]

In Bentley's own edition 'Stood trembling' is in the event offered as the replacement for 'Resounding, and'.[15] Similarly at viii. 508 in his copy of the 1720 text Bentley underlines 'I follow'd her: she what was Honour knew' and conjures up three alternatives, '~~courted~~', 'made Address', and 'I her cares't [sic]';[16] his own 1732 text offers a more radical revision still: 'I made addresses: she what's Honour knew'.[17] All Bentley's proposed improvements were confined to the margin, yet, given this degree of creativity, the widespread ridicule which they attracted is scarcely surprising; as late as 1743 Bentley's text was still being mocked in James Bramston's The Crooked Six-Pence, a parodic Bentleian 'edition' of John Philips's own Miltonic parody The Splendid Shilling.[18] However, as R. G.

[13] 1733, p. xxix.
[14] The Poetical Works of Mr. John Milton (London, 1720); Cambridge University Library copy, shelfmark Adv. b. 52. 12, p. 239.
[15] Milton's Paradise Lost: A New Edition, ed. Richard Bentley (London, 1732), 189.
[16] Cambridge University Library Adv. b. 52. 12, p. 332.
[17] Paradise Lost, ed. Bentley, 259. For a further instance see John K. Hale, 'Notes on Richard Bentley's Edition of Paradise Lost', Milton Quarterly, 18 (Mar. 1984), 46–50 (p. 48).
[18] James Bramston, The Crooked Six-Pence: With a Learned Preface Found Among Some Papers bearing Date the same Year in which Paradise Lost was publish'd by the Late Dr. Bently (London, 1743).

Moyles has pointed out, it was Bentley's intervention alone which directed renewed attention to the textual problems of *Paradise Lost* and led, via the work of such figures as Pearce, the Richardsons, and Peck, to Thomas Newton's 1749 text, the first to abandon the use of the latest previous edition to provide copy.[19] The immediate response to Bentley concentrated its fire on his emendatory licence. *Milton Restor'd, and Bentley Depos'd*, a hostile pamphlet purporting to be by Swift, objected despite its epigraph ('Sing Heav'nly Muse, from Pedantry be free')[20] not, as the Christ Church Wits had done, to any excessively minute labour, but to the lack of such labour:

To regulate the Work of a deceased Author from various Readings in Manuscripts or printed Copies is a laborious, but useful Undertaking: But this way of restoring, *i.e.* interpolating by Guess, is so sacralegious an Intrusion, that, as it had its rise, so it is to be hoped it will have its Fall with you.[21]

The interest in collation and assessment of earlier copies which was a feature of Bentley's classical philology was deserted in favour of emendatory display in his text of Milton. Bentley claimed in his 1732 text that no manuscript of the poem existed, although, as John K. Hale remarks, 'he himself had entered variant readings from the still extant manuscript of Book One into his copy of Tickell['s edition]'.[22] Zachary Pearce was also to comment on Bentley's limited interest in bibliographical matters; his *Review of the Text* pointed out that Bentley had mistaken the date of the first edition of *Paradise Lost*.[23]

The controversy over Bentley's first and only attempt at vernacular editing aroused scarcely less interest than its earlier counterpart, the dispute over Pope's text of Shakespeare. The edition was much discussed in contemporary periodicals, and Bentley's emendations were thought of sufficient interest to merit their publication in a separate volume.[24] Theobald's own advertised attention to bibliographical matters thus

---

[19] R. G. Moyles, *The Text of* 'Paradise Lost*': A Study in Editorial Procedure* (Toronto, 1985), 59. The contributions in question are Zachary Pearce, *A Review of the Text of Milton's Paradise Lost* (London, 1732); Jonathan Richardson, father and son, *Explanatory Notes and Remarks on Milton's Paradise Lost* (London, 1734; repr. New York, 1970); Francis Peck, *New Memoirs of the Life and Poetical Works of Mr. John Milton* (London, 1740); *Paradise Lost*, ed. Thomas Newton, 2nd edn. (2 vols., London, 1750).

[20] *Milton Restor'd, and Bentley Depos'd* (London, 1732), title-page.

[21] Ibid., pp. vii–viii.   [22] Hale, 'Notes', 49.

[23] Pearce, *Review of the Text*, p. vi.

[24] *Dr. Bentley's Emendations on the Twelve Books of Milton's Paradise Lost* (London, 1732); see Michael M. Cohen and Robert E. Bourdette, jun., 'Richard Bentley's Edition of *Paradise Lost* (1732): A Bibliography', *Milton Quarterly*, 14/2 (May 1980), 37–49.

allows him further to distinguish himself from the editorial procedures for which Bentley's Milton had become notorious. Theobald takes over in part the bibliographical theories put forward by the 'stroling Player' in *An Answer to Mr. Pope's Preface to Shakespear*, to suggest that it is not the generalized low interestedness of the players and player-editors but the material circumstances in which the texts were produced and transmitted that are responsible for their inadequacies. Like the 'Player', he suggests that many of the Quartos were surreptitiously published, whether from stenographic transcripts or individual parts,[25] although his account of the categories of Folio copy is less extensive than the author of *An Answer*'s.[26] Theobald also explains the current lamentable condition of the text as the accumulation of successive errors.[27] Such an explanation might lead us to expect an explicit discussion of the use by modern editors of a *textus receptus* for copy; but Theobald, significantly for his own practice, as we shall later see, is silent on this question.

Theobald is not prepared, however, to argue that textual criticism is an entirely self-justifying activity, or one whose justifications lie entirely in its contributions towards a historical understanding of language and culture. Just as the final defence of classical philology is that, by it, 'the Grammarians have been enabled to write infinitely better in that Art than even the preceding Grammarians, who wrote when those Tongues flourish'd as living Languages',[28] so the highest commendation of vernacular textual criticism is that

a Path might be chalk'd out, for abler Hands, by which to derive the same Advantages to our own Tongue; a Tongue which, tho' it wants none of the fundamental Qualities of an universal Language, yet as a *noble Writer* says, lisps and stammers as in its Cradle; and has produced little more towards its polishing than Complaints of its Barbarity.[29]

The aspiration to make an edition of Shakespeare a contribution towards the polishing of the language contrasts sharply with the historical understanding of language with which, as we have seen earlier, Theobald is especially concerned. Indeed, there are elsewhere indications that Theobald regarded the language as less Shakespearian in so far as it was more polished. Arguing that 'pray' should be emended to read 'prate' in a passage from Act V of *Coriolanus*, Theobald remarks (before appending a catalogue of Shakespearian uses of the word):

---

[25] *1733*, i, pp. xxxvii–xxxviii.   [26] Ibid., p. xxxviii.   [27] Ibid., p. xliii.
[28] Ibid., p. lxii.   [29] Ibid.

Prate, 'tis true, is a Term now ill-sounding to us, because it is taken only, as the Grammarians call it, *in malam partem*. Our Language was not so refin'd, tho' more masculine, in *Shakespeare*'s days; and therefore (notwithstanding the present suppos'd κακοφωνια,) when he is most serious, he frequently makes use of the Word.[30]

Such a note insists that the polishing or refining of the language would necessarily take place at the expense of a historical understanding of it. Theobald's determination (here) to judge Shakespeare's English by historically relative, rather than absolute, criteria necessarily contradicts the claims made in his preface for the public usefulness of his work as a contribution to the polishing of the language.

2

Far from being an external consideration, whose effects might be confined to Theobald's public characterization of his work, such a contradiction can be seen in Theobald's editorial practice itself. The extent to which this practice is influenced by the existing culture of opinion about textual criticism, rather than defined by systematic opposition to previous textual-critical theory and practice, is perhaps most clearly seen with respect to the crucial question of his choice of copy-text. As we saw earlier, the use of the most recent edited text (or *textus receptus*) for copy had been challenged by Bentley's proposals for his intended edition of the New Testament, and Theobald's own *Shakespeare Restored* had strongly supported Bentley's position against what he took to be Pope's hostility to it. Yet, as Richard Corballis has shown, Pope's duodecimo set of 1728 provided the copy-text for Theobald's own edition.[31] Although Theobald made many silent, as well as annotated, restorations of First Folio and early Quarto readings to his text, his choice of copy-text often allowed readings introduced by accident or design since 1623 to remain. The bluntness of this contradiction has recently prompted a startling solution: Peter Seary has suggested that Theobald was obliged by his publisher, Tonson, to take Pope's second edition as his copy-text, so that Tonson could reinforce his claim to copyright in Shakespeare's works.[32] The attractions of such an account are clear: it would explain not only

[30] *1733*, vi. 109.
[31] Richard Corballis, 'Copy-Text for Theobald's Shakespeare', *The Library*, 6th ser. 8 (1986), 156–9.
[32] Seary, 133–5.

Theobald's use of Pope's text for copy but also, as Seary points out, Theobald's failure to include in his edition certain plays which he at various points considers to be Shakespeare's work in whole or in part: *Locrine*, *Pericles*, *Two Noble Kinsmen*, and *Double Falshood*.[33]

Seary's argument falls well short of proving that Tonson insisted upon Theobald's use of Pope for his copy-text. The basis of Theobald's text in Pope's is nowhere advertised in Theobald's edition, for obvious reasons. Nor is it clear, in the absence of any such advertisement, how the use of Pope's text for copy could be presented to any court as strengthening Tonson's claims to his rights in the text: it is hard to imagine a magistrate sufficiently bored, insane, or malicious to have the texts collated with each other, or to hear such evidence were it presented. More importantly, even if we accept the hypothesis of Tonson's intervention, it is unlikely that Theobald would, if left to his own devices, have used early Quartos and the First Folio for copy. The evidence of his notes and bibliographical table shows that his attitude towards the received text, and towards questions of bibliographical authority in general, was an ambiguous one. On the one hand, the degree of attention given by Theobald to bibliographical authority distinguishes his edition from all previous attempts at English textual criticism. Seary shows that some of Theobald's notes indicate his awareness that certain plays in the First Folio were set up from Quarto copy;[34] and Theobald's metaphors for textual history lend support to the idea that he generally considered that history stemmatically rather than eclectically: 'Thus the whole Stream of the Copies, from the first downwards'[35] and 'a Blunder of Inadvertence, which has run thro' the whole Chain of Impressions'[36] are typical instances. Other notes provide fuller evidence of Theobald's critical attitude to the idea of a received text. A note on a passage from *The Merry Wives of Windsor* reiterates the insistence of *Shakespeare Restored* that a blind adherence to the received text is superstitiously unenlightened: in preferring the Quarto reading of 'Brook' as Ford's alias (in place of 'Broom' which had been retained in the text and on the stage since the First Folio), Theobald remarks that the theatrical successors to the First Folio player-editors '(like the old Priest, who had read *Mumpsimus* in his Breviary, instead of *Sumpsimus*, too long to think of altering it;) continue to this day to call him, Master *Broom*'.[37] A collation of Theobald's text of *Hamlet* with Pope's 1728 text does show that

---

[33] Ibid. 135.   [34] Ibid. 137–8.   [35] *1733*, i. 418.   [36] Ibid. iv. 413.

[37] Ibid. i. 248; see also e.g. vii. 42, where Theobald attacks Pope's supposed appeal to Rowe's authority in defence of Pope's own substitution of 'Aristotle' for 'graver sages' in *Troilus and Cressida*.

Theobald often silently emended his copy-text to restore a First Folio or early Quarto reading for no apparent reason other than to restore the best attested reading to the text.[38] On one occasion, indeed, Theobald goes so far in his insistence upon following the reading of the most authoritative text as to argue that all material given in the First Folio text should be reprinted, regardless of whether or not it can be considered to be Shakespeare's work. Discussing a passage (from Act V of *Cymbeline*) which Pope had entirely omitted from his text, Theobald insists upon its restoration, remarking that

All this intermediate Scene, from the Instant that *Posthumus* falls asleep to the *Exit* of the *Goaler* here, I could be as well content, as Mr. *Pope* is, should be left out. But as 'tis found in the earliest *Folio* Edition, tho' it should have been an Interpolation, and not of SHAKESPEARE's Writing, I did not think, I had any Authority to discard it.[39]

But there is also evidence to suggest that Theobald's view of the idea of a received text was intermittently, rather than systematically, critical. In particular, several of Theobald's annotations suggest that, in cases of indecision, the reading of the received text, rather than that of whichever copy has been evaluated as most authoritative, should be allowed to stand. In discussing the expression 'Masterless Passion' in Act IV of *The Merchant of Venice*, Theobald, having pointed out that the phrase was introduced by Rowe without any authority, nevertheless remarks that 'I have not disturb'd the Text'.[40] Here 'the' text in question is not that of the First Folio or of an early Quarto, but Pope's (following Rowe): Theobald on this occasion implies that deviations from the received text, rather than from that evaluated as most authoritative, are those which demand justification. A parallel implication is made when Theobald discusses a passage from *Othello*:

Let him command,
And to obey shall be in me Remorse,
What bloody Business ever.] Thus all the old Copies, to the manifest Depravation of the Poet's Sense. Mr. *Pope* has attempted an Emendation, but with his old Luck and Dexterity.
Not *to obey shall be in me Remorse,* &c.
I read, with the Change only of a single Letter;
Nor, *to obey, shall be in me Remorse,* &c.[41]

---

[38]   See, for examples, *1733*, vii. 297, 'And as my love is *siz'd*, my fear is so' (*1728*, viii. 265: 'fix'd'; Furness 246); 300, 'With Hecate's *ban* thrice blasted, thrice infected' (*1728*, viii. 267: 'bane'; Furness 257); 306, 'To keep those *many, many* Bodies safe, that live' (*1728*, viii. 271: 'many'; Furness 275).
[39]   *1733*, vi. 449.   [40]   Ibid. ii. 62.   [41]   Ibid. vii. 443–4.

Theobald advertises his use of the *ductus litterarum*, implying that his emendation is justified because it might plausibly have been mistaken for the supposedly corrupt reading given. However, this technique is of relevance only when the emended reading differs from that of an authoritative text by a single letter. Here, Theobald implies that changing only a single letter by comparison with the *received* text (described as an edition of no authority in Theobald's own bibliographical table)[42] lends probability to emendation. These are not moments typical of Theobald's textual criticism, but that they can occur at all suggests that Theobald's hostility to the idea of a *textus receptus* does not work systematically.

Theobald's own bibliographical table, and his use of the texts there listed, provides further evidence that his approach to bibliography was often eclectic rather than systematic. The First and Second Folios are listed together as 'EDITIONS *of Authority*' without any attempt to distinguish between them; likewise the 1597, 1598, and 1602 Quartos of *Richard III*, for example, are listed as of equal authority.[43] Moreover, Theobald introduces an intermediate category of 'EDITIONS *of middle Authority*' in which he places not only the Third Folio but a variety of mid-seventeenth-century Quartos published after Shakespeare's death. Seary's response to this difficulty, that 'his classification in his "Table" reflects primarily his sense of their [post-1623 texts'] importance to him when he was engaged in forming his collection'[44] does not explain why an editor with a supposedly well-developed understanding of textual relationships between the various printed copies should publish such a generalized account of their relative authority. Nor is the whole story told when Seary remarks that, whatever the implications of Theobald's bibliographical table, he in practice uses post-1623 texts not as authoritative, but only as helpful sources of possible emendations. Theobald does indeed often use post-1623 texts in this way, and Seary quotes several instances as 'representative';[45] at one point Theobald goes out of his way to insist that an emendation of his which happens to coincide with the Fourth Folio reading has not been drawn from the 1685 text but is the editor's own work.[46] Yet counter-examples of the use of such texts as if they were authoritative are not lacking. Theobald's text of *Henry VIII*, for which only a Folio tradition exists, continually refers to the authority of 'All the Old Copies'.[47] Theobald will often cite the First and Second Folios together as if they are of equal value: 'The first *Folio*'s agree in

---

[42] Ibid. vii, 'A Table of the several Editions of Shakespeare's Plays, Collected by the Editor', sig. 2I4ʳ.

[43] Ibid., sig. 2H8ʳ; sigs 2I1ᵛ, 2I2ʳ.   [44] Seary, *Theobald*, 137.   [45] Ibid. 136–7.

[46] *1733*, vii. 309.   [47] See, for examples, *1733*, v. 57, 77.

would-woman . . .';[48] 'Thus the two first *Folio*'s, and all the other Impressions of any Authority, that I have seen, exhibit the Text: . . .'.[49] The authority of post-1623 Quartos is also occasionally brought to bear upon the text:

Another *Ship* of Venice
Hath seen a grievous Wreck, &c.] But no Ship, before this, has arriv'd, or brought any Account of the *Turkish* Fleet's Distress: How then can This be call'd *another* Ship? Oh, but The eldest *Quarto* has call'd it so; and, if there be a various Reading, Mr. *Pope* is pretty good at taking the wrong one. The two Elder *Folio*'s and the *Quarto* in 1630 read, as I have restored to the Text;
——A noble *Ship* of Venice.[50]

This is an instance of just the kind of generalized amassing, rather than systematic evaluation, of authorities which is implied by Theobald's bibliographical table. The 1630 Quarto of *Othello* is there listed as a text '*of middle Authority*': here its weight and that of the Second Folio are added on to that of the First Folio to outvote the First Quarto, regardless of the fact that neither post-1623 text is likely to furnish independent evidence of any authoritative reading.

An examination of Theobald's conception of the relationship between early Quartos and the First Folio text, as indicated by his textual-critical practice, raises further objections to the idea that Theobald was in possession of a coherent theory as to how to fix upon his copy-text, and was only prevented from doing so by Tonson's intervention. Although Seary argues that Theobald's 'faith in the 1604–5 Quarto' of *Hamlet* is 'very much in advance of his time',[51] any such faith would be surprising in the light of Theobald's remark about 'the Ignorance of the first Editors' of *Hamlet*,[52] and the idea of his devotion to the 1604–5 Quarto is not one consistently borne out by Theobald's text. Theobald does replace many Folio readings given by Pope with Quarto readings,[53] and includes in his text almost all the Quarto passages omitted from the First Folio.[54] But, in the first place, it is not clear either from the evidence of Theobald's bibliographical references in his commentary, or from the evidence of alterations which he made silently, how thoroughly Theobald had in fact collated the 1604–5 Quarto. It is clear that he must have consulted it upon occasion: defending his reading in the Player Queen's speech, for exam-

[48] See, for examples, *1733*, i. 171.   [49] Ibid. i. 30.   [50] Ibid. vii. 403–4.
[51] Seary, *Theobald*, 148.   [52] *1733*, vii. 306.
[53] See, for examples (deviations from Pope's text are italicized), *1733*, vii. 252 ('That *roots* itself in ease on *Lethe*'s wharf'; *1728*, viii. 228, 'rots'), 267 ('pity *'tis*, *'tis* true'; *1728*, viii. 240, 'it is'), 239 ('*Hast* ta'en with equal thanks'; *1728*, viii. 262, 'Hath').
[54] See App. 2.

ple, 'And as my love is siz'd, my fear is so' (for Pope's 'fix'd'), Theobald correctly notes that 'the Quarto of 1605 reads, *ciz'd* . . .'.[55] On many other occasions, when Theobald's commentary refers to the Quartos it becomes clear that he has not consulted the Quarto of 1604–5. When discussing the notorious crux at the end of Hamlet's long speech immediately before the ghost's entry in Act 1, Theobald quotes the passage in question thus:

> ———*The Dram of* Ease
> *Doth all the noble Substance of* a Doubt
> *To his own Scandal.*[56]

The 1604–5 Quarto, however, reads 'the dram of eale':[57] the only texts listed in Theobald's bibliographical table which read as he quotes are the Quartos of 1611 and 1637, from one of which Theobald must here be quoting, whilst giving the impression that he is quoting from the earliest Quarto available.[58] Theobald's proposed emendation, 'the dram of Base', is certainly closer to the 1611 and 1637 reading than to the 1604–5 text. Further doubts as to the extent of Theobald's collation of the 1604–5 Quarto emerge later: Theobald replaces Pope's 'You laying *these slight sallies* on my son'[59] with 'these slight sullies' and notes that 'All the old Copies, which I have seen, read as I have reform'd the text.'[60] Yet the Quarto of 1604–5 in fact supports Pope's 'sallies'.[61] The implication is that Theobald has not seen or not consulted the 1604–5 text of this passage. Elsewhere Theobald appears to use the term 'elder' Quartos not to designate pre-First Folio Quartos, but all those before the performance texts beginning with the 1676 Quarto. The 'elder *Quarto's*' are said to read 'The time invests you' in Polonius's address to Laertes: this is the reading of all Quartos before 1676.[62]

On other occasions Theobald's commentary can be still more misleading: replacing the line which Pope's text gives to Fortinbras, 'What feast is tow'rd in *thine eternal cell*' with 'thy infernal cell', Theobald comments: 'I have chose the Reading of the old *Quarto* Editions, *infernal*.'[63] In fact the first text to read 'infernal' is the 1637 Quarto.[64] Another example of a reading from a later performance text inserted as though quarried from the older Quartos is to be found in Theobald's text of Ophelia's report to Polonius:

---

[55] *1733*, vii. 297; Allen and Muir 638. [56] *1733*, vii. 248.
[57] Allen and Muir 622. [58] *1637*, sig. C2ᵛ. [59] *1728*, viii. 234.
[60] *1733*, vii. 260. [61] Allen and Muir 626; Furness 121.
[62] Furness 70; *1733*, vii. 244. [63] *1733*, vii. 366.
[64] Furness 455; but no copy of the 1637 Quarto was available to Furness: cf. *1637*, sig. N3ᵛ.

————*his Stockings* foul'd,
Ungarter'd, and down-gyved to his Ancle.] I have restored the Reading of the Elder
Quartos—*his Stockings* loose.—The Change, I suspect, was first from the Players,
who saw a Contradiction in his Stockings being *loose*, and yet *shackled* down at
Ancle. But they, in their Ignorance, blunder'd away our Author's Word, because
they did not understand it.
    Ungarter'd, and down-gyred,
i.e. turn'd down.[65]

The reading 'loose', although Theobald describes it as given by the 'Elder
Quartos' in fact appears in no text before the Quarto of 1676; 'foul'd', for
which Theobald provides a history of error, is not only the reading of the
First Folio (which Theobald here regards as the Players' edition) but also
(as 'fouled') of all Quartos before 1676.[66] Moreover, 'down-gyred', the
expression whose difficulty Theobald uses to explain this supposed error
on the part of the First Folio editors, appears not in the Quarto of 1604–
5, but only in subsequent Quartos.[67]

The evidence of Theobald's practice concerning silent departures from
his copy-text confirms the case against his supposed faith in the 1604–5
Quarto. There are no instances in which Theobald restores a reading to be
found only in that Quarto. But on several occasions he silently adopts a
reading whose earliest source is a later Quarto. Pope's 'A man may fish
with the worm that hath eat of a king, and eat of the fish . . .'[68] is abbrevi-
ated in Theobald's text to 'A man may fish with the worm that hath eat of
a king, eat of the fish', the earliest authority for which is the 1611 Quarto;[69]
the same situation applies in the case of Theobald's unnoted alteration of
'The cat will mew, and dog will have his day' to 'The cat will mew, a dog
will have his day'.[70] His silent alteration in Lucianus's speech, 'Confederate season, *and* no creature seeing' (for 'else') is based on the 1676 Quarto
alone.[71] It is clear that Theobald either often collated without consulting
the 1604–5 Quarto or (less probably) chose to ignore it in many instances
despite having collated it.

Moreover, leaving aside Theobald's treatment of texts in the Quarto
tradition, there are many occasions on which Quarto alternatives to Pope's
Folio readings are ignored,[72] as well as (more decisively) occasions on

[65] *1733*, vii. 261.
[66] Furness 125; Allen and Muir 626; Hinman, p. 767, l. 975; *1637*, sig. D3ʳ; *1676*, 24.
[67] *1733*, vii. 261.   [68] *1728*, viii. 284.   [69] *1733*, vii. 324; Furness 319.
[70] *1733*, vii. 353; Furness 411.   [71] *1733*, vii. 299; Furness 257; *1676*, 47.
[72] *1733*, vii. 251 ('Like quills upon the fretful porcupine'); Allen and Muir 623 ('fearefull
Porpentine').

which neglected Folio readings are preferred to Quarto readings already present in Pope's text, even where there are apparently no reasons for Theobald to prefer the Folio reading.[73] What this evidence shows is that Theobald's editorial theories and practices are in many respects still eclectic ones: as much material as possible from early Quartos and the First Folio is to be gathered and used to correct a text whose basis is Pope's second edition of 1728; decisions as to whether Quarto or Folio readings should have priority in disputed cases are often made on the basis of a variety of aesthetic or linguistic, rather than bibliographical, criteria. Accordingly, Theobald's assessments of the provenance of the pre-1623 Quartos and the First Folio are liable to vary with the circumstances in which these texts are discussed. In Theobald's preface, where he wishes to emphasize the importance of the editor's task, he draws upon the ideas about Quarto copy for the First Folio set out in the 'stroling Player's' *Answer to Mr. Pope's Preface to Shakespear*, in a manner calculated to heighten the reader's sense of these texts' unreliability: of the four categories of Quarto copy mentioned by the 'stroling Player',[74] Theobald mentions only the two least reliable, short-hand transcriptions from performances and printing from individual actors' parts.[75] Similarly, Theobald emphasizes that the First Folio was prepared by 'Players', and discusses the sorry consequences of this provenance in terms which owe more to Pope's feral Elizabethan stage than to the professional actors described by the 'stroling Player': 'Scenes were frequently transposed, and shuffled out of their true Place, to humour the Caprice or suppos'd Convenience of some particular Actor.'[76]

The bibliographical discussion in Theobald's preface serves the tactical purpose of indicating the need for a critical editor of the text, and Theobald's characterization of those responsible for the early Quartos and First Folio in his notes is often no less tactically chosen: where he wishes to restore or defend a First Folio reading, for example, that text is described simply as the 'old' or 'first' Folio;[77] but where a First Folio reading is to be replaced, Theobald often describes the First Folio as the players' edition.[78] Nor are players responsible only for false readings in the Folio:

---

[73] *1733*, vii. 260 ('You laying these slight *sullies* on my son'), 262 ('I'm sorry that with better *speed* and judgment'), 311 ('I took thee for thy *Betters*'), 338 ('first asking *your* pardon thereunto').

[74] *An Answer to Mr. Pope's Preface to Shakespear . . . By a stroling Player* (London, 1729), 32–3.

[75] *1733*, i, pp. xxxvii–xxxviii.   [76] Ibid., p. xxxviii.

[77] See, for an example, iv. 70.   [78] Ibid. v. 286; vii. 306.

they can also be called to account for mistakes in Quarto texts. Thus in *Hamlet* the description of Duke Gonzago and his wife as a 'King and Queen' in the stage direction instructing them to enter (which appears in the Quarto of 1604–5) is attributed to the actors: '*Regal* Coronets being at first order'd by the Poet for the *Duke* and *Dutchess*, the succeeding Players, who did not strictly observe the *Quality* of the Persons or *Circumstances* of the Story, mistook 'em for a King and Queen'.[79]

The players become a flexible source for a wide variety of histories of error corresponding to scribal histories of error in classical textual criticism. Thus they are liable not only to remove passages for their own convenience, as is suggested in the preface,[80] but also to replace difficult or unusual words by more familiar ones,[81] or to insert inauthentic readings by association with the immediate context.[82] Moreover, the failings of transcribers or compositors can also be used to provide histories of error, whether acting alone[83] or in spectacular concert with the players: in emending 'I shall sing it at her death' to 'I shall sing it after death' in Act 4 of *A Midsummer Night's Dream*, Theobald explains that

The Source of the Corruption of the Text is very obvious. The *f* in *after* being sunk by the vulgar Pronunciation, the Copyist might write it from the Sound,— *a'ter*; which the wise Editors not understanding, concluded, two Words were erroneously got together; so splitting them, and clapping in an *h*, produced the present Reading——*at her*.[84]

3

This last instance indicates how easily the use of hypothetical histories of theatrical and scribal error might return us to Pope's depiction of a largely gentlemanly poet corrupted by vulgar and interested players and editors; and the complexity and contradictions of Theobald's approach to bibliographical problems are indeed replicated in his approach to his stated aspiration to chalk out a path for the polishing of the English language. As can be seen in *Shakespeare Restored*, Theobald's concern (unprecedented in the criticism of English texts) for proper bibliographical justification for particular readings led him to insist that constructions rejected as ungrammatical were properly Shakespearian, and hence to imply that

[79] *1733*, vii. 295.   [80] Ibid. i, p. xxxviii.
[81] Ibid. i. 455 ('Approof').
[82] Ibid. ii. 95: 'As God *grant us Patience* immediately preceded, they thought, Heaven of Consequence must follow.'
[83] Ibid. iv. 38.   [84] Ibid. i. 133.

standards of linguistic correctness would necessarily be historically variable. Theobald's interest in the dependence of a polished language upon
settled texts of the authorities adduced in its support did not, accordingly,
generally lead him to the conclusion that archaic, provincial, or vulgar
words and constructions should be removed from the text of such authorities, but rather to believe that works of reference would need to incor-
porate such words and constructions. Thus a defence of a Shakespearian
metaphor against the charge of catachresis can lead Theobald to indicate
the inadequacies of current dictionaries: 'Tho' there may seem no Conso-
nance of Metaphors betwixt a *single Ten* and a *Deck*, the latter Word being
grown obsolete, and not acknowledg'd by our Dictionaries in the Sense
here required; yet *Deck*, in all our *Northern* Counties, is to this day used
to signify a *Pack* or *Stock* of Cards.'[85] This instance illustrates some of the
ambiguities at work in Theobald's ideas of the English language: although
the word 'deck' is 'to this day' used in the '*Northern* Counties', it is
nevertheless 'obsolete', since provincial usage alone is insufficient to justify its admission to the body of current English words.

But there is no suggestion that such allegedly obsolete language should
have no place in the text of a writer an edition of whose work is to
contribute to the polishing of the language. Indeed, Theobald's sense of
the priority of authoritative English texts over the works of reference
dependent on them leads him to restore and defend apparent archaisms of
lexicon and syntax throughout his edition. Thus '*sacring* bell' in *Henry
VIII* is restored (Pope had emended to 'scaring'), with the support of
parallel passages from Scot's *Discovery of Witchcraft* and *The Merry Devil
of Edmonton*.[86] Similarly, 'scotch'd' is restored to *Macbeth* in place of
'scorch'd', 'however the Generality of our Dictionaries happen to omit the
Word'.[87] Theobald is prepared not only to defend expressions which have
no support in early eighteenth-century usage, but even, on occasion, those
for which he can find no support in other Renaissance texts. Thus when
glossing 'Lunes' in *The Winter's Tale* Theobald admits that 'I have no
where, but in our Author, observ'd this Word adopted in our Tongue to
signify *Frenzy, Lunacy*'.[88] Although he here goes on to add the mitigating
circumstance that 'it is a Mode of Expression with the *French*', elsewhere
no collateral authority whatsoever is found necessary:

. . . as it is most frequent with our Author as well to coin Words, as to form their
Terminations *ad libitum*; he may have adopted *Stricture* here to signify *Strictness*;
as afterwards, in this very Play, he has introduced *prompture*, the Usage of which

[85] Ibid. iv. 379.   [86] Ibid. v. 64–5.   [87] Ibid. v. 425–6 (p. 426).
[88] Ibid. iii. 90.

Word I no where else remember in our Tongue; neither have we *promptura* or *prompture*, from the *Latin* or *French*, that I know of.[89]

Shakespeare's English is to be taken as self-licensing rather than as authorized by the usage of others, whether contemporary with Shakespeare or with the editor: Theobald's preparedness to admit as authentic a text found nowhere else in the language anticipates Johnson's provision in his *Plan of a Dictionary* for a special category of words appropriated to particular writers.[90]

Theobald's apparent determination to apply historical, rather than supposedly absolute, criteria of linguistic correctness is evident not only in his treatment of individual words, but also in his approach to Shakespeare's syntax. In restoring the double comparative 'more better' (emended away by Pope) to Act I of *The Tempest*, Theobald's refusal to judge early seventeenth-century grammar by early eighteenth-century rules is clear: 'This is the genuine Reading, which the last Editor has sophisticated, not observing, I suppose, how frequent it is with *Shakespeare*, and the other Writers of that Age, to add the *Termination* to Adjectives of the *comparative* and *superlative* Degrees, and at the same time prefix the *Signs* showing the Degrees.'[91] Other double comparatives and double superlatives removed by Pope are likewise restored to the text. Thus in *Henry VIII* Theobald reads 'there is no *English* Soul | More stronger to direct you than your self', whereas Pope had been prepared to incur some awkwardness in order to remove the double comparative: 'there is no English | Soul stronger to direct you than your self'.[92] Similarly, where Pope removes a double negative from Act 4 of *The Comedy of Errors*, to read 'First he deny'd you had in him a right', Theobald restores 'no Right'.[93]

It is clear that Theobald's historical understanding of Shakespeare's language must severely modify any project of using the edition as a preparatory help to the polishing of the language. But the element of eclecticism in Theobald's bibliographical procedures furnishes the opportunity, at his discretion, for linguistic corrections introduced by Pope or other post-1623 editors to remain in Theobald's text. The most celebrated double superlative in Shakespeare, for example, Antony's 'This was the most unkindest cut of all', in *Julius Caesar*, stands in Theobald's text, as it had stood in Pope's, 'This, this was the

---

[89] *1733*, i. 320–1; for a further example see iii. 532 ('Proface').
[90] Samuel Johnson, *The Plan of a Dictionary* (London, 1747), 28–9.
[91] *1733*, i. 6.   [92] Ibid. v. 10; *1728*, vi. 12.
[93] *1733*, iii. 38; *1728*, ii. 37.

unkindest cut of all',[94] despite the fact that Theobald has only a few pages earlier restored 'With the most boldest, and best hearts of *Rome*' to the text in place of Pope's 'With the most bold, and the best hearts of *Rome*'.[95] Similarly, in cases where a plural subject governs a singular verb, Theobald follows the received reading: 'the walls are thine' (rather than 'is thine'), just as the 'clamors of a jealous woman | Poison more deadly than a mad dog's tooth' (for 'Poisons').[96] The use of 'it' as a possessive pronoun is everywhere regularized to 'its' in Theobald's text as well as in Pope's: '*it had its* [it] *head bit off by its* [it] *young*', 'The innocent milk in its [it] most innocent mouth', and 'Woman its [it] pretty self' are instances.[97]

Theobald's textual-critical theory and practice are certainly no more self-contradictory than those of other early eighteenth-century editors: indeed they are less self-contradictory than most, and it is easy to see why most of those who have discussed his work in the past have been eager to emphasize its 'pioneering' aspects. But it is also worth considering those aspects of his work which demonstrate the persistence of older and less systematic practices of textual criticism, not simply in order to arrive at a more 'balanced' assessment of Theobald, but in order better to understand the implications of the relations between his practice and his cultural and political circumstances. After Peter Seary has justly remarked that 'the close study of English language and literature is connected with the politics of increasing national self-consciousness', he goes on to insist that 'These generalizations are, however, far removed from the personalities of the critics and scholars themselves, who were caught up in a web of assumptions and disputes determined by their social class, education, ambition, and their stature among their peers'.[98] He is right to suggest that the relationship between the politics of national self-consciousness and editorial practice is complex, and his warning against the simple identification of relatively autonomous intellectual practices with particular political positions is important. But what the complexities and contradictions of Theobald's editorial practice indicate is that the gulf implied by Seary's phrase 'far removed' is illusory. Political 'generalizations' and interested constructions of literary personality do not take place in spheres irrevocably separated from one another; rather, each is mediated through the

[94] *1733*, vi. 176.   [95] Ibid. 165.
[96] Ibid. v. 209 (*1728*, iii. 446); iii. 51 (*1728*, ii. 50).
[97] *1733*, v. 127 (*1728*, iii. 374); iii. 103 (*1728*, iii. 292); vi. 404 (*1728*, viii. 56).
[98] Seary, *Theobald*, p. vii.

other. Such a view of Theobald's work suggests that the development of a historical understanding of language and culture is not the progress of lonely pioneers towards a fixed goal, but a contested struggle which has left its mark on the work of those who have taken part in it.

5

The 'Art of Criticism': Shakespearian Editing as the Display of Comprehensive Taste and Learning

FEW EIGHTEENTH-CENTURY editions of Shakespeare can have been so little illuminated by chroniclers of the subject as William Warburton's. McKerrow devotes only a single paragraph to Warburton's edition,[1] and such brief accounts of his editorial work as exist elsewhere are often concerned principally to insist upon his low rank in a notional league table of early eighteenth-century editors: for Ernest Walder, Warburton was 'decidedly the worst' of such editors, as he is 'surely the worst' for Arthur Sherbo.[2] Even a more balanced account such as that by Brian Vickers nevertheless expresses puzzlement as to 'what Warburton thought he was doing, and why'.[3] It is not the purpose of this discussion to right an imaginary wrong, but to suggest that Warburton's supposed vanity and ignorance do not of themselves explain either the claims made in his preface or the character of his edition. Discussions from which Warburton emerges as no more than a laughable eccentric leave the contemporary reputation of the writer whom Pope described as 'the greatest general critic I ever knew', whom Gibbon thought of as 'the tyrant and dictator of

---

[1] R. B. McKerrow, 'The Treatment of Shakespeare's Text by his Earlier Editors (1709–1768)', in P. Alexander, ed., *Studies in Shakespeare: British Academy Lectures* (Oxford, 1964), 103–31 (p. 127).

[2] Arthur Sherbo, *The Birth of Shakespeare Studies* (East Lansing, Mich., 1986), 12; Ernest Walder, *Shakespearian Criticism* (Bradford, 1895; repr. New York, 1982), 109. For further examples, see D. N. Smith, *Shakespeare in the Eighteenth Century* (Oxford, 1928), 44; Allardyce Nicoll, 'The Editors of Shakespeare from First Folio to Malone', in Israel Gollancz, ed., *1623–1923: Studies in the First Folio* (London, 1924), 174. Fuller accounts appear in Robert M. Ryley, *William Warburton* (Boston, Mass., 1984) and in A. W. Evans, *Warburton and the Warburtonians* (London, 1932).

[3] Brian Vickers, ed., *Shakespeare: The Critical Heritage, 1733–1752* (London, 1975), 15.

literature', and of one of whose Shakespearian emendations Johnson could say that it 'almost sets the critick on a level with the authour', looking like an inexplicable accident.[4] Warburton's edition represents an attempt to go beyond the complementary inadequacies of the two kinds of verbal criticism satirized in the fourth book of the *Dunciad* and criticized in Warburton's own preface. Warburton wishes to display his command both of the attention to literal detail and bibliographical learning of the merely professional critic, and of the taste and more discriminating learning which the gentleman of letters may possess. Warburton himself had mentors of both kinds. We have already seen how closely he was involved with the new case against verbal criticism made by his literary mentor Pope in Book IV of the *Dunciad*; but another of his patrons was Bishop Hare, whom we earlier discovered vehemently defending the value of minute scholarship, and who had himself gone on to edit scriptural and classical texts.[5] Yet Warburton's new conception of an art of textual criticism uniting broad taste with minute learning, no less than Theobald's explicit advocacy of the qualified specialist, presented obstacles to his own avowed project of using settled texts of English classics to help settle the English language.

I

There are several indications of Warburton's interest in the necessary features of, and the difficulties facing, any authoritative English dictionary. He discussed the topic in some detail with Spence in 1744;[6] and he formulated in the preface to his edition of Shakespeare, more explicitly than had any previous editor, the dependence of any establishment of a settled and pure national language upon the availability of properly edited canonical texts:

[4] Maynard Mack, *Alexander Pope: A Life* (New Haven, Conn., 1985), 743; Edward Gibbon, *Memoirs of My Life*, ed. Betty Radice (Harmondsworth, 1984), 149 (quoted in Clifton Cherpack, 'Warburton and the *Encyclopédie*', *Comparative Literature*, 7 (1955), 226–39 (p. 227)). For Johnson, see Arthur Sherbo, ed., *Johnson on Shakespeare* (2 vols., New Haven, Conn., 1968), ii. 975. The emendation was 'A God, kissing carrion' for 'A good kissing carrion' in *Hamlet*.

[5] Hare recommended Warburton to Queen Caroline shortly before her death in 1739 as a 'man of learning' suitable to entertain her: Evans, *Warburton*, 46; Warburton prefixed an encomium on Hare to vol. iii of the 4th edn. of his *Divine Legation of Moses Demonstrated* (5 vols., London, 1764–5), iii, pp. xxxi–xxxii).

[6] Joseph Spence, *Observations, Anecdotes and Characters of Books and Men*, ed. James M. Osborn (2 vols., Oxford, 1966), i. 374.

we have neither GRAMMAR nor DICTIONARY, neither Chart nor Compass, to guide us through this wide sea of Words. And indeed how should we? since both are to be composed and finished on the Authority of our best established Writers. But their Authority can be of little use until the Text hath been correctly settled, and the Phraseology critically examined.[7]

Warburton here points out the circular nature of the difficulties facing English philology: editors need authoritative dictionaries and grammars in order to help them settle their text, but grammarians and lexicographers in their turn need settled texts in order to make their reference works authoritative. One of the 'Philologic dissertations' with which Warburton described his *The Divine Legation of Moses Demonstrated* as being 'interspersed'[8] confirms Warburton's sense of the close reciprocal relationship between adequate textual criticism and commentary and adequate reference works. In a dispute over the significance of the word ὑς in a passage of Herodotus, Warburton maintains that it signifies 'swine', against Gale's opinion that it means 'cows' or 'heifers':

His authority for this use of the word is *Hesychius*. But *Plutarch* is a much better for the other signification . . . The truth of the matter seems to be this, *Hesychius* found that ὑς, in some obscure province or other, meant a *Heifer* . . . and so put it down to inrich his dictionary with an unusual signification.[9]

Such remarks indicate Warburton's belief in the importance of a canon of established authors to an adequate national dictionary: Hesychius's lexicon is seen as an untrustworthy guide because its authorities are likely to be provincial. It may therefore itself vitiate the semantic interpretation (and thus, potentially, the text) of a linguistic authority such as Herodotus. Such a lexicon can offer only 'unlicens'd Greek', as Suidas is said to do in Book IV of the *Dunciad*.[10]

It follows from Warburton's view of the mutual interdependence of dictionaries and grammars, on the one hand, and edited texts of canonical authors, on the other, that the textual critic's task is, for him, one of public and national significance. The closing pages of his preface attempt to illustrate from precedents the public importance of the textual critic's work. Thus, 'The famous University of OXFORD . . . thought good Letters so much interested in correct Editions of the best *English* Writers, that they, very lately, in their public Capacity, undertook one, of this very

[7] *1747*, i, p. xxv.
[8] *The Divine Legation of Moses Demonstrated*, 4th edn. (5 vols., London, 1765), iii, sig. 2A3ʳ.
[9] Ibid. i, p. xlv.
[10] Alexander Pope, *The Dunciad*, ed. James Sutherland (London, 1963), 365.

Author, by subscription.'[11] Whereas in the *Dunciad* Pope and Warburton had implied that Sir Thomas Hanmer's 1744 edition was to be a vanity publication,[12] Warburton here chooses to emphasize Oxford University's public beneficence in undertaking the edition. This emphasis upon the public importance of editions of the vernacular classics is subsequently further developed from classical precedent. Warburton argues that 'the greatest men of Antiquity never thought themselves better employed than in cultivating their own country [*sic*] idiom. So *Lycurgus* did honour to *Sparta*, in giving the first compleat Edition of *Homer*; and *Cicero*, to *Rome*, in correcting the Works of *Lucretius*.'[13] The significance of Warburton's instancing Lycurgus becomes more apparent when considered in the context of his discussion of the Spartan legislator in *The Divine Legation of Moses Demonstrated*. Lycurgus (like Moses) is considered not merely as a lawgiver, but as the founder of a deliberately separatist national polity: 'the end, which Moses and Lycurgus pursued in common, (tho' for different purposes) of keeping their people *separate*, occasioned such a likeness in several parts of the two Institutions as was, in my opinion, the real origin of that tradition mentioned in the first book of Maccabees, That there was a Family-relation between the two People'.[14] The attempt of Lycurgus the lawgiver to endow his nation with distinctive political institutions in perpetuity[15] is mirrored by that of Lycurgus the editor to settle the text of the greatest writer in his language. The significance of such an analogy for Warburton is only emphasized when it is remembered that Homeric Greek can in no sense be said to be specifically 'Spartan': Warburton is prepared to stretch this point in order to establish Lycurgus as a national lawgiver-editor.

Who might be fit to follow in these heroic footsteps? Oxford University's act of public virtue, after all, has been compromised by an unfit editor 'who thrust himself into the employment'.[16] Indeed, the antithesis between Bentley and Hanmer in Book IV of the *Dunciad*,[17] with its simultaneous assault upon the merely amateur and the merely professional verbal critic, would seem to rule out altogether the possibility that modern verbal criticism could ever be a disinterested or publicly virtuous activity, and thus to insist that verbal critics could not be trusted to legislate over national cultural institutions such as the texts of canonical authors and the settled and pure language which those texts were to support and illustrate. Warburton's appearance as just such a critic, not only (in 1747) as an

---

[11] *1747*, i, p. xxiii.   [12] *Dunciad*, p. 352 n.   [13] *1747*, i, pp. xxiv–xxv.
[14] *Divine Legation*, iv. 118.   [15] Ibid. i. 111.   [16] *1747*, p. xxiii.
[17] *Dunciad*, pp. 352–3, 362–71.

editor of Shakespeare but also (editing individual poems throughout the 1740s and the complete works in 1751) of Pope himself, was potentially, therefore, the occasion of considerable embarrassment on Warburton's part.[18] Warburton could hardly escape from this dilemma simply by recanting the position which he had helped Pope to work out: indeed, he developed and substantiated the *Dunciad*'s antithesis between the merely amateur and merely professional critic in both the preface and the notes to his edition. Rather, he sought to present his work as uniting the taste and genius unavailable to the laborious scholar with the scholarly labour scorned by the gentlemanly dabbler in letters; Johnson's later remark that Warburton 'at once exerted the powers of the scholar, the reasoner and the wit' is thus just the praise at which Warburton's literary self-construction aims.[19] Such a presentation certainly could not provide Warburton with any really disinterested social standpoint: the last book of the *Dunciad* had already recognized that there were no such standpoints available, and accordingly Warburton's preface shows him to be as anxious as any other editor in the century about the social and intellectual status of editing. But it was able to engage with the criticism that social partiality was accompanied by epistemological partiality, that the interested critic's eye examines bit by bit and consequently fails to understand the whole: Warburton's edition continually attempts to show that correct adjustment of the minute particulars of the text demands comprehensive thought and knowledge.[20]

2

Warburton's sense of the disapproval to which he might expose himself by his appearance as a verbal critic would have been confirmed by his previous experience. When, in 1736, he had published a specimen of a projected edition of Velleius Paterculus in the *Bibliothèque britannique, ou histoire des ouvrages des savans de la Grande-Bretagne*,[21] his then friend

[18] For Warburton's edns. of Pope, see R. H. Griffith, *Alexander Pope: A Bibliography* (1 / 2; Austin, Tex., 1927), 471–536.

[19] Samuel Johnson, *Prefaces, Biographical and Critical, to the Works of the English Poets* (10 vols., London, 1779–81), vii. 'Life of Pope', 165.

[20] Compare *Dunciad*, p. 366, l. 234. See also William Warburton, ed., *The Works of Alexander Pope* (9 vols., London, 1751), i. 170, where Warburton himself alludes to this line to illustrate a passage from *An Essay on Criticism*.

[21] 'Gi. Warburton A. M. in C. Velleii Paterculi. Historias, Emendationes', *Bibliothèque britannique, ou histoire des ouvrages des savans de la Grande-Bretagne* (n.pl., July–September 1736), 256–94.

Conyers Middleton (who had in the 1720s responded with such hostility to Bentley's proposal for a new edition of the New Testament) had written to him urging that, while conjectural emendation might be 'a laudable and liberal Amusement', it could 'hardly be thought a Study, fit to employ a life upon; at least, not worthy, I am sure, of your Talents and Industry, which instead of trifling on Words, seem calculated rather to correct the Opinions and Manners of the World'.[22] Middleton's response to Warburton's plan for an edition suggests that publication is the point at which a praiseworthy ornament to the character of a man of letters threatens to become the vain devotion of a life to mere trifling.

Indeed, Warburton's declared intention of publishing an edition of Shakespeare, advertised in his specimen notes and emendations in the ninth volume of Thomas Birch's *General Dictionary* of 1739,[23] and in the 'Advertisement' to the 1745 reprint of Hanmer's text (which the Tonsons and Wellingtons had produced as a response to what they saw as Hanmer's piracy), had already afforded him some indication of what he might expect once his edition appeared.[24] One controversialist had indicated the possibilities for anti-Warburtonian adaptations of Scriblerian satire upon pedantry by signing himself 'Martinus Scriblerus Junior' in a hostile pamphlet.[25] Zachary Grey's pamphlet of 1746, *A Word or Two of Advice to William Warburton: A Dealer in many Words*, carries a suggestion in its title that Warburton is a merely commercial literary tradesman, and on its first page refers to the 'pretty *second-hand* Goods, retailed by [Warburton]' in *The Divine Legation of Moses Demonstrated*.[26] Grey hints further at the inappropriateness of work on Shakespeare for a clergyman when, drawing upon a tradition stemming from Rowe's preface, he warns Warburton that 'Thy Remarks upon that profane *Deer-stealer*, *William Shakespear*, afford thee no more Credit than those upon *Pope's Essay* . . .'.[27] Such hits at Warburton's implied interestedness and lowness

[22] Evans, *Warburton*, 50–1.

[23] Thomas Birch *et al.*, eds., *A General Dictionary, Historical and Critical*, ix (London, 1739), 190.

[24] See Giles E. Dawson, 'Warburton, Hanmer, and the 1745 Edition of Shakespeare', *Studies in Bibliography*, 2 (1949–50), 35–48 (p. 43); Arthur Sherbo, 'Warburton and the 1745 "Shakespeare"', *Journal of English and Germanic Philology*, 51 (1952), 71–82.

[25] *Proposals for Printing by Subscription . . . a Commentary Critical and Theological upon the learned Mr. Warburton's apologetical dedication to the Reverend Dr. Henry Stebbing . . . by Martinus Scriblerus Junior* (London, 1746).

[26] Zachary Grey, *A Word or Two of Advice to William Warburton: A Dealer in many Words* (London, 1746; repr. New York, 1975), 1; the first part of *The Divine Legation of Moses Demonstrated* had appeared in 1738.

[27] Grey, *A Word or Two*, 2.

(recalling the *Dunciad*'s literary poacher, Bentley) are accompanied by attacks upon his vanity cast in terms reminiscent of that poem's portrayal of Sir Thomas Hanmer as a courtly fop. Arguing against Warburton's proposed reading 'gemell' for the received reading 'jewel' in a passage from *A Midsummer Night's Dream*, Grey comments 'I cannot allow him the Foppery of this Alteration';[28] and proposing an alternative ('panted') to Warburton's reading ('pantlered') for 'pannelled' in a passage of *Antony and Cleopatra*, Grey ironically admits that 'in thy [Warburton's] vain Way of Writing, "it may not give the Expression an Air of Gallantry" '.[29]

Warburton occasionally, and uncharacteristically, attempted to pre-empt or deflect such satire by developing the idea that verbal criticism might be simply 'a laudable and liberal Amusement'. 'Mr. Warburton has bestowed some of those leisure hours which he could spare from the duties of his sacred function', explains *The History of the Works of the Learned*, introducing a reprint of his specimen emendations and commentary.[30] Even the preface to Warburton's edition at one point refers to his labours on Shakespeare (much against the tenor of the remainder of the document) as 'these amusements'.[31] But, as Middleton's objection to Warburton's planned edition of Paterculus suggests, publication implies larger claims, which require public justification. Without such support, the publication of private 'amusements' becomes merely an instance of amateur vanity. Accordingly, the main burden of Warburton's self-justification rests upon a firm assertion of the comprehensive, rather than merely particular, abilities and learning requisite to a fit editor of Shakespeare, and upon an attempt to display such comprehensive capacities in the text and commentary. This is supported by a history of Shakespeare's editorial reception which gives a negative account of the two principal kinds of unfit editor. Theobald and Hanmer are taken to exemplify these (as the *Dunciad* had taken Bentley and Hanmer) and this characterization of their work in the preface is pursued throughout Warburton's commentary.

Warburton had an obvious motive for choosing Theobald and Hanmer to exemplify inadequate textual criticism: he had quarrelled with both of them in the 1730s over privately communicated emendations of his, many of which they had used, with varying degrees of permission from Warburton, in their editions.[32] But the way in which Warburton chooses to discuss their respective deficiencies shows that there is more than

---

[28] Ibid. 3–4; Warburton, *1747*, i. 154; *1723–5*, i. 135.   [29] Grey, *A Word or Two*, 5.
[30] Quoted in Evans, *Warburton*, 155.   [31] *1747*, i, p. xxii.
[32] See Evans, *Warburton*, 143–55.

personal enmity at stake in his account. Although the contrasting accounts of Theobald and Hanmer do not dwell upon their status to the same extent as the portrayals of Bentley and Hanmer in the *Dunciad*, the social underpinning of their antithetical failings as editors is clearly indicated when Warburton first introduces the topic of his literary relations with his fellow critics: 'The One was recommended to me as a poor Man, the Other as a poor Critic'.[33] Theobald's use of Warburton's work is graciously excused as prompted by poverty and consequently permitted by Warburton himself: 'As to Mr. *Theobald*, who wanted Money, I allowed him to print what I gave him for his own Advantage'.[34] Hanmer's plagiarism, however, is more severely dealt with: 'But, as to the *Oxford Editor*, who wanted nothing, but what he might very well be without, the Reputation of a Critic, I could not so easily forgive him for trafficking with my Papers without my Knowledge'.[35] Theobald's motives for wishing to edit Shakespeare are represented as merely interested, Hanmer's as merely vain. The respective deficiencies of Theobald and Hanmer as editors are distinguished in accordance with these social characterizations: 'They separately possessed those two Qualities which, more than any other, have contributed to bring the Art of Criticism into disrepute, *Dulness of Apprehension*, and *Extravagance of Conjecture*.'[36] Warburton's account of Theobald's incapacity as a low and interested editor draws upon ideas familiar both from the *Dunciad* and from Pope's preface to his own edition (reprinted in Warburton's edition, which claimed misleadingly to be the joint work of Warburton and Pope, although in fact Warburton's text was based on Theobald's).[37] The only merit allowed to Theobald is the diligence of the bibliographical specialist:

> Mr. *Theobald* was naturally turned to Industry and Labour. What he read he could transcribe: but, as what he thought, if ever he did think, he could but ill express, so he read on; and, by that means got a Character of Learning, without risquing, to every Observer, the Imputation of wanting a better Talent. By a punctilious Collation of the old Books, he corrected what was manifestly wrong in the *latter* Editions, by what was manifestly right in the *earlier*.[38]

Just as Pope regards Hemings and Condell as capable only of correcting obvious literal errors, so Theobald's ability to discern textual corruption is claimed to extend only to what is 'manifestly wrong' in the received text. Furthermore, in the same way that Pope's dunces are often portrayed

---

[33] *1747*, i, p. x.   [34] Ibid.   [35] Ibid., pp. x–xi.   [36] Ibid., p. xiii.
[37] R. B. McKerrow, 'Treatment', 127; Peter Seary, *Lewis Theobald and the Editing of Shakespeare* (Oxford, 1990), 134.
[38] *1747*, i, p. xi.

as treating intellectual products as mere physical material (lumber or frippery, for example), Theobald's use of his books is presented as a thoughtless and simply mechanical one: 'What he read, he could transcribe'.[39]

Thus far, Theobald's unsuitability as an editor is cast in recognizably Scriblerian terms: he lacks the talent which might make learning more than lumber. But Warburton subsequently pursues the suggestion in the words 'he got a Character of Learning', that Theobald cannot even be regarded as genuinely learned. 'For where the Phrase was very obsolete or licentious in the *common* Books, or only slightly corrupted in the *other*', claims Warburton, 'he wanted sufficient Knowledge of the Progress and various Stages of the *English* Tongue, as well as Acquaintance with the Peculiarity of *Shakespear*'s Language to understand what was right . . .'.[40] These are accusations with little to support them: it was just Theobald's attention to the peculiarity of Shakespeare's language in his extensive deployment of parallel passages that led him to edit with an unprecedented awareness of the historical mutability of English; and instances both of Theobald's defending apparently obsolete or licentious readings, and of his deploying apparently corrupt variants from Elizabethan and Jacobean copies in emended form, are legion.[41] What is significant here is that Warburton wished to indicate a kind of learning which would be beyond the powers of the merely laborious critic, and which Warburton himself could be represented as commanding: the genuinely learned editor, for Warburton, does not require merely a narrow bibliographical knowledge, but a comprehensive understanding of the history of the language.

Warburton's commentary develops in detail the view of Theobald's work outlined in the preface. Theobald's supposedly mechanical transcription of readings from the (here unspecified) 'old books' is held to lead him into an unthinking reverence for such variants. It is in this vein that Warburton criticizes Theobald's restoration of a First Folio reading ('breeds') in *Measure for Measure*. Warburton's text, like Pope's, reads 'She speaks, and 'tis such sense, | That my sense bleeds with it', and he comments that 'The first Folio reads *breeds*, which tho' it have no meaning, yet Mr. *Theobald* adopts, and discards a very sensible word, to make room for it.'[42] Later in the same play another reading restored by Theobald from the First Folio is found wanting: Warburton follows the received reading 'my intention, hearing not my tongue, | Anchors on

[39] See e.g. *Dunciad*, pp. 279–81.   [40] *1747*, i, p. xi.
[41] See above, e.g. Ch. 2, s. 4.   [42] *1747*, i. 386; *1740*, i. 323; Hinman, p. 86, l. 901.

Isabel: 'Nothing can be either plainer or exacter than this expression. But the old blundering Folio having it, *invention*, this was enough for Mr. *Theobald* to prefer authority to sense.'[43] As in the *Dunciad*, an insistence upon the superior authority of earlier copies is taken as a return to a pre-enlightened preference for 'authority' over the requirements of 'sense'.[44] Warburton's notes, moreover, develop a parallel between Theobald's editorial work and that of the low and partially sighted First Folio editors, and of the low and interested players, invoked by Pope. Just as Hemings's and Condell's sphere of expertise is confined by Pope to corruptions of single letters, so Theobald's major contributions are implied by Warburton to be similarly restricted. The minuteness of the details to which Theobald attends is the topic of recurrent ironic notes: 'A comma here set exactly right, by Mr. *Theobald*'; 'A point set right by Mr. *Theobald*'.[45] In each of these instances Theobald had given substantial notes claiming that his reform of the punctuation made the passages in question comprehensible for the first time.[46] The comparison of Theobald's impact upon the text to that of the players is made implicitly: both are prepared to alter it for the sake of such supposedly low satisfactions as the provision of a rhyme,[47] or of a pun or other witticism ('A pun, in an *ill angel*, which Mr. *Theobald* here tells us, he has restored and brought to light').[48]

Hanmer's unsuitability derives from opposite and complementary deficiencies:

> How the *Oxford Editor* came to think himself qualified for this Office, from which his whole Course of Life had been so remote, is still more difficult to conceive. For whatever Parts he might have either of Genius or Erudition, he was absolutely ignorant of the Art of Criticism, as well as of the Poetry of that Time, and the Language of his Author.[49]

Although Theobald and Hanmer are alleged to share an ignorance of Elizabethan language in general and of Shakespeare's idiosyncrasies in particular, they fall short of competence on different sides. Theobald is seen as unqualified because he 'lacks a better talent' than that of the

---

[43]   *1747*, i. 390; *1740*, i. 326; Hinman, p. 89, ll. 1005–6.   [44] *The Dunciad*, p. 59 n.

[45]   *1747*, ii. 148; iii. 459. Cf. Pope, 'Epistle to Dr. Arbuthnot', l. 161: *Imitations of Horace*, ed. John Butt (London, 1939), 108.

[46]   *1740*, ii. 134; iii. 402.

[47]   For an alleged instance of the players altering for the rhyme, see *1747*, v. 302; for the same charge against Theobald, see i. 150. *1740*, i. 120.

[48]   *1747*, iv. 218; *1740*, iv. 196. For alleged instances of Theobald altering for wordplay, see *1747*, ii. 164; iv. 225.

[49]   Ibid. i, pp. xi–xii.

specialist collator; Hanmer may, it is conceded, be a man of parts, but this cannot compensate for his ignorance of the specialized 'Art of Criticism'. Where Theobald mechanically follows the readings of the 'old books', Hanmer is 'so far from a Thought of examining the *first* Editions, that he even neglected to compare Mr. *Pope*'s, from which he printed his own, with Mr. *Theobald*'s', thereby surrendering the fruits of Theobald's mechanical collation.[50]

Whereas Theobald's alleged historical ignorance is taken to lead him into sins of omission rather than of commission, Hanmer's leads him greatly to alter the text: 'in spite of that extreme Negligence in Numbers, which distinguishes the first Dramatic Writers, he hath tricked up the old Bard, from Head to Foot, in all the finical Exactness of a modern Measurer of Syllables'.[51] Warburton's metaphor here reinforces the social distinction between Theobald and Hanmer: where the former attempts to introduce or restore low rhymes and puns, the latter foppishly adjusts Shakespeare's metrical clothing. If Theobald is claimed to emend the received text unnecessarily in order to follow the 'old books', Hanmer also errs as a result of his bibliographical ignorance. Warburton appeals against Hanmer (with some bibliographical imprecision on his own part) to 'the old books (which our Editor appears never once to have look'd into, as trusting all to his own sagacity)'.[52] The unqualified man of parts who regards the drudgery of bibliographical labour as unnecessary inflicts no less damage upon the text than the collator who regards it as the one thing needful.

Warburton's commentary frequently reproaches Hanmer with such historical-linguistic ignorance and insensitivity. Defending 'state of floods' in *Henry IV, Part 2*, Warburton glosses 'state' as 'assembly' and remarks that 'the *Oxford Editor* much a stranger to the phraseology of that time in general, and to his author's in particular, out of mere loss for his meaning reads it backwards,—*the floods of state*'.[53] Elsewhere, Hanmer's alterations of what Warburton regards as characteristically Shakespearian expressions are implied to be the result, not simply of a failure to understand the text, but of a wish to make it conform to present correct usage. When Hanmer alters 'competitors' to 'complices' in a passage from *Richard III*, Warburton remarks that 'the *Oxford Editor* will make *Shakespear* speak like other people'.[54] In the opening scene of *Measure for*

---

[50] Ibid., p. xii.   [51] Ibid., pp. xii–xiii.

[52] Ibid. iv. 99. *1723–5*, iii. 191; *1744*, iii. 282. Warburton is likely to have found the reading 'did' not in 'the old books' but in his copy-text, *1740*, iv. 93.

[53] *1747*, iv. 302; *1744*, iii. 457.   [54] *1747*, v. 317; *1744*, iv. 385.

Measure Warburton defends the reading 'To one that can my part in him advertise', and attacks Hanmer for his willingness to 'extirpate' such 'quaintnesses of expression'.[55]

3

Warburton's claim that Hanmer is ignorant of 'the Art of Criticism' (or, as he puts it subsequently, of 'every Rule of Criticism')[56] begins to provide a fuller indication of what he might mean by these terms. Warburton objects, in particular, to Hanmer's failure to provide conjectural histories of particular instances of textual corruption, as in the following passage from *Richard II*:

> *To wake our Peace———which thus rouz'd up———*
> *Might fright fair Peace.*] Thus the sentence stands in the common reading, absurdly enough: which made the *Oxford Editor*, instead of, *fright fair Peace*, read, *be affrighted*; as if these latter words could ever, possibly, have been blundered into the former by transcribers. But his business is to alter as his fancy leads him, not to reform errors, as the text and rules of criticism, direct.[57]

Warburton here implicitly invokes a combination of two related rules familiar from classical philology (and also from Theobald's Shakespearian textual criticism).[58] Conjectural emendations, first, are to differ physically from the text of available copies as little as possible, if the readings of such copies are to be attributable to scribal error. Secondly, if they differ from the copies so widely as to make such slips an inadequate explanation of the divergence, the reading(s) of the copies must be explicable as the paraphrase or vulgarization of a more difficult authorial reading, on the assumption that where scribes consciously alter the text they will do so in order to make it more easily understood or to remove unusual linguistic features which they dislike. In this case, Warburton points out, 'fright fair Peace' can be regarded neither as a physical slip for Hanmer's 'be affrighted' (the two readings are too dissimilar) nor as a banalization of it (the 'common reading' is more distinctive and difficult). Warburton himself goes on to explain the absurdity of the received text as the result of an inattentive conflation of Quarto and Folio texts, and argues that the lines from the Quarto inserted by Pope were deliberately left out by Shake-

---

[55] *1747*, i. 357; *1744*, i. 296.   [56] *1747*, i, p. xii.
[57] *1747*, iv. 16–17; *1744*, iii. 205.
[58] E. J. Kenney, *The Classical Text* (Berkeley, Calif., 1974), ch. 2.

speare in revision. Hanmer's unfitness to edit lies not only in his failure to do the necessary work, claims Warburton, but in his unfamiliarity with a range of techniques and principles indispensable to any candidate for the office of a critical editor.

Warburton's attempt to go beyond the complementary varieties of editorial unfitness represented for him by Theobald and Hanmer is, then, to rely on an idea of critical expertise which, by virtue of its comprehensive learning and its methodological rigour, would go beyond the simple accumulation of specialist knowledge. Both the similarity of Warburton's position to that of Pope, and his development beyond it, are clearly indicated when Warburton first begins explicitly to discuss his own textual-critical methods:

> The first sort [of notes] is employed in restoring the Poet's genuine Text; but in those Places only where it labours with inextricable Nonsense. In which, how much soever I may have given Scope to critical Conjecture, where the old Copies failed me, I have indulged nothing to Fancy or Imagination, but have religiously observed the severe Canons of literal Criticism; as may be seen from the Reasons accompanying every Alteration of the common Text.[59]

As so often in early eighteenth-century discussions of Shakespearian textual criticism, the idea of the authority of a *textus receptus*, and a recommendation of the eclectic editorial procedures which accompany such a notion, are at the heart of this passage. 'Reasons' are to be produced, not for departures from 'the old Copies' but for 'every Alteration of the common [i.e. received] Text'. It is implied that the Quartos and Folios need only be consulted where the received text is incomprehensible, and that where they fail to provide sense, conjecture must be attempted. A collation of Warburton's text of *Hamlet* with Theobald's 1740 text shows that Warburton rarely deviated from his copy-text, except on occasions where he had a conjectural emendation to recommend. It was no accident that the Latin author Warburton had earlier planned to edit was Velleius Paterculus: as Richard Bentley had pointed out in one of his most widely read works, Paterculus survived in only a single faulty manuscript, so that there was no scope for improving the text by collation of manuscripts and a correspondingly greater scope for conjectural emendation.[60] But where Pope referred to a 'religious abhorrence of innovation' in the text itself, and thereby incurred Theobald's charge of superstition, Warburton ad-

---

[59] *1747*, i, p. xiv.
[60] Richard Bentley, *Remarks upon a Late Discourse of Free-thinking*, 5th edn. (London, 1716), 65.

vertises his religious reverence, instead, for a body of methodological principles.

Warburton had been interested for some time in the possibility of vindicating textual criticism by the provision of a coherent methodology: in 1736 he wrote to Hanmer (before the two men quarrelled) that 'Your last touched upon a very nice subject the settling a true Canon of Criticism, the adjusting the bounds of it, and vindicating an useful Art from the discredit which has been brought upon it'.[61] It is certainly true, as Warburton himself admits, that he fails to provide the '*body of Canons*, for literal Criticism, drawn out in form; as well such as concern the Art in general, as those that arise from the Nature and Circumstances of our Author's Works in particular', which he 'once intended to have given'.[62] But Warburton's subsequent remark that the same purpose may be served by theoretical notes to the text is more than a simple excuse for a breach of promise.[63] Although Warburton's annotatory reflections do not amount to an organon of textual criticism, they do indicate the textual–critical principles which Warburton has in mind, some (as in the case of those invoked against Hanmer) familiar from classical philology and hence from Theobald's work, others original to Warburton. These principles were to lead Warburton to experiments in critical conjecture which have provoked the understandable derision of subsequent commentators, but whose justification is less arbitrary than has sometimes been thought.

The influence of classical textual criticism upon Warburton's editorial practice is significant. Warburton often makes a point of providing histories of error, whether of scribal slips or of intentional banalization. Both a slip and a scribal emendation are conjectured at in the complicated history of error which accounts for the alleged corruption of 'maple' to 'female' in Warburton's text of *A Midsummer Night's Dream*: 'The corruption might happen by the first blunderer dropping the *p* in writing the word *maple*, which word thence became *male*. A following transcriber, for the sake of a little sense and measure, thought fit to change this *male* into *female*; and then tacked it as an epithet to *Ivy*.'[64] Although Warburton's conjectural histories of error generally bear the marks of their classical-philological origins in their postulating successive acts of transcription as

[61] Evans, *Warburton*, 159.   [62] *1747*, i, p. xiv.

[63] For the accusation of a breach of contract, see Thomas Edwards, *The Canons of Criticism*, 7th edn. (London, 1765; repr. 1970), 15. For Warburton's promise, see Birch *et al.*, eds., *A General Dictionary*, ix. 190.

[64] *1747*, i. 148. For a further instance, cf. ibid. iii. 443.

a principal source of textual corruption, he occasionally anticipates later uses of this principle by explaining corruption from typographical, rather than scribal, accident. Thus 'a virtue of a good wing, and I like the wear well' in *All's Well That Ends Well* is allegedly a corruption of 'a virtue of a good ming ['i.e. mixture, *composition*']': 'The *M* was turn'd the wrong way at the press, and from thence came the blunder.'[65]

Principles familiar from classical philology, such as the provision of parallel passages from an author's work or from that of his or her contemporaries, however, can be found more thoroughly applied in Theobald's edition. They are, accordingly, less well adapted for Warburton to display the principled and theoretical expertise (as distinct from the purely specialist labour allegedly represented by Theobald) which he advertises in his preface, than are those ideas original to Warburton about the theory of editing in general and about Shakespearian language in particular. Especially significant in this respect are Warburton's discussions of integrity of metaphor, and of the extent to which such violations of integrity can be taken as grounds for emendation. Annotating the line 'This is the flower, that smiles on ev'ry one' from *Love's Labour's Lost*,[66] Warburton argues that a strict attention to the point at which a metaphor becomes so familiar as to lose its figurative quality is essential. Whereas Theobald had objected to the line in a letter to Warburton on the grounds that 'A Flower shewing its teeth is a very odd image', and had suggested emending 'flower' to 'fleerer',[67] Warburton argues that 'The broken disjointed metaphor' is here acceptable because this is a metaphor which has 'grown so common as to desert, as it were, the figurative'.[68] Warburton concedes that, in the case of 'solemn, less-used metaphors', such a descent from the figurative to the literal plane becomes shocking, but maintains that an attempt to enforce the figurative quality of dead metaphor 'would have as ill an effect on the other hand'[69] by reminding a reader or listener unnecessarily of a redundant image. He underlines the consequences of his observations for classical textual criticism: 'Grammarians would do well to consider what has been here said when they set upon amending *Greek* and *Roman* writings. For the much-used hacknied metaphors being now very imperfectly known, great care is required not to act in this case temerariously.'[70]

---

[65] Ibid. iii. 11. [66] Ibid. ii. 266; Hinman, p. 157, l. 2256.

[67] John Nichols, *Illustrations of the Literary History of the Eighteenth Century* (8 vols., London, 1817–58; repr. New York, 1966), ii. 327. Theobald eventually retained 'flower', on Warburton's advice, and printed an early version of Warburton's defence of that reading in his 1st edn.: *1733*, ii. 163. Warburton's note disappears entirely from Theobald's 2nd edn.: *1740*, ii. 243.

[68] *1747*, ii. 266. [69] Ibid. 267. [70] Ibid.

The modern critic, that is, is unlikely to be able to determine, at a historical distance from the chosen author, which metaphors were living and which dead, and consequently is likely to emend unnecessarily, as Theobald proposes to emend the Shakespearian text here despite the fact that 'a very complaisant, finical, over-gracious person, was so commonly called the *flower*, or as he elsewhere expresses it, the *pink of courtesie*, that in common talk, or in the lowest stile, this metaphor might be used without keeping up the image'.[71]

Warburton's view of the correct editorial treatment of metaphor does indeed act as an informing methodological principle. He argues against Theobald's emendation to a line from *Henry IV, Part 2*, ('And consecrate Commotion's Civil Edge?'): 'Mr. *Theobald* changes *edge* to *page*, out of regard for the *uniformity* (as he calls it) of the metaphor.'[72] Warburton glosses 'edge' as an allusion to papal consecrations of crusaders' swords and then extends his argument against mechanical uniformity of metaphor by arguing that 'the dwelling overlong upon *one* occasions the discourse to degenerate into a dull kind of allegorism'.[73] The flexibility with which Warburton can apply his theory of metaphor is indicated in his discussion of an earlier passage from the same play: he identifies 'metal' in the lines 'For from his metal was his party steel'd | Which once in him abated' as a dead metaphor of the kind discussed in his note to *Love's Labour's Lost*, 'So that it may with elegance enough be said, *his metal was abated*, as well as *his courage was abated*'.[74] But he goes on to point out that other metallic metaphors in the context reactivate this dead metaphor and require that 'what he predicates of metal, must be then convey'd in a term conformable to the metaphor'.[75] Warburton therefore reads 'REBATED, ——*i.e.* blunted' in place of 'abated'.[76]

Warburton's discussion of Shakespeare's alleged stylistic 'incorrectness' also indicates that his claim to have given his canons of criticism in his notes is less unjustified than has been thought. In a note to *King Lear*, Warburton insists upon a distinction between two kinds of incorrectness, 'an inconsistency of the terms employed with one another; and an incongruity in the construction of them. In the first case he is rarely faulty; in the second, negligent enough.'[77] From this stylistic observation Warburton does indeed draw a canon of Shakespearian textual criticism: 'where we find gross inaccuracies, in the relation of terms to one another, there we may be confident, the text has been corrupted by his editors:

[71] *1747*, ii. 267.   [72] Ibid. iv. 268; *1740*, iv. 241; Allen and Muir 348.
[73] *1747*, iv. 269.   [74] Ibid. 209.   [75] Ibid. 210.
[76] Ibid.   [77] Ibid. vi. 66–7.

and, on the contrary, that the offences against syntax are generally his own'. The principle is immediately applied to startling effect. Warburton reads:

> Those wrinkled creatures yet do look well-favour'd,
> When others are more wrinkled . . .[78]

(where Theobald's 1740 text reads, with the First Quarto and First Folio texts, 'wicked . . . wicked') on the grounds that 'wicked', unlike 'wrinkled', is not a true contrary to 'well-favour'd'.[79] Once more this extended discussion does indeed provide a guiding principle of Warburtonian editorial practice. Queen Mab's arrival 'in shape no bigger than an agate-stone', in *Romeo and Juliet*, becomes '*In* SHADE; *no bigger than an agate-stone*' since '*Shape* not signifying *quantity* but *quality, in shape no bigger*, must needs be a great inaccuracy of expression'.[80] A similar (but more extreme) logic governs the emendation of Westmorland's 'they know your Grace hath cause' in *Henry V* to 'They know your Race had cause', so that his words may refer back to Exeter's 'As did the former Lions of your blood'.[81] Conversely, Warburton's defence (against Hanmer's tidying of the syntax) of the Duke's lines, in the opening scene of *Measure for Measure* discussed above, is an instance of his willingness to regard apparently incongruous syntax as Shakespearian rather than editorial. Where the syntax of the Elizabethan and Jacobean copies has been 'corrected', such corrections are generally already present in Warburton's copy-text. Thus the double superlative 'This was the most unkindest cut' in *Julius Caesar* had stood 'This, this, was the unkindest cut' in all editions since Pope's;[82] and the double comparative 'some more fitter place' in *Measure for Measure* had from the same date read 'some more fitting place'.[83] Even where Warburton himself emends so as to 'correct' points of grammar there are often other reasons for the emendation: thus his emendation of 'his phis'nomy is more hotter in *France*' to 'his phis'nomy is more honour'd in *France*' in *All's Well that Ends Well* is made to remove the 'nonsense' of the description of a physiognomy as 'hot' (although the removal of the double comparative may be a subsidiary motive to emendation).[84]

---

[78] Ibid. 66.   [79] *1740*, vi. 50; Hinman 803; Allen and Muir 682.

[80] *1747*, viii. 23–4; *1740*, viii. 23.   [81] *1747*, iv. 329; *1740*, iv. 292.

[82] *1723–5*, v. 270; *1733*, vi. 176; *1740*, vii. 53; *1744*, v. 248; *1747*, vii. 61.

[83] *1723–5*, i. 344; *1733*, i. 334; *1740*, i. 319; *1744*, i. 317; *1747*, i. 381.

[84] Ibid. iii. 93. The emendation first appeared in Hanmer's edn. (*1744*, ii. 404), although this does not preclude its being Warburton's own work. See Dawson, 'Warburton, Hanmer', 42.

Warburton's extended methodological notes exemplify his display of an art of criticism which claims to draw simultaneously on learning, on wider theoretical reflection, and on taste, qualities which the simply professional or simply amateur critic may separately possess but cannot combine. Such display is still more strikingly instanced in the aspect of his edition which has most attracted ridicule, his emendatory coinages. These range from the conversion of old words by their transfer from one part of speech to another (as in the case of substantive verbs) to the creation of altogether new English words from Latin words or from foreign vernaculars. The first of these categories of emendatory coinages illustrates the way in which an aspect of Theobald's learning can be implied to be the mechanical basis for an art of Warburtonian criticism which demands a genius unavailable to the mechanical drudge. Where Theobald had used his collection of examples of Shakespeare's substantive verbs principally as a defence for Folio and Quarto readings once thought to be corruptions of the text, Warburton uses it as a basis for emendatory conjecture. Thus he comments on a passage from *The Two Gentlemen of Verona* 'My substance should be statue in thy stead' that 'It is evident this noun should be a participle STATUED, *i.e.* placed on a pedestal, or fixed in a shrine to be adored', without adducing any further instances of the use of 'statue' as a verb.[85]

Warburton's coinages from other languages, especially those from Latin, also offer him the opportunity to display his sensitivity to the peculiarities of Shakespearian style. Warburton argues at a number of points (as Monboddo was later to argue of Milton) that Shakespeare uses English words with an acute sense of their etymology.[86] Thus Warburton argues that in Prospero's instruction to Ariel to 'bring a corollary, | Rather than want a spirit'[87] in *The Tempest*, the word 'corollary' 'has here a singular propriety and elegance' because it alludes to the Latin expressions 'corollaria', gifts given to the public at Roman theatrical festivals, and 'corollae', crowns awarded to the best actors.[88] Such remarks serve as an implicit justification for a series of emendatory coinages from Latin words. Thus Warburton emends 'And beauty's crest becomes the heavens well' in his text of *Love's Labour's Lost* (which he dislikes because 'he who is contending for the *white*, takes for granted the thing in dispute,

[85]   *1747*, i. 239; *1740*, i. 200.

[86]   James Burnet, Lord Monboddo, *Of the Origin and Progress of Languages* (6 vols., London, 1772–93; repr. Menston, 1967), iii. 25.

[87]   *1747*, i. 63.

[88]   Ibid. Compare also Warburton's discussion of the word 'suggestion': ibid. v. 424.

by saying, that *white* is the *crest of beauty*') to '*And beauty's* CRETE *becomes the heavens well*', 'i.e. beauty's white from *creta*'.[89] The emendation attacked by Zachary Grey, '*I have found* Demetrius *like a* GEMELL' ('From *Gemellus* a *Twin*', in place of Pope's reading 'jewel'),[90] was one of those sent by Warburton to Theobald for use in his edition. Characteristically, Warburton leaves Theobald to append there what weak support exists for such a reading: this supporting material is found surplus to requirements in Warburton's own edition.[91]

4

By this stage it should have become evident that any text settled according to Warburton's 'Art of Criticism' must create as many problems as it solves for any would-be settler of the language. If 'offences against syntax' are generally Shakespearian rather than editorial, how can Shakespeare supply an authoritative source of correct grammar to the grammarian? If a significant proportion of Shakespeare's lexicon consists of words never used before or since, how can the lexicographer use Shakespeare as an authority on the limits of the English vocabulary? These difficulties are also seen to be pressing ones in the account given in Warburton's preface of the peculiarities of Shakespeare's language, as when Warburton broaches the topic of Shakespeare's '*licentious Use of Terms*': 'To common Terms he hath affixed Meanings of his own, unauthorised by Use, and not to be justified by Analogy. And this Liberty he hath taken with the noblest Parts of Speech, such as *Mixed-modes*; which, as they are most susceptible of Abuse, so their Abuse most hurts the Clearness of the Discourse'.[92] Shakespeare's idiosyncratic usage differs from the general 'Use' (whether of Shakespeare's or of Warburton's contemporaries is not here specified), nor can it always be justified by its similarity to some aspect of that 'Use' (by 'Analogy'). And yet 'our best established Writers' are to have lexicographical authority precisely in order that disputes as to what correct usage is may be determined by reference to such writers. Accordingly Warburton rejects what he claims to be Theobald's and Hanmer's solution of regarding '*Shakespear*'s Anomalies' as 'amongst the Corruptions of his Text',[93] and he later supports this rejection by finding what he regards as an instance of such anomalous signification certified as authentically Shakespearian by its context: Warburton claims that Paulina's 'I could

[89] Ibid. ii. 243; *1740*, ii. 222.   [90] *1747*, i. 154; *1723–5*, i. 135.
[91] *1733*, i. 131–2; *1740*, i. 123.   [92] *1747*, i, p. xv.   [93] Ibid., p. xvi.

afflict you further' in *The Winter's Tale* uses 'afflict' in the sense of 'affect'
and that did not Leontes himself mention 'affliction' in his reply to
Paulina 'one should have concluded the Poet had wrote, affect you . . .
This is only observed to shew, that when we find words to which we must
put an unusual signification to make sense, that we ought to conclude
Shakespear took that liberty, and that the text is not corrupted.'[94] Shakespeare's linguistic peculiarities must be understood as licensed by his own
authority, paralleling Johnson's admission into his *Plan of A Dictionary*
(which appeared in the same year as Warburton's edition) of 'the peculiar
sense, in which a word is found in any great author'.[95]

The consequences of Shakespeare's linguistic idiosyncrasy are especially acute because they concern 'Mixed-modes', which Warburton
here describes as 'the noblest Parts of speech' and which he regarded as
offering a central problem to any proposed English dictionary. When discussing the possibility of such a dictionary with Spence in 1744, Warburton remarked that 'The chief difficulty in a work of this kind would lie
in giving the definitions of the names of mixed-modes.'[96] The importance
of this difficulty is indicated by the aims of the projected 'large Glossary'
to his future edition (which, like the promised 'rules' of criticism, did not
in the event appear there) announced in the *General Dictionary*:

> It will be a Glossary of the words in Shakespeare, which require explanation; not
> of *terms of art* or *obsolete expressions*, for these every common Dictionary or Gloss-
> ary will supply; but of such words [*'chiefly mixed modes', Warburton later explains*]
> as Shakespeare has affixed peculiar significations of his own to, unauthorized by
> use, and unjustified by analogy . . .[97]

It is not the place of the editor of Shakespeare, Warburton implies, to
provide what may be supplied by mechanical consultation of 'common'
reference works, but to provide glosses for just that selection of Shakespeare's lexicon which may only be detected and explained by the art of
the qualified critic. Despite Warburton's emphasis on the lexicographical
usefulness of a correctly edited text of Shakespeare, such a text will, it

---

[94]   *1747*, iii. 382.

[95]   Samuel Johnson, *The Plan of a Dictionary* (London, 1747; repr. Menston, 1970), 24.

[96]   Spence, *Observations*, i. 374. For the source of Warburton's term 'Mixed-modes', and
a definition of it, see John Locke, *An Essay Concerning Human Understanding*, ed. P. H.
Nidditch (Oxford, 1975), 288: 'the Complex *Ideas*, we mark by the names *Obligation*,
Drunkenness, a *Lye*, etc., which Consisting of several Combinations of simple *Ideas* of
different kinds, I have called *Mixed Modes*, to distinguish them from the more simple
Modes, which consist only of simple *Ideas* of the same kind.'

[97]   Birch *et al.*, eds., *A General Dictionary*, ix. 190 n.

appears, be of little assistance in offering other than purely Shakespearian sense for that part of speech which constitutes the 'chief difficulty' for any lexicographer.

Shakespeare poses equal difficulties as an authority for the grammarian. Warburton argues that a 'hard and unnatural Construction' adopted so as to 'disguise a vulgar expression'[98] is typical of the dramatist, and that here even the drastic solution allegedly adopted by Theobald and Hanmer with respect to Shakespeare's licentious usage is of no avail, since 'the arbitrary change of a Word doth little towards dispelling an obscurity that ariseth, not from the licentious use of a single Term, but from the unnatural arrangement of a whole Sentence'.[99] None the less, that Warburton still wishes to retain Shakespeare as a model of correct construction is indicated by his subsequent qualification of this judgement: he concedes that 'in his best works, we must allow, he is often so natural and flowing, so pure and correct, that he is even a model for stile and language'.[100] Once more the advertised blessings of a settled Shakespearian text to those who would settle the English language turn out to be mixed. Even were the grammarian to resolve to admit only Shakespeare's 'best works' as models of correctness, the grammarian must first decide (on his or her own grammatical grounds) which those works are: an authority in whose canon only those works approved by a grammarian are authoritative is no longer more than a subsidiary authority.

Warburton's edition, then, and his attempt to enlist Shakespearian textual criticism in the service of a more settled and correct English language, illustrate at length the circular nature of the notion of linguistic authority with which Warburton works. The provision of a canon of correct texts of good authors is intended to obviate disagreement about the correctness or otherwise of particular expressions, but such a canon, and the details of its texts, are themselves determined by those who wish to refer to such authorities in case of dispute. Yet it would be wrong to think of Warburton's predicament as a trivial one, or to regard his attempts at dealing with it as merely idiosyncratic; as Randall McLeod has pointed out, it is a problem which persists (albeit in a different form) for contemporary lexicographers.[101] Warburton's edition did indeed make its own small impact upon the language: Johnson marked up a copy for illustrative

---

[98] *1747*, i, pp. xvi–xvii.   [99] Ibid.   [100] Ibid.
[101] Randall McLeod (as 'Random Clod'), 'Information on Information', *Text*, 5 (1991), 241–82 (pp. 249–50).

quotations to his dictionary, and several of Warburton's subsequently ridiculed coinages consequently appear there;[102] 'behowls', a word invented by Warburton, can still be found in current editions of *A Midsummer Night's Dream* and in the *Oxford English Dictionary*.[103] Such occasional survivals are the traces of a broader set of critical methods which, whilst far from systematically coherent, are by no means as random as has sometimes been thought. Furthermore, the problems of linguistic authority which Warburton faced had also to be struggled with by Samuel Johnson. The two contrasting ideas of literary labour with which Warburton's edition had so anxiously negotiated were to remain of central importance to Johnson's work as a textual critic and lexicographer.

[102] A. Cuming, 'A Copy of Shakespeare's Works which Formerly Belonged to Dr. Johnson', *Review of English Studies*, 3 (1927), 208–12; Arthur Sherbo, 'Dr. Johnson's "Dictionary" and Warburton's "Shakespeare" ', *Philological Quarterly*, 33 (1954), 94–6. See Samuel Johnson, *A Dictionary of the English Language* (2 vols., London, 1755): BEHOWL; STATUE (v.a.); GAUDE.

[103] See e.g. Harold F. Brooks, ed., *A Midsummer Night's Dream* (London, 1979), 124; *The Oxford English Dictionary*, 2nd edn. (20 vols., Oxford, 1989), ii. 79. The word was subsequently used by Emerson and Kingsley in the 19th cent.

6

Johnson's Authorities:
The Professional Scholar and
English Texts in Lexicography
and Textual Criticism

THE FULLEST account of the social and political significance of Johnson's writings about language—that by John Barrell in his *Equal, Wide, Survey*—points to an apparent contradiction in Johnson's account of English usage. Who may be said to use the language properly? Barrell argues that Johnson 'regards the national language as derived from a world apart from and above the languages of those who follow particular callings', but also refuses to specify any group of language users who might be thought to inhabit such a world. This may indicate, Barrell goes on, 'either that the writer, at least one who lives in the world and not in the cloister, is now the only authority, or . . . that perhaps no one can now claim that his own language is the national language'.[1] These last two suggestions are significant, both for the way in which Johnson thought about and used the illustrative quotations which were the decisively new feature of his *Dictionary*, and for the close relationship in Johnson's philological career between lexicography and textual criticism. A problem of circularity attends any attempt to define a community of authoritative users of a language, and Johnson's is no exception: authority necessarily devolves upon the figure responsible for selecting the authorities, so that those authorities themselves may come to appear the bearers of a merely supplementary authority. Moreover, Johnson's own position as a professional writer and scholar, who was happy (unlike many of his predecessors) to acknowledge that he wrote for money, made him unable to assent to any notion that a 'qualification necessary to the authoritative users of the

---

[1] John Barrell, *English Literature in History, 1730–1780: An Equal, Wide, Survey* (London, 1983), 134.

language was a private income substantial enough to free them from the need to work for a living'.[2]

Johnson's own expository statements on such questions, as Donald T. Siebert has pointed out, have too often been considered in isolation from his philological practice.[3] The best way of answering any question as to which group of writers or speakers Johnson imagined to be authoritative users of the language is to examine the wide variety of texts adduced in support of individual words in the main body of the *Dictionary* itself. A large mass of commentary on questions of linguistic propriety lies buried in the many occasional comments which Johnson adduced to particular words or senses of words, and while these remarks have often been quarried for evidence as to Johnson's opinions on particular issues, less interest has been shown in considering the linguistic implications of this body of commentary as a whole. An examination of this material shows not only the breadth of sources quoted by Johnson but also the complexity of the ways in which they are cited. Quotation of a source does not in all cases imply its authoritativeness, since Johnson's commentary frequently qualifies or undermines the source's authority. Such qualifications reinforce Barrell's sense that, for Johnson, no speaker or writer can be considered an unproblematically authoritative user of the language. What is more, the same material also complicates any attempt to identify those who are taken to threaten the language with any single social or cultural group.

I

Johnson first publicly discussed the project of a dictionary that might both settle and purify the English language in the *Plan of a Dictionary* (1747). He renounced from the outset the possibility of achieving the ends of such a dictionary by the reduction of linguistic irregularities to an analogical conformity: 'OUR syntax . . . is not to be taught by general rules, but by special precedents'.[4] Consequently, 'the credit of every part of this work must depend' upon the authorities cited in support of it.[5] Johnson is aware, however, that such a solution leaves several questions unanswered.

---

[2] John Barrell, 134.
[3] Donald T. Siebert, '*Bubbled, Bamboozled*, and *Bit*: "Low Bad" Words in Johnson's *Dictionary*', *Studies in English Literature*, 26 (1986), 485–96 (p. 486).
[4] Samuel Johnson, *The Plan of a Dictionary* (London, 1747; repr. Menston, 1970), 19.
[5] Ibid. 30.

Which writers are to be taken as authoritative, and by what criteria or according to whose judgement is the selection to be made? Johnson considers this in terms of a metaphor from law:

IT has been asked, on some occasions, who shall judge the judges? And since with regard to this design a question may arise by what authority the authorities are selected, it is necessary to obviate it, by declaring that many of the writers whose testimonies will be alleged, were selected by Mr. Pope, of whom I may be justified in affirming, that were he still alive, solicitous as he was for the success of this work, he would not be displeased that I have undertaken it.[6]

Johnson's reply is an ironic admission that the notion of authority in language is at some point a necessarily arbitrary one. Pope's name will in itself, it is expected, 'obviate' further questioning, including any question as to how Pope himself has been selected. Meanwhile, Pope is made to endorse Johnson's suitability on Johnson's own testimony. Final authority over the dictionary, this passage makes clear, rests with the lexicographer himself, however much he may be buttressed by the testimony of others; Johnson's claims on the previous page, merely to be 'exercising a kind of vicarious jurisdiction' as Chesterfield's delegate, are made as a rhetorical apology for his decision 'to interpose my own judgment'.[7]

Once the *Dictionary* has been completed, it is still clear even from Johnson's 'Preface' that the lexicographer's authority cannot be dispensed with, despite Johnson's pains there to discount any ambitions thoroughly to regularize the language. From the pre-Restoration writers whose work represents 'the wells of English undefiled', Johnson remarks, 'a speech might be formed adequate to all the purposes of use and elegance' by selecting particular kinds of vocabulary from particular writers: for use and elegance to be served the lexicographer must first filter out whatever might obstruct such purposes.[8] Such an interposition of the lexicographer's judgement necessarily raises the possibility that an interested or partial representation of the language may be given by the *Dictionary*, especially since Johnson begins the 'Preface' to his work by describing lexicography as one of the 'lower employments of life'.[9] As in the *Plan*, but more drastically so, Johnson resorts in the face of this difficulty to an ironic stoicism which takes any hope of complete disinterestedness as a vain illusion. His discussion of the question of living authorities epitomizes this procedure:

---

[6] Ibid. 31.   [7] Ibid. 30.
[8] Samuel Johnson, *A Dictionary of the English Language* (2 vols., London, 1755), i, sig. C1^r.
[9] Ibid., sig. [A]2^r.

My purpose was to admit no testimony of living authours, that I might not be misled by partiality, and that none of my cotemporaries might have reason to complain; nor have I departed from this resolution, but when some performance of uncommon excellence excited my veneration, when my memory supplied me, from late books, with an example that was wanting, or when my heart, in the tenderness of friendship, solicited admission for a favourite name.[10]

Johnson's self-collapsing disclaimer ends bathetically, by admitting into the catalogue of exceptional deviations from his rule that very partiality which the exclusion of living writers is designed to obviate. Such an admission intimates that any attempt to exclude the lexicographer's partiality is bound to fail.

The mutual interdependence of a dictionary-maker whose legitimacy rests upon a body of authoritative quotations, on the one hand, and authorities contingent upon the lexicographer's selection, on the other, is evident in the main body of the 1755 *Dictionary* itself. Johnson's use of illustrative quotations was what critically distinguished his *Dictionary* from previous English dictionaries and invited comparison with the della Crusca and Académie française dictionaries; and many features of the *Dictionary* emphasized its character as a collection of precedents rather than of prescriptions. Charles Richardson, a follower of Horne Tooke who was committed to Tooke's etymological approach to semantics, believed that Johnson had merely provided 'A collection . . . of usages, quoted from (in general) our best English authors, and those usages explained to suit the quotations'.[11] This view of Johnson's work as a commentary upon a body of selected precedents (consistent with the metaphor from English common, rather than Roman, law in the *Plan*) is certainly confirmed by the content of many of Johnson's entries. In many cases the numeral denoting a further sense of the word is followed not by a definition but by a commentary on a given passage from one of Johnson's authorities. On several occasions, words of whose meaning Johnson confesses himself ignorant are included in the *Dictionary* because they occur in one of Johnson's sources. On URIM (n.s.), for example, Johnson cites Thomas Newton, the editor of Milton, to the effect that '*Urim* and thummim were something in Aaron's breastplate; but what, cricks and commentators are by no means agreed' and appends a quotation from Newton's text of Milton. Still blunter are some of Johnson's other admissions of ignorance: of both STAMMEL (n.s.) and TROLMYDAMES (n.s.), to take only two

---

[10]   Samuel Johnson, sig. B2ᵛ.
[11]   Quoted in Allen Reddick, *The Making of Johnson's Dictionary 1746–1773* (Cambridge, 1990), 48.

instances, from Shakespeare and Ben Jonson respectively, Johnson confesses 'Of this word I know not the meaning'. He remarks tersely that the
noun CLINK 'seems in *Spenser* to have some unusual sense' and then simply
reprints the passage in question.

In cases where Johnson provides a conjectural definition based on a
single passage, the sense that the dictionary may become a series of scholia
is still stronger. SERE, supported by a quotation from Chapman's translation of the *Odyssey*, is defined as 'Claw; talon', but within parentheses
Johnson admits that 'Of this word I know not the etymology, nor, except
from this passage, the meaning'. Nor does such treatment apply only to
Johnson's pre-Restoration sources: the verb TO TORE, despite Johnson's
admission that 'Of this word I cannot guess the meaning', is included,
even though it is authorized only by John Mortimer's *The Whole Art of
Husbandry*.[12] In all these cases an idea of the dictionary as a collection of
precedents, and only secondarily as a system of definitions, is implied: so
that even where no definition of a word is to be given, it must nevertheless
be included as belonging to one of the authorities used. Johnson did not,
of course, actually include the entire vocabulary of each source quoted
from; even in the case of Shakespeare, the most extensively cited author in
the 1755 edition, there are clearly many words available in Warburton's
text alone which Johnson does not include. The point is, rather, that the
inclusion of undefined words implies to readers of the *Dictionary* that any
words appearing in the chosen sources must be listed.

Other aspects of Johnson's lexicographical practice seem to confirm the
priority given to recording the usage of authorities over prescription. The
categories of the 'peculiar sense, in which a word is found in any great
author' and of 'words which are found only in particular books', already
announced in the *Plan*, are often called upon in the *Dictionary*, most often
for Shakespeare, but also for a surprising variety of other authorities.[13]
Such a category emphasizes the *Dictionary*'s function as a commentary
upon the usage of its authorities. The words listed thus form 'part of
the durable materials of a language', not in the sense that they will continue to be written or spoken, since they are appropriated to particular
authors or texts, but only in the sense that they will continue to be
read.[14] TO ILLIGHTEN (v.n.) is 'A word, I believe, only in *Raleigh*'; whilst

---

[12] John Mortimer, *The Whole Art of Husbandry: Or, the Way of Managing and Improving
of Land*, 5th edn. (2 vols., London, 1721). For further instances of words listed whose
meaning is unknown or conjectured at from the passage given, see TO COTE (v.a.) (Chapman),
and SKILT (n.s.) (Cleveland).

[13] *Plan*, 24; 28.   [14] *Dictionary*, i, sig. C1ᵛ.

SUFFICIENCY (n.s.) 'is used by *Temple* for that conceit which makes a man think himself equal to things above him': in each case the implication is that these senses are not available for general use but are a record of usage proper in works by Ralegh and Temple respectively. This is still more clearly the case with words appearing only in particular passages, or nonce-words, such as Milton's ADAMANTEAN (adj.), Shakespeare's INCARNADINE (v.a.), or Bacon's BEEMOL (n.s.). Nor, despite Johnson's reference to 'any great author' in the *Plan*, is the range of authorities selected for such treatment especially restricted. Thus Thomson's use of LUCULENT (adj.) to mean 'Clear; transparent; lucid' is received, even though 'This word is perhaps not used in this sense by any other writer', and despite the fact that Johnson elsewhere casts doubt on Thomson's authority; similarly, the testimony of John Norris, a writer infrequently quoted by Johnson, supports a sense of the adjective ECSTATICAL 'only to be found once'.

But if the accumulation of commentary such as this appears to imply that the lexicographer's primary task is to collect and annotate the materials at his disposal, there are also occasions on which Johnson shows himself hostile to ἅπαξ λεγομενα as well as to words or senses of words peculiar to individual authors, and in a way which qualifies the linguistic authority of the writers in question. The noun CITESS is noted as 'A word peculiar to *Dryden*' without any adverse comment: the implication is that Dryden is licensed to employ his own vocabulary. But on other occasions, Johnson takes vigorous issue with expressions peculiar to Dryden: 'MACKEREL-GALE seems to be, in *Dryden*'s cant, a strong breeze, such, I suppose, as is desired to bring *mackerel* fresh to market.' Here the peculiarity of Dryden's word classifies it not as part of a licensed idiolect, but as 'cant', a term whose complexities we shall need to investigate later, but one which certainly implies disapproval. Still more striking is Johnson's procedure in the case of sense 4 of TO FALSIFY, 'To pierce; to run through', defended by Dryden on analogy with the Italian *falsare*. Johnson quotes Dryden's defence at length and then remarks that '*Dryden*, with all this effort, was not able to naturalise the new signification, which I have never seen copied, except once by some obscure nameless writer, and which indeed deserves not to be received.' Although elsewhere a single appearance in the text of an authoritative writer (amongst whom Dryden is numbered) is sufficient in itself to constitute the reception of a word, here TO FALSIFY is regarded as not received, despite its use not only by Dryden but also by another, albeit 'nameless', writer. Dryden's presentation of his word as a conscious innovation is probably what prompts Johnson's scepticism: but it is none the less clear that Dryden's authoritiveness varies from case to case, to be supplemented, as here, by Johnson's own authority.

The extent to which the authoritative status of the sources cited may be qualified is seen still more clearly in the case of Johnson's quotations from James Thomson's *The Seasons*. Thomson is sometimes given as the sole authority for certain words without this fact implying that those words are less fully authorized than others.[15] But a number of notes call into question whether Thomson can really be considered an authority on English usage at all. The verb TO TUFT (v.a.), for example, is described as 'a doubtful word, not authorised by any competent writer': Thomson's is the sole testimony cited in favour of the word. TO CULTURE (v.a.) is, similarly, described as 'used by *Thomson*, but without authority'; Thomson's use of TO DRILL (v.a.) as 'To drain; to draw slowly' (sense 6) 'wants better authority'. At one point Thomson is taken as a Scottish writer likely to introduce Scotticisms: TO FREAK (v.a.) is described as 'A word, I suppose, Scotch, brought into England by *Thomson*.'[16]

Indeed almost all the sources quoted, not only those who, like Thomson, are of recent or supposedly peripheral provenance, are liable to Johnson's censure. Of Johnson's list of pre-Restoration writers representing 'the wells of English undefiled', for example, scarcely any is free from occasional criticism. Bacon is responsible for low[17] and vulgar[18] expressions and for Latinisms;[19] Hooker's sense of TO EXAGITATE (v.a.) to mean 'To reproach; to pursue with invectives' is 'now disused, being purely Latin'.[20] Shakespeare provides examples for most of the available categories of disapproval;[21] Spenser is frequently convicted of using Latinisms[22] and of inventing words to serve the 'poor convenience of his rhyme';[23] Ralegh uses the adjective WONDROUS 'barbarously' as an adverb.[24] The

[15] For examples see, in addition to LUCULENT (adj.), TO BROADEN (v.n.) and TO MEEKEN (v.a.).

[16] Allen Reddick has pointed out that the number of quotations from Thomson is substantially reduced in the 4th edn.: see *Johnson's Dictionary*, 136–40. For other points at which Thomson's authority is called into question, see TO GIRT (v.a.), INFUSIVE (adj.), TO SAVAGE (v.a.), SKYED (adj.), and SITE (n.s.).

[17] See GREAT (adj.) (sense 11) and POSSE (n.s.).

[18] See PRETTY (adj.) (sense 4).

[19] See EXPEDITE (adj.) (sense 4) and TO PREVENT (v.n.).

[20] See TO EXAGITATE (v.a.) (sense 2).

[21] For a few of many examples see QUIDDIT (n.s.) ('low'), FULHAM (n.s.) ('cant'), TO PEAL (v.a.) (sense 2) ('used . . . improperly'), IMMOMENT (adj.) ('barbarous'), and FRAUGHTAGE (n.s.) ('bad').

[22] See, for examples, TO COMPARE (v.a.) (sense 4), PRINCIPAL (adj.) (sense 1), TO TEMPER (v.a.) (sense 8).

[23] QUAID (part.). See also TO LEAVE (v.a.) ('To levy; to raise').

[24] WONDROUS (adj.) (sense 2).

King James Bible is cited at one point to show how '*Way* and *ways*, are now often corruptly used for *wise*'.[25] Given that Johnson's most highly commended authorities are liable not only, as the 'Preface' has already suggested, to selection, but also to censure, the significance of the authorities takes on a rather different complexion. No authority, however good, is exempt from criticism, so that Johnson's own authority is constantly required to supplement that of his sources.

This is clear in the many instances where Johnson claims that authorities have misused a word as a result of not understanding its 'true' meaning. Thus under the noun WARLOCK or WARLUCK it is claimed that Dryden 'did not understand the word': nevertheless the only authority given for the word is a quotation from Dryden. Elsewhere Swift,[26] Samuel Garth,[27] John Philips (the author of *Cider*),[28] and Thomson[29] are all presented as having misunderstood the words for whose usage they stand as authorities. In many instances, indeed, authorities become altogether dispensable: as Johnson himself admits in the 'Preface', the only authority given for a word is often '*Dict.*', referring to Bailey's *Dictionarium Britannicum* (1730). On other occasions, no authority whatsoever is provided for a particular word or sense of a word, and consequently such words are suffered to stand upon Johnson's own attestation;[30] more rarely, the testimony of 'Anonymous' is brought to bear.[31] For some words a quotation from Johnson's own writings provides the only support.[32]

The circularity of authoritative usage means that much of Johnson's philological commentary is able to become surprisingly prescriptive. One instance of this is provided by Johnson's frequent insistence that, where possible, words should be spelt so as to indicate their derivations. At times such an insistence leads Johnson into direct conflict with the authorities upon whose testimony the credit of every part of his dictionary had once been expected to depend. Under CIMETER (n.s.), for example, Johnson quotes a derivation from '*cimitarra*, Span. and Portug. from *chimeteir*, Turkish' and then comments that 'This word is sometimes erroneously

---

[25] WAY (n.s.) (sense 25). The passage cited is Num. 30: 15.

[26] See INCARNATE (adj.) (sense 2) and MENIAL (adj.) (sense 2).

[27] See HAGGARD (n.s.) (sense 3).

[28] See TO INTERLARD (v.a.) (sense 4) and IRRIGUOUS (adj.) (sense 2).

[29] See TO SCOOP (v.a.) (sense 2).

[30] See, amongst many other examples, ATTENUANT (adj.), TO EXAMINE (sense 3), and PORTERAGE (n.s.).

[31] See BREECH (n.s.) (sense 3) and SHIN (n.s.).

[32] See TO DISJOINT (v.a.) (sense 2) and SULTANESS (n.s.). For Johnson's self-quotation in general see W. K. Wimsatt, jun., and Margaret H. Wimsatt, 'Self-Quotations and Anonymous Quotations in Johnson's Dictionary', *English Literary History*, 15 (1948), 60–8.

spelt *scimitar*, and *scymeter*; as in the following examples.' Indeed, no examples whatever of Johnson's proposed spelling are provided: here credit clearly rests, not with the authorities (Shakespeare and Dryden) but with a prescriptive preference for etymological orthography. In Johnson's remark on sense 2 of the adjective HAGGARD, the text of a source is effectively rewritten to provide Johnson's preferred spelling. An analogous case is represented by the instances in which Johnson objects to individual words on the grounds that they are internally tautologous or self-contradictory. Thus of TO DISSEVER (v.a.) Johnson notes that 'In this word the particle *dis* makes no change in the signification, and therefore the word, though supported by great authorities, ought to be ejected from our language'. Here the internal tautology of 'dis' and 'sever' is held to outweigh the admittedly great authorities (Sidney, Ralegh, Shakespeare, and Pope), although the status of the word remains ambiguous, since whilst its ejection from the language has been recommended, it is nevertheless retained in the *Dictionary*.[33] Yet Johnson is not always willing in such instances to set his own judgement above those of his chosen authors. In many instances Johnson's own preference and those of his sources are left in unresolved tension. Of the adjective OUTRAGIOUS Johnson remarks 'It should, I think, be written *outrageous*, but the custom seems otherwise', just as ODDLY (adv.) 'and *oddness* should, I think, be written with one *d*; but the writers almost all combine against it'. The failure to resolve a conflict between usage and prescription is still more starkly evident in Johnson's comments under TO GHESS (v.n.): '*Ghess* is by criticks considered as the true orthography, but *guess* has universally prevailed'. When an abridged version of the *Dictionary* was published in 1756 this tension remained unresolved: one of the 1756 edition's advertised advantages over previous concise dictionaries was that 'The words are more correctly spelled, partly by attention to their etymology, and partly by observation of the practice of the best authors.'[34]

The detailed evidence of Johnson's continuous commentary upon his sources, then, suggests that the notion of linguistic authority is one which works in complex and variable ways within the main body of the *Dictionary* itself. The illustrative quotations provide the basis of the dictionary's substance and organization, and where several authorities are collected together Johnson is reluctant to contradict them. Nevertheless, Johnson's remarks upon the usages of his authorities are a constant reminder that

---

[33] Cf. also TO UNLOOSE (v.a.); HENCE (adv. or interj.) (sense 8).

[34] Samuel Johnson, *A Dictionary of the English Language . . . Abstracted from the Folio Edition* (2 vols., London, 1756), i, sig. π 1ᵛ.

their authoritative status is itself dependent upon Johnson's selection, and also that such status is relative rather than absolute: different texts are authoritative in differing degrees, and are variously liable to have their authority suspended and replaced by Johnson's own judgement.

2

It is not in any case clear that a putative authoritative user of the language, for Johnson, need be leisured or disinterested. Johnson's explicit self-presentation as a literary professional is accompanied throughout his work by an understanding of the national language and culture which sees leisured vanity as a threat equal to professional interestedness. Consequently neither Johnson's lexicographical writings nor his philological practice wish to identify a single social or economic group as indisputable correct users of the language. Conversely, no section of the population is in practice presented as automatically incorrect in its usage. The impossibility of mapping linguistic correctness on to social provenance means once more that many cases are settled by the intervention of a lexicographer who is himself the self-declared follower of a particular calling.

It is obvious that the authority over language offered in the *Dictionary* is an authority of writers, not of those who are only speakers of the language; more significantly, conversation is repeatedly seen in Johnson's commentary as a corrupting influence on the language, which is thereby represented as primarily written. Thus the adjective COMPATIBLE is declared to have arrived at an unetymological spelling by the influence of spoken English: the word has been 'corrupted, by an unskilful compliance with pronunciation, from *competible*, from *competo*, Latin, to *suit*, to *agree*'. Similarly HOBNOB is 'probably corrupted from *hab nab* by a coarse pronunciation', whilst LIMBECK (n.s.) 'has been corrupted by popular pronunciation from *alembick*'. ROUNDABOUT 'is used as an adjective, though it is only an adverb united to a substantive by a colloquial license of language, which ought not to have been admitted into books'. The first difference listed in the 'Preface' to the 1756 abridgement between the likely users of that abstract and those of the full text was that the former were 'seldom intending to write'.[35] For such readers, the names of writers alone were sufficient authorization: the 1756 title-page described

---

[35] Samuel Johnson, sig. π 1^r.

the *Dictionary*'s word-stock as 'Authorized by the NAMES of the WRITERS in whose Works they are found'.[36]

At one level, of course, the distinction between the imagined readership of the abridged *Dictionary* and that of the first edition is a distinction in social status: the former are likely to 'turn over books only to amuse their leisure, and to gain degrees of knowledge suitable to lower characters, or necessary to the common business of life'.[37] But it is also clear that, for Johnson, the distinction between those who write and those who merely read is not to be reduced to a distinction between the polite and the vulgar, or one between the disinterested man of leisure and those who follow a particular calling. Alvin Kernan has recently re-emphasized the extent to which Johnson's literary persona was built around an explicit writerly professionalism.[38] Whereas Pope could write in the preface to his 1717 *Works* that 'I writ because it amus'd me' and insist that he aspired to the character of a good man more than to that of a good writer,[39] Johnson found such disclaimers unconvincing and deplored the 'despicable foppery' of wishing to be considered as a gentleman first and an author second.[40] The same contempt for the leisured dabbler is evident in Johnson's remarks that Somerville 'writes very well for a gentleman'.[41] Johnson's explicit self-construction as a professional writer was one recognized by his opponents. For Archibald Campbell, attacking Johnson as 'Lexiphanes', it was an important charge against Johnson and the change he had brought about in the tone of the literary world that 'those Lexiphaneses . . . are all, excepting the boys just raw from the university, authors by profession; and they reckon a gentleman who writes, or in the language of the shop, makes a book, an interloper who takes so much of their trade out of their hands'.[42] As we have seen, Johnson's own authority as a lexicographer inevitably figures largely in the pages of the *Dictionary*, although lexicography itself has already been described as one of 'the lower employments of life'.[43]

Such considerations certainly did not mean that Johnson wholly abandoned any notion that interestedness could pose a threat to a legitimate

---

[36] Ibid., title-page. [37] Ibid., sig. π 1ʳ.
[38] Alvin Kernan, *Printing Technology, Letters, and Samuel Johnson* (Princeton, NJ, 1987).
[39] Alexander Pope, *The Prose Works of Alexander Pope*, ed. Norman Ault and Rosemary Cowler (2 vols., Oxford, 1936–86), i. 292; 295.
[40] Samuel Johnson, *Prefaces, Biographical and Critical, to the Works of the English Poets* (10 vols., London, 1779–81), vi. 'Life of Congreve', 23.
[41] Ibid. ix. 'Life of Somerville', 4.
[42] Archibald Campbell, *Lexiphanes, A Dialogue. Imitated from Lucian, and suited to the present Times* (London, 1767), p. xviii.
[43] *Dictionary* (1755), i, sig. A2ʳ.

national language and culture. Johnson, instead, develops further the position implicit in the *Dunciad* and in much of Warburton's editorial work, that the language and its monuments are as liable to be damaged by amateur vanity as they are by venal interestedness. It is startling to find how frequently Johnson uses the antithetical pairing of 'vanity and interest' as a way of summarizing all possible motives to writing. When reviewing Soame Jenyns's *Free Enquiry into the Nature and Origin of Evil* in 1757 Johnson asked, 'I am told, that this pamphlet is not the effort of hunger; What can it be then but the product of vanity?'[44] A dedication written by Johnson for a *Dictionary of the English and Italian Languages*, which appeared in 1760, described the generality of dedications as 'dictated by interest or vanity'.[45] Indeed, the pairing of interest and vanity recurs not only in Johnson's considerations of motives to writing but also in his moral and political thought more generally. Johnson's *Observations on the Present State of Affairs* questions the need for secrecy about policy insisted upon by 'ministers, and those whom vanity or interest makes the followers of ministers'.[46] In *Rambler*, no. 79, Johnson refers to 'the two great seducers of the world, vanity and interest',[47] and other *Ramblers* repeat this formulation;[48] in his 'Introduction' to *The World Displayed* (1760) Johnson refers to the way in which 'Interest and pride harden the heart'.[49]

A more extensive examination of the way in which vanity can constitute as serious a threat as interest to the nation's culture is offered by the sketch in *Rambler*, no. 82, of the collector, or virtuoso. The virtuoso inherits a small estate whose revenues he expends in forming a collection of rarities. In the *Dunciad*, 'Tibbald' amasses a large collection of supposedly obsolete literature only to convert it into a sacrificial pyre. Here too the unreflective collector is taken as a destroyer, rather than a preserver, of cultural monuments: 'I never entered an old house, from which I did not take away the painted glass, and often lamented, that I was not one of that happy generation who demolished the convents and monasteries, and broke windows by law.'[50] But here the collector-as-destroyer is not an impoverished hack, but a propertied prodigal, whose own collection is finally dispersed when he arrives at financial ruin, having mortgaged his estate in

---

[44] *The Literary Magazine: or, Universal Review: for the Year MDCCLVII: Vol. II* (London, 1757; repr. Newark, NJ, 1978), 171.

[45] *Samuel Johnson's Prefaces and Dedications*, ed. Allen T. Hazen (New York, 1937), 8.

[46] Samuel Johnson, *Political Writings*, ed. Donald J. Greene (New Haven, Conn., 1977), 186.

[47] Johnson, *The Rambler*, ed. W. J. Bate and Albrecht B. Strauss (3 vols., New Haven, Conn., 1969), no. 79, ii. 51.

[48] Ibid., no. 64, i. 344; no. 77, ii. 44.   [49] *Johnson's Prefaces*, ed. Hazen, 227.

[50] *Rambler*, no. 82, ii. 65.

order to purchase medals from the Harleian collection. The discussion of collectors in the following *Rambler* describes the virtuoso as one who has 'discovered a method of gratifying his desire of eminence by expence rather than by labour, and known the sweets of a life blest at once with the ease of idleness, and the reputation of knowledge'.[51] Here it is just that obligation to work for a living experienced by the unpropertied scholar which renders such a scholar more likely to produce valuable work than any man of property who takes his wealth as sanctioning idleness. In *Rambler*, no. 108, Erasmus's life is taken to exemplify the general truth that 'among those who have contributed to the advancement of learning, many have risen to eminence in opposition to all the obstacles which external circumstances could place in their way, amidst the tumult of business, the distresses of poverty, or the dissipations of a wandering and unsettled state'.[52] Poverty need by no means disqualify the scholar: indeed, it is here taken as characteristic of the true scholar's life.

Johnson lays far less emphasis than Pope and Warburton either upon the low social provenance of minute criticism or upon its epistemological partiality of view. The extended discussion of scholarship in *Rambler*, no. 137, illustrates this point. Certainly a notion of the gentleman–scholar akin to that of Warburton's self-presentation is still available to Johnson, together with its attendant insistence upon simultaneous comprehensiveness and minuteness of attention. Johnson wishes 'that they who devote their lives to study would at once believe nothing too great for their attainment, and consider nothing as too little for their regard; that they would extend their notice alike to science and to life, and unite some knowledge of the present world to their acquaintance with past ages and remote events'.[53] Here we can see once more an implicit parallel at work between the pattern of intellectual endeavour and the scholar's social position: the scholar who will succeed in uniting the great with the little, the comprehensive with the minute, will be the scholar who can successfully participate in the sphere of 'life'. 'Life' and 'science' appear as opposites. But Johnson's discussion of the question elsewhere indicates that the appearance of the scholar uniting broad comprehension with minute attention would be a prodigy hardly to be hoped for. In *Rambler*, no. 43, he sets out a view of two contrasting kinds of intellectual endeavour which hardly seems to allow for their possible unification in one mind: 'There seem to be some souls suited to great, and others to little employments; some formed to soar aloft, and take in wide views, and

---

[51] Ibid., no. 83, ii. 75.   [52] Ibid., no. 108, ii. 213.   [53] Ibid., no. 137, ii. 362.

others to grovel on the ground, and confine their regard to a narrow sphere. Of these the one is always in danger of becoming useless by a daring negligence, the other by a scrupulous solicitude . . .'[54]

Comprehensive views and attentiveness to particulars are unlikely to be found together in the same person. But they may, for Johnson, be found together in a single work, because of the essentially syncretic character of intellectual inquiry. Whereas for Pope any number of minute criticisms could never add up to a comprehensive idea of the whole, comprehensiveness is, for Johnson, potentially obtainable by the accretion of minute particulars. Earlier in *Rambler*, no. 137, Johnson presents a surprising extended comparison between the world of scholarship and a factory, a comparison which lays greater emphasis on the need for attention to the little than on aspiration to the great:

Among the productions of mechanic art, many are of a form so different from that of their first materials, and many consist of parts so numerous and so nicely adapted to each other, that it is not possible to view them without amazement. But when we enter the shops of artificers, observe the various tools by which every operation is facilitated, and trace the progress of a manufacture thro' the different hands that, in succession to each other, contribute to its perfection, we soon discover that every single man has an easy task, and that the extremes however remote of natural rudeness and artificial elegance, are joined by a regular concatenation of effects, of which every one is introduced by that which precedes it, and equally introduces that which is to follow.

The same is the state of intellectual and manual performances.[55]

This passage offers a striking contrast with the surveys of the world of learning which we have previously examined. It is unlikely that such a comparison could have been made by either Pope or Warburton: for the earlier writers, it is just the distorted partiality of vision which divided intellectual labour imposes on each critic that renders such criticism mutilating by its insufficient attention to the whole. Nor could Johnson have shared Goldsmith's horror at the 'fatal revolution whereby writing is converted to a mechanic trade'.[56] Johnson, instead, is here able to take the artificer's shop as a model for the smooth operation of the world of learning. Comprehensiveness of understanding, according to such a model, is not a goal to which the individual critic either need or can reasonably aspire, but one which inheres in the completed product made up of the partial contributions of divided intellectual labour. Johnson's remarks to Boswell on a similar topic in 1763 emphasize this point:

[54] *Rambler*, no. 43, i. 233.   [55] Ibid., no. 137, ii. 360–1.
[56] Quoted in Kernan, *Printing Technology*, 77.

A system, built upon the discoveries of a great many minds, is always of more strength, than what is produced by the mere workings of any one mind, which of itself, can do little. . . . The French writers are superficial, because they are not scholars, and so proceed upon the mere power of their own minds; and we see how very little power they have.[57]

To be a scholar is to refuse to proceed upon the power of one's own mind alone: it is to renounce the vanity of supposed intellectual self-sufficiency in favour of a truth which is the sum of true particular enquiries. It is because the French writers 'are not scholars' that they believe themselves intellectually self-sufficient. Johnson takes reason itself, indeed, to be syncretic: 'reason . . . exhibits the collective knowledge of different ages, and various professions'.[58] This is not to say that Johnson cannot imagine excessive minuteness as a danger for scholarly enquiry: many of the meditations on scholarship in the *Rambler* explicitly warn against it. But whereas such warnings in the work of Pope and Warburton are accompanied by a fear that the excessively minute enquirer will impinge narrowly and partially upon a public culture, in *Rambler*, no. 103, Johnson warns against 'trivial employments and minute studies'[59] as damaging to the enquirer rather than to the public. They are identified with a failure to work hard *enough*: such minuteness, for Johnson, is a 'luxury' which is likely to be the product of 'ease and novelty' rather than of genuinely laborious interestedness.

Johnson's willingness to use the division of labour in an artificer's shop as a model for the division of intellectual labour should lead us to wonder whether he need take the language of those pursuing partial callings or professions as the gravest threat to the national language. It is evident from the 'Preface' to the *Dictionary* that the leisured, no less than the 'laborious' classes, are for Johnson an important cause of linguistic change and thereby of the acknowledged impossibility of settling and purifying the language. Johnson's insistence that the *Dictionary* must inevitably be deficient in the 'terms of art and manufacture' appropriated to particular trades or callings, and that many such terms constitute a 'fugitive cant' unworthy of preservation, is well known. Yet 'politeness' itself, far from being the lexicographer's unambiguous goal, is a source of linguistic instability. Johnson remarks that the most favourable location for a permanent language would be 'that of a nation raised a little, and but a little, above barbarity, secluded from strangers, and totally employed in procuring the conveniences of life':

[57] *Boswell's Life of Johnson*, ed. G. B. Hill, rev. L. F. Powell (6 vols., Oxford, 1934), i. 454.
[58] *Rambler*, no. 41, i. 223.   [59] Ibid., no. 103, ii. 187.

But no such constancy can be expected in a people polished by arts, and classed by subordination, where one part of the community is sustained and accomodated by the labour of the other. Those who have much leisure to think, will always be enlarging the stock of ideas, and every increase of knowledge, whether real or fancied, will produce new words, or combinations of words . . . As politeness increases, some expressions will be considered as too gross and vulgar for the delicate, others as too formal and ceremonious for the gay and airy; new phrases are therefore adopted, which must, for the same reasons, be in time dismissed.[60]

Such sentiments indicate how far Johnson is from imagining a putatively pure and stable language as requiring a community of the leisured and consequently disinterested. On the contrary, the nation in which the language might remain stable is one in which all must work to secure the necessities of life. In this passage, linguistic innovation is not, as it was earlier, the consequence of the working practices of the laborious part of the people, but of the luxury of intellectual leisure, some of whose 'advances' may be merely imaginary. The final sentence, moreover, shows the diction of politeness to be no less 'casual and mutable' than that of the laborious and mercantile part of the people: indeed, it is here the very desire of the polite to avoid vulgarity which leads them to a practice of linguistic innovation which is taken to be necessarily transient. The polite need not be proper users of the language, nor need the vulgar use it improperly; discussing the verb TO CRAUNCH (v.a.), 'To crush in the mouth', Johnson remarks that 'the vulgar say more properly to *scraunch*'.

Once more Johnson's handling of such questions needs to be examined not only in the pronouncements of his 'Preface' but also in the practice of the main body of his *Dictionary*. The remarks on innovation made in Johnson's comments upon particular words generally provide little evidence that such innovations might be thought of as the result of the unwarrantable imposition of the language of a particular calling upon the language of the nation as a whole. GAS, for example, is described as 'A word invented by the chymists'; but since there is no indication of disapproval in Johnson's note, its reception as an entry must be taken to imply that it falls into the category of new words really needed to match advances in knowledge. The invention of new words is more often attributed to the needs or mistakes of individual polite writers than to the encroachments of any trade, and to proceed by what is implied to be a vain display of linguistic learning; Johnson's scorn, discussed earlier, for Dryden's TO FALSIFY (sense 4) is a case in point. The adjective CLOUDCOMPELLING (supported by quotations from Waller and Dryden) is 'A word formed in

---

[60] *Dictionary* (1755), i, sig. C2r.

imitation of νεφεληγερετης, ill understood'; whilst the 'Preface' mentions Milton's coinage '*highth*' (not entered in the *Dictionary* itself) as a result of his 'zeal for analogy'.[61]

A more important obstacle to any notion of Johnson's canon of authoritative writers as representing a leisured and disinterested culture is provided by the sheer variety of sources which Johnson brings to bear in the *Dictionary*. Amongst these are texts which explicitly set themselves outside any notion of an exclusively polite readership. John Mortimer declares in the preface to his *The Whole Art of Husbandry: Or, the Way of Managing and Improving of Land* (1721), frequently quoted by Johnson, that 'I have endeavoured, throughout the whole Book, to express my self in as few Words and plain a Stile as I could, for the Benefit of Vulgar Readers, the Culture of Lands being left almost intirely to their Management.'[62] Similarly, *The Builder's Dictionary* was addressed, if not to the 'vulgar', then to readers professionally engaged in the building trade: it described itself as 'chiefly for the Assistance of such, who study the Mechanical Part of Building, and will be of the greatest Service to all Professions that have any Relation to it'.[63] Other such sources included a 'Sea Dictionary',[64] a 'Military Dictionary',[65] and a 'Farrier's Dictionary'.[66] Still others amongst Johnson's source texts took themselves as introducing technical topics to a gentlemanly audience. Joseph Moxon's *Mechanick Exercises* (1683), often quoted by Johnson, felt it necessary to account for its choice of an apparently low subject ('though the Mechanicks be by some accounted ignoble and scandalous; yet it is very well known, that many Gentlemen in this Nation of good Rank and high Quality are conversant in Handy-Works')[67] and often presents itself as introducing technical jargon to a reader assumed innocent of it: 'in Smiths Language', [68] 'as Workmen phrase it',[69] are typical expressions. Many of these technical terms are to be found in the *Dictionary*.[70] Equally significantly, the technical manuals from which Johnson quotes are not cited in

---

[61] *Dictionary*, i, sig. [A]2ʳ. For further examples of innovations assigned to the responsibility of particular authorities, see MODERNISM, (n.s.) (Swift), PERFECTIONATE (v.a.) (Dryden), and SORTAL (adj.) (Locke).

[62] Mortimer, *Husbandry*, i, sigs A3ᵛ–A4ʳ.

[63] *The Builder's Dictionary, or Gentleman and Architect's Companion* (2 vols., London, 1734), i, sig. A1ᵛ.

[64] See the nouns BOLTSPRIT or BOWSPRIT and LOOF.

[65] See COUNTERGUARD (n.s.).   [66] See BOW (n.s.) (sense 6).

[67] Joseph Moxon, *Mechanick Exercises, or the Doctrine of Handy-Works* (2 vols., London, 1683), i, p. [i].

[68] Ibid. 1.   [69] Ibid. 12.

[70] See, for examples, TO RED-SEAR (v.n.), SLICE (n.s.) (sense 3), RIGLET (n.s.), and TEWEL (n.s.). These words appear in Moxon, *Mechanick Exercises*, i. 12, ii. 25, i. 7, and i. 2 respectively.

support of technical terms alone: quotations from Moxon, for example, are used to illustrate such non-technical words as ARMPIT (n.s.), BULGE (v.n.) (sense 2), HARDNESS (n.s.) (sense 7), and TO REFINE (v.a.) (sense 1), amongst others.

The variety of eighteenth-century authors used by Johnson is also hard to reconcile with any notion of his rigorously insisting upon authors recognized as polite. The first edition of the *Dictionary* included ninety-six quotations from Richardson's *Clarissa* and three from *Pamela*:[71] when Johnson asked David Garrick for his impression of the *Dictionary*'s reception, Garrick reported that 'it was objected that he cited authorities which were beneath the dignity of such a work, and mentioned Richardson'.[72] Several of the writers characterized as dunces in the *Dunciad* became authorities on English usage in the *Dictionary*: Defoe, Welsted, Broome, Dennis, and Concanen were all quoted there, often as the sole authority for a given word.[73] Richard Bentley himself, whose supposedly clownish and pedantic English had often been ridiculed by the wits in the Phalaris controversy, was frequently cited, principally from his sermons but also from his edition of Milton.[74] In several cases, words used by Bentley which the wits had ridiculed as pedantic coinages were included in the *Dictionary*.[75] Moreover, the living authorities cited by Johnson were a miscellaneous collection apparently united by little more than Johnson's personal acquaintance with them, and hardly conforming to any notion that current best usage could only be judged by the disinterested: amongst them were the poem *Agriculture* by Dodsley the bookseller, Charlotte Lennox's *Female Quixote* and *Shakespeare Illustrated*, David Garrick, and one of Johnson's assistants in the preparation of the *Dictionary*, the Scot

[71] W. R. Keast, 'The Two *Clarissa*s in Johnson's *Dictionary*', *Studies in Philology*, 54 (1957), 429–39 (p. 430).

[72] *Boswell's Life of Johnson*, iv. 4.

[73] *Robinson Crusoe* is the only source given in support of IRONWOOD (n.s.) and LOCKER (n.s.); a passage of Welsted's verse is quoted under HERO (n.s.) (sense 1); Broome's notes to the tr. of the *Odyssey* in which he participated are the only authority for sense 2 of CIRCUM-STANTIALLY (adv.); Dennis is the sole authority given for AVOIDLESS (adj.) and LATINITY (n.s.); Concanen is the sole authority for TRIBUTARY (adj.) (sense 3). The writers appear in Alexander Pope, *The Dunciad*, ed. James Sutherland (London, 1963), 302, 306, 280, 167, and 301 respectively.

[74] The edn. of Milton is cited under DEFOEDATION (n.s.).

[75] For examples, see COMMENTITIOUS (adj.) (supported by a quotation from Glanville), PUTID (adj.) (under which L'Estrange is quoted), CONCEDE (v.a.) (authorized by a quotation from Bentley himself and by one from Robert Boyle) and REPUDIATE (v.a.) (supported by quotations from Bentley and *The Government of the Tongue*). The words are attacked in *Dr. Bentley's Dissertations . . . Examin'd* (London, 1699), 94, 287; and in William King, *Dialogues of the Dead: Relating to the present Controversy concerning the Epistles of Phalaris* (London, 1699).

Alexander Macbean.[76] Richard Savage, whose desperate career as an impoverished hack Johnson himself had previously chronicled, was quoted under TO GLOW (v.a.) (sense 4).[77]

Nor does Johnson's commentary provide much evidence of censure for words or combinations of words appropriated to a particular calling. Johnson's description of certain parts of the language of the laborious and mercantile part of the people as a 'fugitive cant' raises the question of the ways in which 'cant' is used as a term of reprobation within the main body of the *Dictionary* itself. It is well known that Johnson thought it 'sufficiently despicable' to be 'infected with the jargon of a particular profession',[78] and much of his literary criticism bears out this dislike. Johnson believed that Cowley's description of the angel Gabriel in his *Davideis* was vitiated by his use of the terms of 'the mercer and the taylor';[79] more startlingly, Macbeth's hope 'That my keen knife see not the wound it makes' was for Johnson a sentiment 'weakened by the name of an instrument used by butchers and cooks in the meanest employments'.[80] But Johnson insisted, as we should expect from his conception of the world of learning, that such particularity was sometimes an unavoidable consequence of the requirement for accurate specialized knowledge: 'it is always difficult, and sometimes scarcely possible, to deliver the precepts of an art, without the terms by which the peculiar ideas of that art are expressed, and which had not been invented but because the language already in use was insufficient'.[81] There are indeed certain occasions in the *Dictionary* upon which labouring-class or professional words are described as a form of 'cant'. DAWK (n.s.) is described as 'A cant word among the workmen for a hollow or incision in their stuff'; FLIMSY (adj.) is described as an instance of 'the cant of manufacturers', whilst DISHING (adj.) is 'a cant term among artificers'. The use of NERVOUS (adj.) to mean 'having weak or diseased nerves' (sense 3) is described as 'medical cant'; FASCINE (n.s.) is 'Military cant'. But such instances are few and far between, and easily

[76] Dodsley's poem is quoted under TEMPERANCE (n.s.) (sense 1), TINKLE (v.n.) (sense 1), and THRESHER (n.s.) (for which it is the only authority given); *The Female Quixote* is quoted under, amongst other entries, VISIONARY or VISIONIST (n.s.), for which it is the only authority, and SOLEMNITY (n.s.) (sense 7), whilst *Shakespeare Illustrated* is the only authority given in support of STARRY (adj.) and UNCLE (n.s.); for Garrick see GIGGLER (n.s.); Macbean is quoted in a lengthy etymological note on LOORD (n.s.) and his verse is quoted in support of SCALE (n.s.) (sense 7).

[77] Johnson's *Life of Savage* itself provides the only quotation for sense 2 of TO DISSIPATE (v.a.).

[78] *Rambler*, no. 99, ii. 168.

[79] *Prefaces, Biographical and Critical*, i. 'Life of Cowley', 136.

[80] *Rambler*, no. 168, iii. 128.   [81] Ibid., no. 86, ii. 89.

outweighed by the number of occasions on which words are described as in use within a particular trade or profession without being accompanied by any mark of disapproval.[82] Indeed, the most frequent comment attached by Johnson to words described as 'cant' is that their etymology cannot be traced.[83] Amongst the sources cited for quotations containing 'cant' words are many of Johnson's most favoured authorities: Bacon, Clarendon, South, Dryden, Locke, Pope, Prior, and Swift (whom Johnson was later to describe as a 'safe' authority in matters of style)[84] all provide instances of such words.[85]

3

The evidence of Johnson's philological practice and of his lexicographical theory, then, is that there is no ideally authoritative user of the language for Johnson, but instead a series of case-by-case judgements to be made, in which the precedents set by linguistic authorities are of various and relative, rather than absolute, importance. Johnson's stoical acceptance of the inevitability of linguistic change or corruption owes as much to the vagaries of authors habitually thought of as polite as to the depredations of low and interested users of the language. The idea of a group of authoritative users of the language is one whose social complexity and internal circularity mean that the *Dictionary* itself can only make use of it in a qualified and often necessarily self-contradictory way. But the notion of authoritative usage is still further complicated when it is remembered that many of the authorities are cited not in their first published form, but from eighteenth-century reprints and edited texts. The use of such texts means that the authorities quoted may be mediated not only through the lexicographer's selection and comment, but also through the editorial practice of a variety of eighteenth-century editors. Once more, only the

---

[82] For a few examples amongst many see CATCHWORD (n.s.) ('With printers'), CLOUGH (n.s.) ('In commerce'), DIVERSION (n.s.) (sense 4) ('In war'), and SKELETON (n.s.) (sense 1) ('In anatomy').

[83] See e.g. TO TRAIPSE (v.a.) ('A low word, I believe, without any etymology'); FLAM (n.s.) ('A cant word of no certain etymology'), and TO CHOUSE (v.a.) ('perhaps a fortuitous and cant word, without etymology').

[84] *Prefaces, Biographical and Critical*, viii. 'Life of Swift', 85.

[85] For such examples of 'cant' words see the following entries: Bacon: TO SOAK (v.a.) (sense 2); Clarendon: PRO (n.s.); South: FLAM (n.s.); Dryden: TO DRIB (v.a.), MACKEREL-GALE (n.s.), and MOBILITY (n.s.) (sense 2); Pope: FIB (n.s.), FLIRTATION (n.s.), and SNIPSNAP (n.s.); Prior: LACE (n.s.) (sense 6) and PRO (n.s.); Swift: CRONY (n.s.), SOS (v.n.), and STOUT (n.s.).

evidence of Johnson's own philological practice within the text of the *Dictionary* itself will enable us to assess the extent to which the notion of authoritative usage was complicated for Johnson by this problem.

Johnson's work necessarily raises the question of the relations between lexicography and textual criticism in a more practical way than that of any of his predecessors. The two activities ran in tandem for much of his career: although the *Dictionary* appeared nine years before Johnson's edition of Shakespeare, he had been considering the possibility of an edition of Shakespeare at least since 1745, when his *Miscellaneous Observations on the Tragedy of Macbeth* were published, and had collected thousands of instances of Shakespearian diction on index slips since that date;[86] substantial revisions both of the Shakespeare edition and of the *Dictionary* were published in 1773, and many of the new alterations to the text of the latter can be shown to have derived from Johnson's editorial work on Shakespeare. Since Johnson's was the first English dictionary to support its definitions with illustrative quotations from authoritative texts, he faced the problem of the mutual interdependence of lexicography and textual criticism indicated by Warburton in an especially acute form; indeed, Johnson alluded to Warburton's very words when writing to Thomas Warton in 1755 of the approaching completion of his dictionary: 'I now begin to see dry land, after having wandered, according to Mr. Warburton's phrase, in this vast Sea of words.'[87] The *Plan* had earlier advertised the benefits of one aspect of the dictionary's proposed method of definition—the explanation of given words 'by their opposition to others'—to textual criticism: it was want of attention to such detail which had led Richard Bentley unwarrantably to emend the text of *Paradise Lost*.[88] When writing to Warton on the deficiencies of Hughes's edition of Spenser and other similar editions of classic English texts, Johnson suggested that his dictionary would be an asset to editors of sixteenth-century texts because it would place the vocabulary of such texts in historical context: 'The Reason why the authours which are yet read of the sixteenth Century are so little understood is that they are read alone, and no help is borrowed from those who lived with them or before them. Some part of this ignorance I hope to remove by my book which now draws towards its end . . .'.[89]

---

[86] Bertrand H. Bronson, 'Introduction', to *Johnson on Shakespeare*, ed. Arthur Sherbo (2 vols., New Haven, Conn., 1968), p. xiv.

[87] To Thomas Warton, 1 Feb. 1755: *The Letters of Samuel Johnson*, ed. Bruce Redford (Oxford, 1992), i. 92.

[88] *Plan*, 26.   [89] To Warton, 16 July 1754: Johnson, *Letters*, ed. Redford, i. 81.

Conversely, the definitions and the word-stock of any dictionary relying on authorities would themselves be dependent on the editors of the texts of those authorities. W. B. C. Watkins showed how often Johnson consulted his pre-Restoration authorities in eighteenth-century texts;[90] and more recently, Allen Reddick has suggested that the appearance in 1772 of an edited text of William Browne's *Works* prepared by Thomas Davies may have been responsible for the inclusion of quotations from Browne in the fourth edition of the *Dictionary*, just as Johnson's acquisition of an edited text of Drayton's *Poly-olbion* (in the 1748 *Works* edited by William Oldys) occasioned the appearance of a number of passages from Drayton in the 1773 edition.[91] Johnson's philological commentary on his word-list and also on the illustrative quotations adduced in support of it bears out his awareness of the dependence of lexicography on textual criticism: on many occasions he pauses to remark that a passage which he has quoted in support of a particular entry may have been misprinted.

Elizabethan texts offer a particularly interesting instance of this difficulty because of Johnson's remarks about the language of Elizabethan authors in the 'Preface' to the *Dictionary*. Johnson's suggestion that a fully adequate language 'might be formed' from 'the authours which rose in the time of *Elizabeth*'[92] indicates both the special authority of those texts as guarantors of the word-stock and the need for the supplementary authority of the lexicographer. Such a language does not fall ready-made into the dictionary, but requires the formative selection of the dictionary-maker. It is instructive to compare these remarks with others in the preface to Johnson's edition of Shakespeare, which also suggest that Shakespeare may have an especially significant place as a linguistic authority, and that such authority might depend upon selection:

If there be, what I believe there is, in every nation, a stile which never becomes obsolete, a certain mode of phraseology so consonant and congenial to the analogy and principles of its respective language as to remain settled and unaltered; this stile is probably to be sought in the common intercourse of life, among those who speak only to be understood . . . The polite are always catching modish innovations, and the learned depart from established forms of speech, in hope of finding or making better; those who wish for distinction forsake the vulgar, when the vulgar is right; but there is a conversation above grossness and below refine-

---

[90] W. B. C. Watkins, *Johnson and English Poetry before 1660* (Princeton, NJ, 1936), 85–113.

[91] Reddick, *Johnson's Dictionary*, 222 n. 2, 135.   [92] *Dictionary*, i, sig. C1r.

ment, where propriety resides, and where this poet seems to have gathered his comick dialogue.[93]

This passage is of central interest for a number of reasons. It raises the possibility that whilst, as we have seen, the ambition to fix the language may be an unattainable one for Johnson, the possibility of isolating a core of this language which 'never becomes obsolete' remains. Such a permanent core, moreover, would for Johnson be identified with a social middle ground, neither excessively polite nor grossly vulgar. But this never-obsolete style is only to be found in Shakespeare's comic dialogue: Shakespeare can be an authority for this permanently just style only in works which have already been selected by the critic.

Taken together, Johnson's view of Elizabethan texts and especially of Shakespeare as authoritative in selection might seem to offer ample opportunities to any philologist with any interest at all in reforming or purifying the language, especially to a scholar who was both dictionary-maker and editor of the text most often cited in that dictionary. But it is important here to take note of the qualified tone of Johnson's declaration: *if* there be a permanently proper English style, this style is 'probably' to be sought in the common intercourse of life. Johnson is intensely aware, moreover, of the difference between noticing (and recommending as models) intimations of such a style in Shakespeare's text, on the one hand, and any project of making this a basis for textual-critical and lexicographical practice on the other. It is the measure of Johnson's sense of the specialized duty of the lexicographer and textual critic that he hesitates to use any position of legislative authority over English dictionaries and texts to mould or re-form the language: the contrast with Warburton's vision of Lycurgus, the textual critic as heroic legislator, could hardly be greater. The evidence of Johnson's philological practice again indicates the need for caution in interpreting his prefatory announcements about the language and its classic authorities. Instead, we need to understand the relationship between Johnson's work on the *Dictionary* and on the text of Shakespeare as a reciprocal one, which cannot be described as part of any straightforward plan 'to rectify and enrich language and literature and inculcate readers with critical values and their social and moral correlatives'.[94] Johnson aspired primarily to supply accurate repositories of the history of the language, repositories which would more often be a

---

[93] *Johnson on Shakespeare*, i. 70.
[94] Margreta de Grazia, *Shakespeare Verbatim* (Oxford, 1991), 71.

resource than a corrective for their readers: 'the history of our language, and the true force of our words, can only be preserved, by keeping the text of authours free from adulteration'.[95]

4

Johnson's references in his commentary to possible textual difficulties with the selected quotations supporting his word-list bear out in detail his awareness of the reciprocal relationship between lexicography and textual criticism. Reproducing a passage of Spenser's *Faerie Queene* in order to illustrate TORTUOUS, Johnson reminds the reader that 'This in some copies is *tortious*, and therefore from *tort*';[96] under TO BEGIRT he quotes Ben Jonson's *Catiline*, but adds the caveat that 'This is, I think, only a corruption of *begird*; perhaps by the printer.'[97] Possible or probable misprints are indicated not only in literary texts, but also in religious documents: under RECKLESSNESS Johnson comments that 'This word in the seventeenth article is erroneously written *wretchlessness*'; quoting Genesis under ENDUE (v.a.), sense 2 ('Leah said, God hath *endued* me with a good dowry'), he comments that 'In the following passage it seems incorrectly printed for *endow*.' Johnson sometimes suggests that the word which a given text is quoted to illustrate may be misprinted in that text, yet continues to give the word in this (supposedly misprinted) form, as an illustration of the word in question. The entry for PRESENTATION offers an example: the fourth 'sense' of the word is Johnson's remark that '4. This word is misprinted for *presension*' in a passage of Sir Thomas Browne's *Vulgar Errors*, which Johnson nevertheless goes on to quote with the reading 'presentation'. The same procedure is applied to DRILL (n.s.), sense 3; Johnson quotes a passage of Sandys containing the word as the sole supporting quotation for this entry, whilst remarking 'This I have found no where else, and suspect it should be *rill*.' The implication of such a procedure, once more, is that the *Dictionary* is often to be taken as a

---

[95]   *Johnson on Shakespeare*, i. 105.

[96]   The source of Johnson's quotation is uncertain, since all the 18th-cent. texts of Spenser printed before 1755, as well as the 1679 Folio and the early edns., read 'tortious': see *The Works of that Famous English Poet Mr. Edmund Spenser* (London, 1679), 62; John Hughes, ed., *The Works of Mr. Edmund Spenser* (6 vols., London, 1715), ii. 209; id., ed., *The Works of Spenser* (London, 1750), ii. 25; *The Faerie Queene. By Edmund Spenser* (3 vols., London, 1751), i. 247; and the variorum edn. of Edwin Greenlaw, Charles Grosvenor Osgood, and Frederick Morgan, *The Works of Edmund Spenser* (11 vols., Baltimore, 1932–57), ii (1933), 23.

[97]   *Dictionary* (1755), TO BEGIRT (v.a.).

commentary on the passages assembled rather than as a collection of words for which suitable passages are then appropriated wherever available. Because there is a reciprocal, rather than a hierarchical, relationship between textual criticism and lexicography the dictionary-maker cannot simply emend, on the spot, passages suspected of containing textual errors. Even where a strong presumption of such errors exists, the possibility of error is to be noted alongside a reproduction of the quotation as it appears in the (very often critically edited) text from which it has been quarried.

Johnson used a number of edited texts of Shakespeare in preparing the *Dictionary*. His marked-up copy of Warburton's edition still survives and shows that the 1747 text was Johnson's primary source for the Shakespearian quotations in the *Dictionary*.[98] But it is clear that Johnson also consulted the work of other editors in the course of preparing the *Dictionary*. Hanmer's name appears under many entries, in each case for words defined in the glossary attached to the 1744 edition: Johnson used Hanmer's glossary both to add to the word-stock and to gloss words accumulated from Warburton's edition.[99] Johnson also referred on occasion to Theobald's work;[100] there is no evidence that he consulted Pope's, since the quotations from Pope's celebrated note on 'a table of Greenfield's' in *Henry V* were taken from Warburton's edition, where the note was reprinted.[101]

The history of a single entry from the *Dictionary* epitomizes the complexities which could arise from the mutual interdependence of textual criticism and lexicography:

ENGLE. n.s. [derived from the French *engluer*, to catch with birdlime.] A gull; a put; a bubble.   *Hanmer.*

> I spied
> An ancient *engle* going down the hill
> Will serve our turn.   *Shakesp. Taming of the Shrew.*

An alteration of Theobald's for *angel*.[102]

---

[98] A. Cuming, 'A Copy of Shakespeare's Works which formerly belonged to Dr. Johnson', *Review of English Studies*, 3 (1927), 208–12. Warburton was also quoted as an authority in his own right: OCCUPANCY (n.s.) is supported in the 1755 *Dictionary* by a quotation from 'Warburton on Literary Property', Warburton's 1747 pamphlet on the copyright controversy.

[99] See, for examples, *Dictionary* (1755), LAND (n.s.) (sense 6) and GIMMAL (n.s.).

[100] See, for examples, ENGLE (n.s.), REVERBERANT (adj.).

[101] See EDITOR (n.s.), PIECEMEAL (adv.), and PRINT (v.a.) (sense 4); the note is marked up in William Warburton, *The Works of Shakespear* (8 vols., London, 1747), Aberystwyth, University College of Wales Library, D1388.PR2572 P8 [microfilm], iv. 349.

[102] *Dictionary* (1755), ENGLE (n.s.).

The passage from *The Taming of the Shrew* is the only supporting authority adduced for 'engle', a word confessedly first introduced into that text by Theobald; the definition of its meaning, moreover, is provided by Hanmer. Consequently, 'engle' is authorized by Shakespeare only as mediated by Theobald and Hanmer, with the result that a scholar described in Johnson's 'Preface' to his edition as 'thus weak and ignorant, thus mean and faithless, thus petulant and ostentatious'[103] is in 1755 the principal authority for the right of 'engle' to take its place in the canon of English words. Johnson's own text of Shakespeare later rejected 'engle' in both the instances where Theobald had emended to read thus.[104] The fourth edition of the *Dictionary* omits 'engle' entirely, since there are no longer any sufficient authorities for the word. Similarly, Warburtonian coinages whose credit rests not on contemporary examples but, at best, on etymological analogy, are transcribed from Warburton's edition into the first edition of the dictionary but rejected in the 1773 revision once they have been considered in Johnson's own text of Shakespeare. Warburton's emendation to a passage in *Coriolanus*, 'I ever NARRIFY'D my friends' (for 'verified') produced an entry in the 1755 *Dictionary* under 'TO NARRIFY (v.a.) To relate; to give account of; not in use.' But Johnson removed Warburton's emendation in his own text, remarking that 'If the commentator had given any example of the word *narrify*, the correction would have been not only received but applauded'; and the word is consequently absent from the 1773 *Dictionary*.[105] Conversely, a word which Johnson had missed whilst marking up Warburton's Shakespeare could be brought to his attention in annotating his own text: 'forgetive', absent from the 1755 *Dictionary*, appears in 1773 defined as 'That may forge or produce. A word, I believe, peculiar to Shakespeare'.[106]

Elsewhere, the definition given in the first edition of the *Dictionary* is altered as a result of further work on the edition of Shakespeare. This can follow as a simple accretion of conjecture: in 1755 Johnson suggests that TO HEND (v.a.) may be a corruption in the passage which he gives from *Measure for Measure*, but in his own text of the play he glosses 'Have hent the gates' as 'Have taken possession of the gates',[107] and in the 1773 *Dictionary* this sense is simply added to those given in 1755 as a further possibility: 'or it may mean *to take possession*'. Johnson's work on the edition of Shakespeare also brings glosses by Hanmer to his attention for

---

[103] *Johnson on Shakespeare*, i. 96.   [104] *1765*, ii. 292; iii. 69.

[105] *1765*, vi. 607; *1747*, vi. 541.   [106] See *1765*, iv. 320; *1747*, iv. 281.

[107] *1765*, i. 360.

the first time. In the 1755 *Dictionary*, WHIFFLER, supported by *Henry V*'s 'deep-mouth'd sea, | Which, like a mighty *whiffler* 'fore the king, | Seems to prepare his way' is defined merely as 'One that blows strongly'; in 1765 Johnson annotates this passage with Hanmer's gloss 'An officer who walks first in processions, or before persons in high stations, on occasions of ceremony',[108] and in the 1773 *Dictionary* the word is redefined as 'An ancient officer of state'.[109]

Just as lexicographical work went on in the edition of Shakespeare, so textual-critical work went on in the *Dictionary*. Johnson quoted from *Twelfth Night*[110] in support of REVERBERANT:

> Hollow your name to the *reverberate* hills,
> And make the babbling gossip of the air
> Cry out, Olivia!

He prefaced the quotation with a remark that 'The reading in the following passage should be, I think, *reverberant*': in the 1765 text Johnson departs from Warburton to read 'reverberant'.[111] Similarly, under OVER-WROUGHT Johnson creates a separate entry for a Shakespearian sense of the word as used in *The Comedy of Errors*[112] which he nevertheless views with suspicion: '3. It has in *Shakespeare* a sense which I know not well how to reconcile to the original meaning of the word, and therefore conclude it misprinted for *overraught*; that is, *overreached* or cheated.'[113] Once again, Johnson's own text of Shakespeare implements an emendation first prompted by lexicographical work.[114] A still more significant instance of this process is Johnson's restoration of 'hugger-mugger' to the text of *Hamlet*:

All the modern editions that I have consulted give it,

> *In* private *to inter him*;—

That the words now replaced are better, I do not undertake to prove; it is sufficient that they are *Shakespeare*'s: If phraseology is to be changed as words grow uncouth

---

[108] *1765*, iv. 470; *1744*, vi. 'A Glossary Explaining the obsolete and difficult words in the Plays of Shakespear'; iii. 549.

[109] *1765*, i. 134; *1744*, vi. 'A Glossary'; i. 107. Cf. also TO LATCH (v.a.), sense 2 and *1765*, i. 134; *1744*, vi. 'A Glossary'; i. 107.

[110] *1747*, iii. 137.

[111] *1765*, ii. 374. For another example of a criticism of Shakespeare's text first put forward in the *Dictionary*, see TO DISPURSE ('It is not certain that the following passage should not be written *disburse*') and *1765*, v. 48, where Johnson silently departs from his copy-text to read 'disbursed'.

[112] *1747*, iii. 217.   [113] *Dictionary* (1755), OVERWROUGHT (adj.) (sense 3).

[114] *1765*, iii. 111.

by disuse, or gross by vulgarity, the history of every language will be lost; we shall no longer have the words of any authour; . . .[115]

Johnson identifies the motives for excising obsolete expressions as those of purifying the language, a project to which previous editors of the dramatist had regarded their work as an important contribution. Lexicography here informs textual criticism in just the way envisaged by Johnson in his letter to Warton: Johnson had already noted the word's use in More, Spenser, Butler, and L'Estrange in his work for the *Dictionary*.[116]

There are, of course, instances of words which are received into Johnson's 1765 text yet are absent from both the 1755 *Dictionary* and the fourth edition in 1773. But it would be difficult to argue that these words are excluded as part of any process of selection such as Johnson's 'might be formed' in his 'Preface' to the *Dictionary* would lead us to expect. Certainly, some of the words omitted from the *Dictionary* are described in the edition of Shakespeare as provincial or cant terms: thus 'pugging', which Johnson describes as 'not now understood' and, following Styan Thirlby, as 'the cant of gypsies' when annotating its appearance in his text of *The Winter's Tale*,[117] appears in neither edition of the *Dictionary*. But the omission can hardly evince a conscious process of selection, since there are many instances of Shakespeare's authority being invoked in the *Dictionary* precisely in support of low or cant terms.[118] Amongst provincial words, 'loach', which Johnson, following Warburton, glosses as a Scottish expression for a lake in 1765, is present in the *Dictionary* (in both 1755 and 1773) only as the (non-Scottish) name of a fish. Once more, many expressions glossed as provincialisms in Johnson's commentary on Shakespeare do appear in the *Dictionary*: SNEAP (n.s.) (described, following Pope, as 'a *Yorkshire* word for *rebuke*' in 1765),[119] TO RAKE (v.a.) (sense 5) ('In *Staffordshire*, to *rake* the fire, is to cover it with fuel for the night'),[120] and TO GALLOW (v.a.) ('a west-country word' according to Warburton),[121] all find a place in both the first and the fourth editions of the *Dictionary*.

An examination of Johnson's marked-up copy of Warburton's edition and its eventual use in the first edition of the *Dictionary* shows that Johnson must have been aware, even whilst drawing up his word-list, of the potential pitfalls of collecting the quotations for his most often-cited

[115] See *1765*, viii. 260; *1757*, viii. 193.

[116] *Dictionary* (1755), HUGGERMUGGER (n.s.). For a further example, cf. *1765*, i. 299; *Dictionary* (1755), TESTED (adj.).

[117] *1765*, ii. 293.

[118] See, for examples, IMMOMENT (adj.), IMPORTANCE (n.s.) (sense 4), FRAUGHTAGE (n.s.); FULHAM (n.s.).

[119] *1765*, iv. 261.   [120] Ibid. vi. 134.   [121] Ibid. vi. 82.

authority from an edited text; and that he took steps to limit the possible impact on the *Dictionary* of the vagaries of previous editors by an intermediate process of selection. Johnson's method was to place the passage to be copied out between vertical lines, to underline the word in support of which the passage was to be quoted, and to write the first letter of that word in the margin. His assistants would then copy the passages in question on to slips of paper.[122] But there are many instances in which Johnson marks a word appearing in the 1747 text for inclusion, only to leave the marked word out of the *Dictionary*, having apparently had second thoughts; many of these instances concern words which only appear in the 1747 text as a result of Warburtonian emendations. Thus 'tire-vailant', 'aglet', 'widgeon', 'vann'd', 'geap', 'impage', 'imbare', 'merchant-venturers', 'lethe', 'conseal'd', 'disseat' are all marked up in the Aberystwyth copy, yet the passages are not included in the *Dictionary* (and where, as for Warburton's coinages, there is no other support, the word in question is left out entirely).[123] Elsewhere, Warburton's spelling of particular words is corrected[124] and his text is disputed.[125]

Johnson's practice in managing the relations between lexicography and textual criticism in his own work, then, oscillates between the two paths to substantial philological achievement which we saw outlined earlier in the *Rambler*. On the one hand, Johnson's unusually strong insistence that good scholarly work was necessarily the sum of particular minute enquiries led him both to view the *Dictionary* as, in general, a collection of variously authoritative precedents rather than as an occasion for linguistic prescription, and to exercise a similar caution in his handling of the reciprocal relationship between textual criticism and lexicography. On the other hand, as we have seen, the idea of a breed of scholars who might 'consider nothing too great for their endeavour, and nothing too little for their regard' was still a lingering hope for Johnson. Johnson was himself, after all, working in an unprecedentedly *un*collaborative way for the maker of a national *Dictionary*: it was a commonplace of subsequent responses to the *Dictionary* that Johnson had done alone, and done better, what in France had required forty Frenchmen.[126] The traces of the tension be-

---

[122] Reddick, *Johnson's Dictionary*, 32.

[123] The readings are marked up in Aberystwyth D1388.PR2752 P8 [microfilm] as follows: 'tire-vailant': i. 303; 'aglet': ii. 41; 'widgeons': ii. 135; 'geap': ii. 239; 'impage': iii. 34; 'imbare': iv. 328; 'merchant-venturers': v. 332; 'lethe': vii. 51; 'conseal'd': viii. 69; 'disseat': viii. 301.

[124] See e.g. ibid. i. 70.   [125] Ibid. iv. 110; viii. 6.

[126] See e.g. *Boswell's Life of Johnson*, i. 300–1.

tween Johnson's two models of scholarship can be found in the movement of his philological practice between conscientious commentary upon textual difficulties in the authorities collected and the prescriptive moments which never wholly disappear from Johnson's lexicography or from his textual criticism. Such a tension was also decisively to influence both Johnson's account of the Shakespearian editor's task and his own editorial practice.

7

Johnson's Theory and Practice of Shakespearian Textual Criticism

JOHNSON, AS we have seen, was no less preoccupied with the effects of interest and vanity as motives to scholarly work than was William Warburton. But Johnson had been engaged in textual criticism in various ways for over twenty years by the time his edition of Shakespeare appeared in 1765, and, like Warburton, he wished to defend its worth from the charges which, as many passages in his preface show, he expected a textual critic even at this date to have to face. Unlike Warburton, Johnson did not think a vehement assertion of the comprehensive capacities which were necessary to textual criticism wholly adequate to the task. Instead, the preface to Johnson's edition of Shakespeare repeats, in its discussion of the work of previous editors, the double manœuvre which we have already seen at work in Johnson's view of scholarship in the *Ramblers* and elsewhere. Johnson offers a Warburtonian insistence upon the comprehensive capacities necessary to the qualified textual critic, in order to rebut any notion that the task is a merely laborious or minute one; and those editors who fail to evince such capacities are taken to task for their failings. As in Warburton's account of scholarship, minute bibliographical labour is admitted to be an unavoidable component of competent textual criticism. But Johnson emphasizes, in a way which none of his predecessors had found possible, the necessarily syncretic character of textual criticism. Such an emphasis admits the partial inefficacy of the Warburtonian attempt to show all necessary qualities and kinds of knowledge united in the editor as laborious genius. For Johnson no one editor can unite these qualities and varieties of learning, whose provision must instead depend on the co-operation of individual minute enquirers. Equally importantly, the syncretic character of competent textual criticism means that no one body of theoretical principles, no 'Art of Criticism', could be allowed to determine editorial method: not only knowledge, but reason itself is syncretic for Johnson.

As we shall see, the complex character of Johnson's defence of the value of textual criticism and his conception of the literary labour of the textual critic is reflected in his editorial practice. Johnson's edition is unprecedented in the extent of its desire to serve less as a display of the editor's own gentlemanly ease, painstaking labour, or comprehensive qualifications, than as a collection and summation of all previous editions. It is partly upon this collective character of Johnson's edition, rather than upon the qualifications of the editor alone or the consistency of the editor's methodological principles, that such claims as he is prepared to make for its authority come to rest. As with other eighteenth-century editors of Shakespeare, Johnson's editing cannot be surveyed as if from the standpoint of a finally scientific understanding of textual criticism and found wanting or merely accidentally inconsistent. Any such survey already takes for granted what was still contested amongst Johnson's predecessors and contemporaries: the idea of textual criticism as a discrete 'field' with its own methodology. Only if we understand Johnson's textual-critical theory and practice in the light of his ideas about the nature of scholarly labour itself will we be able to understand their complexities as more than merely accidental.

I

At first glance, Johnson's idea of the editor's task has much in common with Warburton's. His depiction of Theobald, for example, is cast in terms surprisingly similar to Warburton's: Theobald is 'a man of narrow comprehension and small acquisitions, with no native and intrinsick splendour of genius, with little of the artificial light of learning, but zealous for minute accuracy, and not negligent in pursuing it'.[1] As in Warburton's account, Theobald lacks not merely taste but anything that could be described as real learning: Johnson regards diligence as Theobald's principal asset. The earlier *Proposals* for an edition to be published by Cave offer a more explicit social subtext for Theobald's intellectual inadequacies, although one which Johnson is careful to qualify as received opinion rather than an independent assessment of Theobald's work: 'Mr. Theobald, if fame be just to his memory, considered learning only as an instrument of gain'.[2] This portrait of Theobald is echoed in the

---

[1] Samuel Johnson, *Johnson on Shakespeare*, ed. Arthur Sherbo (2 vols., New Haven, Conn., 1968), i. 95.
[2] Ibid. 56.

ambiguous references, in the commentary to the edition, to 'Poor Theobald'.[3] The primary meaning is usually that Theobald is poor in learning or wit, but the literal meaning remains present. When Theobald wishes to emend a line in *The Winter's Tale*, on the grounds that the existing reading makes Paulina speak excessively bluntly to her king, for example, the epithet is used to point up the disparity between Theobald's own obscurity and the concern of his note for courtly etiquette: 'Poor Mr. *Theobald*'s courtly remark cannot be thought to deserve much notice.'[4] It is not difficult to see why Joseph Ritson, writing in 1783, believed that Johnson had ranked his predecessors according to their social standing rather than according to their editorial competence.[5]

Conversely, Johnson's defence of proper textual criticism often relies on an assertion of the mental capacities indispensable to the fit textual critic. Paul Korshin has noted Johnson's admiration for Bentley's *Dissertation* on Phalaris:[6] the scholar who was for Pope the archetypally minute and narrow critic is for Johnson one of the 'mighty minds' of his age.[7] Far from believing that Pope's taste could compensate entirely for his lack of scholarly understanding,[8] Johnson continued throughout his career to rebuke Pope for scorning verbal minuteness. In his 'Life of Pope' Johnson takes Pope's complaint of Theobald's excessive minuteness as a mere cover for his own incompetence: Pope 'hoped to persuade the world, that he miscarried in this undertaking only by having a mind too great for such minute employment'.[9] Johnson's dismissal of Pope's phrase about the 'dull duty of an editor' in his 'Preface' is conducted in highly Warburtonian terms:

The duty of a collator is indeed dull, yet, like other tedious tasks, is very necessary; but an emendatory critick would ill discharge his duty, without qualities very different from dulness. In perusing a corrupted piece, he must have before him all possibilities of meaning, with all possibilities of expression. Such must be his comprehension of thought, and such his copiousness of language. Out of many readings possible, he must be able to select that which best suits with the state,

---

[3] *1765*, ii. 281, 341.   [4] Ibid. ii. 281.

[5] Joseph Ritson, *Remarks, Critical and Illustrative, on the Text and Notes of the Last Edition of Shakespeare* (London, 1783), p. vii.

[6] 'Johnson and the Scholars', 63. Johnson's attitude to Bentley may not always have been so approving: for a suggestion that Bentley may be satirized in *Marmor Norfolciense* see Samuel Johnson, *Political Writings*, ed. Donald J. Greene (New Haven, Conn., 1977), 22.

[7] *Johnson on Shakespeare*, i. 109–10.

[8] Peter Seary, 'The Early Editors of Shakespeare and the Judgements of Johnson', in Paul Korshin, ed., *Johnson after two hundred years* (Philadelphia, 1986), 175–86 (p. 177).

[9] Samuel Johnson, *Prefaces, Biographical and Critical, to the Works of the English Poets* (10 vols., London, 1779–81), vii. 'Life of Pope', 117.

opinions, and modes of language prevailing in every age, and with his authour's particular cast of thought, and turn of expression. Such must be his knowledge, and such his taste. Conjectural criticism demands more than humanity possesses, and he that exercises it with most praise has very frequent need of indulgence. Let us now be told no more of the dull duty of an editor.[10]

Here the emphasis, for Johnson as for Warburton, is on the comprehensiveness of powers necessary to the textual critic: verbal learning, far from being the partial and narrow-sighted matter for which it was so often taken by its eighteenth-century despisers, requires both intellectual breadth of vision and broad learning. Like Warburton's ideal editor, that is, the just emendator unites qualities which, for the *Dunciad*, were unlikely to appear together in any single textual critic: 'knowledge' and 'taste'.

Yet, at the same time, the opening and closing words of this passage indicate Johnson's difference from Warburton. The worth of the editor's task cannot be allowed to rest entirely upon an assertion of the powers necessary to its completion, because there are dull duties to be carried out by the editor, duties which require little but diligence yet which are indispensable to the editor's task. Theobald's laborious collation is more often presented in his defence than as a limitation upon the praise that can fairly be granted him. Johnson at one point takes the trouble to dissent from an unfavourable judgement passed by Warburton on the results of Theobald's critical labours as a whole: 'I cannot concur to censure *Theobald* as a critick very *unhappy*. He was weak, but he was cautious: finding but little power in his mind, he rarely ventured far under its conduct. This timidity hindered him from daring conjectures, and sometimes hindered him happily.'[11] For Johnson, a low estimate of Theobald's intellect need not disqualify his editorial work. Zachary Grey's work is understood in a comparable way in Johnson's preface to the edition. Grey deserves only limited praise because his learning is merely mechanical: 'he employs rather his memory than his sagacity'.[12] But he has nevertheless done useful service by virtue of knowing his own limitations: 'It were to be wished that all would endeavour to imitate his modesty who have not been able to surpass his knowledge.'[13]

Such a characterization of the more diligent labourers amongst eighteenth-century Shakespearian textual critics implies not a single editor continually exercising a comprehensive genius upon the minutest details of the text, but a division of editorial labours: some of which require

---

[10] *Johnson on Shakespeare*, i. 94–5.   [11] *1765*, vi. 245.
[12] *Johnson on Shakespeare*, i. 101.   [13] Ibid.

comprehensive genius whilst others are simple yet necessary drudgery. In a complementary way, the resounding declaration of the qualities which conjectural emendation requires is followed not by an earnest assurance that the present editor is ready to reveal such qualities in his own edition, but by an admission which leaves Johnson's gathering encomium upon the powers necessary to conjectural emendation poised at the brink of bathos: 'Conjectural criticism demands more than humanity possesses'. As in *Rambler*, no. 43, the ideal Warburtonian critic would for Johnson be an unexampled prodigy: certainly Johnson is neither willing to concede Warburtonian comprehensiveness to Warburton, nor prepared to claim it for himself.

Johnson takes editing itself, instead, as a specialized discipline amongst others, rather than as a display of capacities comprehensive enough to embrace all learning. One of the occasions on which Johnson imagines a reply to those who criticize the whole activity of editing as excessively minute illustrates this point: 'To these I answer with confidence, that they are judging of an art which they do not understand; yet cannot much reproach them with their ignorance, nor promise that they would become in general, by learning criticism, more useful, happier or wiser.'[14] For Pope it could never have formed part even of such an unenthusiastic defence of the value of textual criticism that it was a field of special expertise which could be judged only by the expert: indeed, in Pope's case, the notion that classic texts might be handed over to supposed experts was precisely what was most troubling about textual criticism. For Warburton it was essential that such learning as the fit editor possessed should precisely not be specialized learning, but a display of those capacities which every reader might wish to have, and which certainly would, for Warburton, promise usefulness, happiness, and wisdom to their owners. Johnson's insistence that textual criticism is a specialism is later reinforced by his remark in the 'Life of Mallet' on Mallet's satirical poem *Of Verbal Criticism* that its author 'either did not understand or willingly misrepresented' his subject. Textual criticism is not a matter upon which any tolerably literate poet may comment, but demands a knowledge peculiar to its competent practitioners.[15] This view of editing may also be implicit in Johnson's failure to use Warburton's 1747 text for copy: Johnson alternates in his choice of copy-text between that edition and a 1757 reprint of Theobald's 1740 text. Arthur Eastman concludes that Johnson's transfers were not generally the result of editorial evalua-

---

[14] *Johnson on Shakespeare*, i. 108.
[15] *Prefaces, Biographical and Critical*, x. 'Life of Mallet', 4.

tion, but Johnson's failure to stick to Warburton's text for copy is in itself revealing.[16] Johnson frequently declared Warburton's intellectual superiority to Theobald: when questioned about the relative merits of the two by Boswell, Johnson replied that Warburton would 'make two-and-fifty Theobalds, cut into slices'.[17] The fact that Johnson, despite this judgement, in many cases abandoned the use of Warburton's text as copy may indicate an implicit recognition that the more competent editor is not necessarily to be identified with the more comprehensive critic.

Johnson's emphasis falls on the syncretic character of scholarship: the abilities which are not to be hoped for in a single editor are more likely, although not certain, to be assembled by collecting the efforts of many. Despite Johnson's remark that editing is an 'art' which 'the greater part of readers' does not understand, he does not imagine this divided intellectual labour as a collection of special sciences, each with its appropriate and fully consistent methodology. For Johnson, no 'Art of Criticism', not even one so fragmentarily and implicitly articulated as Warburton's own, could stand in for the comprehensive capacities of the Warburtonian critic. Any set of critical rules would imply a rationalist methodology which Johnson is unable to accept: in the conjectural critic's 'art', for example, 'there is no system, no principal and axiomatical truth that regulates subordinate positions'.[18]

In particular, any systematic rules for preparing a commentary, for example, on Shakespeare would be as inappropriate to the irregularity of his text as Johnson had earlier found the application of analogical consistency to the irregularities of English:

The compleat explanation of an authour not systematick and consequential, but desultory and vagrant, is not to be expected from any single scholiast. All personal reflections, when names are suppressed, must be in a few years irrecoverably obliterated; and customs, too minute to attract the notice of law . . . are so fugitive and unsubstantial, that they are not easily retained or recovered . . . Of this knowledge every man has some, and none has much; . . .[19]

The minuteness of the details with which a commentator on Shakespeare must inevitably be concerned renders them historically transient. Once again the contrast with Pope is instructive. For Pope the body of English letters was sufficiently unified and transparent for a single editor to be

[16] See G. B. Evans, 'The Text of Johnson's Shakespeare (1765)', *Philological Quarterly*, 28 (1949), 425–8 (p. 426); Arthur Eastman, 'The Texts from which Johnson Printed his *Shakespeare*', *Journal of English and Germanic Philology*, 49 (1950), 182–91 (p. 191).

[17] *Boswell's Life of Johnson*, ed. G. B. Hill, rev. L. F. Powell (6 vols., Oxford, 1934), i. 329.
[18] *Johnson on Shakespeare*, i. 109.   [19] Ibid. 103.

adequate to the care of a classic text: what threatened English letters with fragmentation and dispersal was less the historically mutable nature of the language and culture itself, than the designs of low and interested specialists on what should be a unified and disinterested public culture. For Johnson the language and culture essential even to understanding Shakespeare are already broken up into details too minute and too transient to be within reach of a single reader or editor. The division of scholarly labour, for Johnson, does not produce the fragmentation of our cultural history, but is a necessary response to a fragmentation which has already occurred.

Yet it would be mistaken to regard Johnson's attitude towards this division of intellectual labour as a straightforwardly enthusiastic one, as though it held out the promise of a simple accumulation of more and better intellectual products. On some occasions, indeed, Johnson can present the division of intellectual labour as an antagonistic, rather than co-operative process, in which competitive interestedness may be just that which makes progress impossible: 'The first care of the builder of a new system, is to demolish the fabricks which are standing. The chief desire of him that comments an authour, is to shew how much other commentators have corrupted and obscured him.'[20] What Johnson later describes as 'the acrimony of a scholiast',[21] bent upon enlarging the bulk of his achievement by rage or exclamation, threatens to turn the division of scholarly labour into a war of all against all, rather than a mutually beneficial co-operation. In this case Johnson goes so far as gloomily to suggest that: 'Thus the human mind is kept in motion without progress'.[22] Occasional remarks in Johnson's commentary also testify to this fear that editorial interestedness may obstruct, rather than further, scholarly progress. Against one emendation suggested by Warburton to the text of *Othello* Johnson urges that 'The old reading will, I think, approve itself to every understanding that has not an interest in changing it';[23] elsewhere Johnson refers to the age of critical editing as that period of time 'since revisal became fashionable, and editors have been more diligent to display themselves than to illustrate their authour'.[24] In such remarks we are once more close to Pope's belief that editors whose professional interest was in emending rather than in preserving the text of Shakespeare were likely to be unfit custodians of it.

Yet it is clear that Johnson nevertheless believes that progress of a kind is being made, even in so notoriously antagonistic a field as textual criti-

---

[20] Ibid. 99.   [21] Ibid. 102.   [22] Ibid. 99.
[23] *1765*, viii. 396.   [24] Ibid. iv. 470.

cism: 'I can say with great sincerity of all my predecessors, what I hope will hereafter be said of me, that not one has left Shakespeare without improvement, nor is there one to whom I have not been indebted for assistance and information.'[25] Johnson's tribute to the work of all his predecessors is indeed a novel feature of his account of Shakespearian editing. Previous editors, both those who thought that the text should be in the care of disinterested gentlemen of letters and those who thought that it should be in the care of qualified specialists, had agreed that editors of the opposite stamp had had a disastrous impact upon the text, leaving Shakespeare further in need of restoration rather than contributing towards a gradual and co-operative process of improvement. It is one of the primary concerns of Johnson's edition, by contrast, not only that the best of all previous editions should be gathered into Johnson's, but that all asperity in literary controversy should be avoided. Johnson remarks that his predecessors have 'all been treated by me with candour, which they have not been careful of observing to one another'.[26] He is not prepared to claim that he himself possesses all necessary qualifications to provide a perfectly adequate edition of Shakespeare, any more than he has earlier been prepared to claim that he has the authority to dictate over the English language: both these must be the tasks of many. But he is prepared implicitly to suggest that he possesses the candour fairly to collect and assimilate those separate labours which had previously been antagonistically divided against each other in scholastic acrimony.[27] The variorum character of Johnson's edition is what supports its claim to be more than another monument to editorial interest or vanity.

2

Johnson's insistence on the authority of the First Folio—'the first is equivalent to all others, and . . . the rest only deviate from it by the printer's negligence'[28]—has often been applauded, usually accompanied by wonder or lament that he did not follow through his unprecedentedly clear statement of this principle by making the First Folio his

[25] *Johnson on Shakespeare*, i. 101.   [26] Ibid. 102.

[27] As Arthur Sherbo has shown, however, Johnson was not equally scrupulous in the acknowledgement of all his debts to other scholars: his use of suggestions by Benjamin Heath, in particular, is often silent. See *Samuel Johnson, Editor of Shakespeare* (Urbana, Ill., 1956), 28–44.

[28] *Johnson on Shakespeare*, i. 96.

copy-text.[29] There are other moments in Johnson's editorial theory which have contributed to such disappointment. His remark that 'the later publishers, with all their boasts of diligence, suffered many passages to stand unauthorized, and contented themselves with Rowe's regulation of the text, even where they knew it to be arbitrary, and with a little consideration might have found it to be wrong',[30] suggests a clear understanding of the effects of the tradition of a *textus receptus* on eighteenth-century editions of Shakespeare. But intimations of an editorial theory critical of the tradition of the received text exist side-by-side with passages which imply the authority of a *textus receptus*. The received text is the most obvious repository of the collective labours of eighteenth-century editors, and as such Johnson is unwilling wholly to abandon it, even though the collation upon which he insisted indicates its inadequacies.

The way in which Johnson goes on to discuss his own editorial practice, after remarking on the worthlessness of the three later Folios, reinforces a point which emerged from Theobald's editorial practice: to perceive the difficulties caused in particular cases by the tradition of the received text is not the same as making a systematic break either in theory or in practice with that tradition. The pervasiveness of *receptus*-thinking, even for those who had understood its deficiencies, is strikingly illustrated when Johnson emphasizes how few have been the occasions on which he has followed the received text (in improvements of the metre or of minute verbal details) against more authoritative copies. Johnson insists that 'this practice I have not suffered to proceed far, having restored the primitive diction wherever it could for any reason be preferred'.[31] Whereas Johnson begins this paragraph by insisting that the received text must justify itself where it differs from more authoritative copies, he ends it by implying that unless the readings of the older copies can be shown to be preferable for some reason, the received text is to stand. Johnson's discussion of the divisions between acts and scenes made in the eighteenth-century editions of the text grants the received text a decisive influence still more bluntly: 'I have preserved the common distribution of the plays into acts, though I believe it to be in almost all the plays void of authority.'[32] It is not that the authority of the copies can be overridden in the face of the rationality of

[29] See e.g. S. K. Sen, *Capell and Malone, and Modern Critical Bibliography* (Calcutta, 1960), 9. In fact, as Matthew W. Black and Matthias A. Shaaber showed in their study of *Shakespeare's Seventeenth-Century Editors, 1632–1685* (New York, 1937), each of the 17th-cent. Folios is revised to the point where it may reasonably be called 'edited'.

[30] *Johnson on Shakespeare*, i. 105.   [31] Ibid. 105–6.

[32] *Johnson on Shakespeare*, i. 107.

the received text's distribution of acts and scenes: Johnson argues that the conventional division of dramas into five acts is in any case 'accidental and arbitrary', and that Shakespeare's own practice bears witness to his awareness that this is so. The reader is left to draw the conclusion that some features of the received text which contradict both bibliographical authority and aesthetic desiderata are nevertheless to be left untouched. In such cases it becomes clear that Johnson's conception of his task as the custodianship of the entire eighteenth-century heritage of Shakespearian textual criticism leads him to look on certain features of that heritage as inalterable.

Although analysts of Johnson's editing have sometimes given the impression that his prefatory remark about the line of descent in the Folio tradition finds no echoes at all in his commentary, Johnson's use of Elizabethan and Jacobean copies is not wholly eclectic. There are indications in the notes of an interest in basing his emendatory practice in a prior evaluation of the sources and reliability of the copies available to him. Such evaluation is admittedly often carried out in an extremely generalized way. Johnson's wish to justify some aspects of the eighteenth-century tradition's divergence from the authoritative copies leads him to concur with previous low estimates of the reliability of the early copies in general, even where he does not wish to endorse the social and epistemological standpoints implicit in earlier eighteenth-century histories of Shakespeare's text. Johnson believes that his predecessors have sufficiently shown 'the negligence and unskilfulness' of the Elizabethan and Jacobean 'publishers',[33] and goes on to remark that 'much credit is not due to the fidelity, nor any to the judgement of the first publishers'.[34] Although Johnson takes the earlier eighteenth-century editors to have demonstrated the unreliability of the early Quartos and First Folio, his terms are in striking contrast to those of some previous accounts of the damage supposedly inflicted upon Shakespeare's text by the Elizabethan and Jacobean 'publishers'. Whereas for Pope it was characteristic of the player-editors Hemings and Condell that they could be trusted only in the narrowest and most literal matters, for Johnson the more minute details are just those which are likely to have been overlooked by the negligent early editors: 'what could be their care of colons and commas, who corrupted words and sentences'.[35]

Where an unfavourable assessment of the reliability of the early copies had for some editors gone hand in hand with an emphasis on the low and

---

[33] *Johnson on Shakespeare*, i, 92.   [34] Ibid. 106.   [35] Ibid. 107.

interested status of the players, Johnson does not usually identify the first 'publishers' with the players,[36] nor does he regard the faults of the early copies as the result of the lowness or interestedness of their publishers. The prospect of regarding the mean or vulgar passages considered unworthy of Shakespeare as just those most likely to have been corrupted by the players and player-editors is thereby closed to Johnson. Instead, he insists, immediately after conceding the poor state of the early copies, that 'they who had the copy before their eyes were more likely to read it right, than we who read it only by imagination'.[37] Whereas in Pope's, Warburton's, and even on occasion in Theobald's editions, a hypothetical 'foolish player' had become a flexible resource (differing in no essential respects from the 'scribe' of classical-philological histories of error), accounting for textual corruption of all kinds, Johnson's commentary, as Robert E. Scholes pointed out,[38] was much more cautious in its use of the theory of theatrical corruption. Johnson does not rule out the possibility of theatrical corruption,[39] but rejects its use as an all-purpose licence to remove whatever might threaten Shakespeare's reputation if charged to him. When Warburton ejects the line 'Up in the air, crown'd with the golden sun' from the text of *Henry V*, as 'A nonsensical line of some player',[40] Johnson responds 'And why of a player? There is yet no proof that the players have interpolated a line.'[41] Where some earlier editors had regarded an anachronism in *Henry VI, Part 1* as the players' responsibility, Johnson notes laconically that '*Machiavel* being mentioned somewhat before his time, this line is by some of the editors given to the players, and ejected from the text.'[42]

Johnson's commentary does frequently take the opportunity to reinforce his unfavourable judgement of the early printers' work, with the explicit intention of showing why attempts at conjectural emendation must sometimes be excused. When defending a reading given in the received text of *Antony and Cleopatra*, 'As matter whole you've not to make it with' Johnson remarks that 'The original copy reads, *As matter whole you have to make it with*. Without doubt erroneously; I therefore

---

[36] Although on some occasions the First Folio is referred to, as so much more often by earlier 18th-cent. editors, as the 'players'' edn.: see, for an example, *1765*, iv. 210, where Johnson refers to the First Folio's division of *Henry IV, Part 1* as the players' responsibility.

[37] *Johnson on Shakespeare*, i. 106.

[38] Robert E. Scholes, 'Dr. Johnson and the Bibliographical Criticism of Shakespeare', *Shakespeare Quarterly*, 11 (1960), 163–71 (p. 166), calculates that Johnson has recourse on 30 occasions to the idea of corruption by a scribe or printer, but on only 7 occasions to that of corruption by a player.

[39] See, for examples, *1765*, iv. 53, 305; v. 205.   [40] *1747*, iv. 353.

[41] *1765*, iv. 401.   [42] Ibid. 582.

only observe it, that the reader may more readily admit the liberties which the editors of this authour's works have necessarily taken.'[43] For Johnson the Folio reading so flatly contradicts the previous line, 'If you will patch a quarrel', that it can be appended as an instance of the extreme unreliability of the copies with which modern editors must work. When annotating the dialogue in French between Katharine and Alice in *Henry V*, Johnson reprints for a similar purpose a specimen from the 1608 Quarto.[44] Such a generalized bibliographical evaluation can also be turned towards specific editorial issues to justify emendatory intervention. In particular, Johnson insists that 'The particles in the old editions are of little credit'.[45] Johnson's understanding of the relationship between copies can fall victim to his belief that all the early texts are in general negligently printed. Johnson appends the following variants to a line in *Richard II* which he gives as 'Fear'd for their breed, and famous by their birth':

The first edition in 4to, 1598, reads,

> *Fear'd* by *their breed, and famous* for *their birth.*

The second 4to in 1615,

> *Fear'd* by *their breed, and famous* by *their birth.*

The first folio, though printed from the second quarto, reads as the first. The particles in this authour seem often to have been printed by chance.[46]

When Johnson finds that the reading in the Folio follows that in the First Quarto this does not prompt him to subject his theory that the Folio text was set up from the 1615 Quarto to further examination, but rather to see yet another example of the extreme casualness of the treatment of Shakespeare's particles by the earlier printers.

But Johnson's attempts at bibliographical evaluation are not always so generalized, and in other respects they show a departure from the straightforwardly eclectic attitude of much earlier eighteenth-century editing. Johnson's bibliographical remarks display a keen interest in the variety of sources of copy for the printed texts available to him, an interest which implies the principle that a bibliographical assessment of the worth of particular copies as a whole is to be made independently of the process of quarrying them for solutions to particular difficulties in whichever

[43] *1765*, vii. 139.
[44] Ibid. iv. 414. For further examples of quotations of early texts by Johnson for the purpose of demonstrating the negligence of the first printers and the need for conjectural emendation, see vi. 42; vii. 472; vii. 532.
[45] Ibid. iv. 47.   [46] Ibid. 28.

copy-text is chosen. Johnson suggests, for example, that the early Quartos of *Henry VI, Parts 2* and *3* and of *Henry V* are 'so apparently imperfect and mutilated, that there is no reason for supposing them the first draughts of Shakespeare': they are instead likely to have been printed from copies taken down by a listener rather than from authorial or playhouse documents.[47] Earlier, Johnson has argued that the publication of Parts 2 and 3 of *Henry VI* without Part 1 'may be admitted as no weak proof that the copies were surreptitiously obtained, and that the printers of that time gave the publick those plays not such as the authour designed, but such as they could get them'.[48] Such bibliographical judgements are then taken into account when considering whether particular readings should be adopted. In a passage of *Henry IV, Part 1* Johnson considers whether the received text's 'We of th'offending side' should read 'We of the off'ring side': 'I cannot but suspect that *offering* is right, especially as it is read in the first copy of 1599, which is more correctly printed than any single edition, that I have yet seen, of a play written by *Shakespeare*.'[49] The evaluations of individual copies are themselves often made on aesthetic rather than on bibliographical grounds, but they imply that assessment of a given copy as a whole may need to precede the case-by-case assessment of its individual readings.

This is particularly the case with those texts for which Johnson believes that the difference between the Quarto and the Folio tradition represents deliberate revision. In many such cases the practice had been simply to gather as much Shakespearian material as possible into a single text and to use Quarto and Folio variants in passages given by both opportunistically, wherever the received text presented difficulties, rather than considering which text might be more authoritative, or the possibility that some of the differences between Quarto and Folio texts might be the result of authorial revision. Johnson's practice, as we shall see later, remained in many respects bound to this tradition; but, as Steven Urkowitz has noted,[50] the bibliographical remarks scattered in Johnson's commentary confirm his awareness that what was likely to be produced by such a procedure was less a close approximation to any ideally authorial state of the texts in question than a conflation of two texts. One of the clearest such indications comes in Johnson's commentary on a line from *Henry IV, Part 1*:

[47] *1765*, v. 225.   [48] Ibid. iv. 589.   [49] Ibid. 197.
[50] Steven Urkowitz, 'The Base Shall to th' Legitimate: The Growth of an Editorial Tradition', in Gary Taylor and Michael Warren, eds., *The Division of the Kingdoms: Shakespeare's Two Versions of King Lear* (Oxford, 1983), 23–43 (pp. 31–3).

In the first editions the passage is read thus, *I could sing psalms or any thing*. In the first folio thus, *I could sing all manner of songs*. Many expressions bordering on indecency are found in the first editions, which are afterwards corrected. The reading of the three last editions, *I could sing psalms and all manner of songs*, is made without authority out of different copies.[51]

The principle implicit in such a passage seems clearly anti-eclectic: it is not enough that the passages now combined in the received text should separately have authorization in the early Quartos and First Folio, since their combination is not authorized by either text, and since the change from Quartos to Folio can be seen to be consistent with a deliberate policy of revision (whether Shakespeare's or another's is not here considered): in this case, the censorship of expressions bordering upon indecency. In his commentary on *Henry V* Johnson protests against the use of readings from inferior copies to mask merely aesthetic emendation under the cloak of attested variants. The principle implicit in Johnson's analysis is clear: the 'authentick' copy is first to be decided upon, and once this judgement has been made, alterations and insertions from other copies cannot be made merely upon aesthetic grounds. Such a principle would seem to be confirmed by Johnson's indications of the cases in which he believes Quarto texts to have provided copy for the First Folio.[52]

An examination of Johnson's commentary in the case of one of the most often discussed instances of Shakespearian revision, *King Lear*, however, makes it clear that this principle can falter where it is not possible firmly to declare that one copy is 'authentick' and the other 'imperfect'. Johnson describes the Folio as 'the better copy' in his bibliographical headnote, and declares that his own text is 'given from the folio'.[53] Such a declaration, of course, is ambiguous: the text is not literally 'given from' the Folio because the copy-text remains Theobald's 1757 edition; presumably, Johnson means that it is given from the Folio in the looser sense that Folio readings are preferred to Quarto unless there is some compelling reason to prefer the Quarto. At moments in Johnson's commentary on *Lear* we find the same hostility to eclecticism and conflation that we have seen elsewhere. At one point Johnson lists the varying suggestions of previous eighteenth-century editors and then points out that 'The true state of this speech cannot from all these notes be discovered. As it now stands it is collected from two editions: . . . The speech is now tedious because it is formed by a coalition of both.'[54] But Johnson's text, although it indicates typographically which passage belongs to which early copy[55] nevertheless

---

[51] *1765*, iv. 157.   [52] See, for an example, ibid. 3.
[53] *1765*, vi. 2.   [54] Ibid. 79.   [55] Ibid.

includes both rather than (as 'given from the folio' might lead us to expect) relegating the Quarto to a footnote or an appendix. This becomes less surprising when we learn that Johnson finds the Quarto version of this passage preferable: where the difference between competing early copies is only that between 'better' and worse copies rather than between 'authentick' and 'imperfect' it seems that eclectic criteria become admissible once more, despite the polemic set out against them. Elsewhere Johnson leaves in place a passage given in the Quarto but omitted from the Folio and 'restored' to the text by Theobald;[56] on another occasion, more surprisingly, he notes that 'This passage, which some of the editors have degraded, as spurious, to the margin, and others have silently altered, I have faithfully printed according to the quarto, from which the folio differs only in punctuation.'[57]

What this evidence suggests, once again, is that Johnson's attitudes towards bibliographical eclecticism are not so straightforwardly hostile as some of his most-often-quoted remarks might lead us to believe. The range of Johnson's attitudes in his commentary towards the post-1623 Folios so firmly regarded as bibliographically valueless in his preface offers a further indication that the assessment given there is not regarded as an inalterable principle. The bibliographical lists given by Johnson before the text of each play are inconsistent in their practice: although in general Johnson lists only the 1623 Folio, which is often described as 'the' Folio,[58] there are also occasions on which he lists later folios. Whilst only the 1623 Folio is listed before *The Tempest*, for example, the bibliographical table preceding *Henry IV, Part 1* includes the Second Folio of 1632 and notes it as one of the texts which Johnson has in his possession;[59] similarly, Johnson thinks it worth listing the Second and Third Folios before his texts of *A Midsummer-Night's Dream*, *The Merchant of Venice*, and *Measure for Measure*.[60] At one point in his text of *The Merchant of Venice* Johnson implicitly invokes the authority of the Second and Third Folios in support of his reading.[61] On other occasions, post-1623 Folios are mentioned in the commentary despite having been omitted from the bibliographical table. A note to *As You Like It*, for which no Quarto tradition exists, refers to a reading given by the 'old editions' of the play, even though the 1623 Folio is the only text noted at the beginning of the play;[62] at one point in Johnson's commentary on *Othello* he notes that he has 'followed the text of the folio, and third and fourth quarto's', as

[56] *1765*, vi. 36.   [57] Ibid. 59.   [58] See, for examples, *1765*, viii. 4 and 318.
[59] Ibid. iv. 108.   [60] Ibid. i. 88, 262 and 384.
[61] Ibid. 435.   [62] Ibid. ii. 36.

though the Third and Fourth Quartos lent additional support to the First Folio's reading, yet they were printed in 1630 and 1650 respectively and derive directly from the Quarto of 1622.[63]

The inconsistency of Johnson's bibliographical commentary leaves his textual-critical stance on many issues following that 'middle way between timidity and presumption' which is recommended in his preface. The question of metrical emendation offers a case in point. Johnson's preface excuses the tradition of making small changes to the text in order to rectify the metre, and even regards silent emendation in this respect as an acceptable practice. At other times, however, the reader is led to regard the practice as an insidious threat to the authenticity of Shakespeare's text. In the course of Johnson's commentary on *King Lear* he pauses to deliver a general denunciation of silent metrical emendation: 'I have given this passage according to the old folio, from which the modern editions have silently departed, for the sake of better numbers, with a degree of insincerity, which, if not sometimes detected and censured, must impair the credit of antient books.'[64] Johnson's editorial practice, as we shall see, reflects the contradiction between this firm assertion of the damage to the history of the language which silent emendation can cause and the opinion of Johnson's preface that such small matters may safely be left to editorial discretion.

3

Only a collation of the text printed by Johnson with his copy-texts can fully demonstrate the extent to which Johnson used his collations of pre-1623 copies to depart from the received text. An analysis of the editorial procedures shows how the idea of a middle way between timidity and presumption influenced Johnson's textual-critical practice. The analysis is based on information provided by a collation of his texts of two plays with their copy-texts: a play for which only a Folio tradition is available (*The Tempest*) and one (*Hamlet*) for which both Folio and Quarto traditions exist. Since Johnson alternated his copy-text in the course of editing Shakespeare, the copy-texts for collation are different: in the former Warburton's 1747 edition, in the latter a 1757 reprint of Theobald's edition.[65]

---

[63] See, for examples, viii. 450.

[64] *1765*, vi. 10. For other occasions on which Johnson's commentary objects to metrical emendation, see ibid. vi. 206; vii. 485.

[65] Evans, 'Text', 425–8.

Johnson's texts of both *The Tempest* and *Hamlet*, in many cases silently, remove some of those emendations which had been introduced into the text (often by Pope) in the interest of a smoother metre. Prospero's 'To me inveterate, hearkens my Brother's Suit'[66] had become in Pope's text the metrically smoother 'hears my brother's suit';[67] Warburton had attempted to save the metrical emendation whilst remaining closer to the First Folio text by reading 'hearks';[68] Johnson restores 'hearkens' despite the risk of a resulting hypermetrical line if 'inveterate' is read, as it is printed, as a quadrisyllable.[69] Hamlet's hypermetrical 'I've heard that guilty creatures, sitting at a play' had become an impeccable pentameter in Pope's text by the simple expedient of removing 'sitting';[70] Theobald, Hanmer, and Warburton had all followed this emendation,[71] but Johnson restores the word excised by Pope.[72] Likewise, Pope and his successors' 'But never the offence. To bear all smooth'[73] becomes once again 'But never the offence. To bear all smooth and even';[74] just as 'The memory be green, and that it fitted'[75] returns to its earlier form, 'The memory be green, and that it us befitted'.[76]

Both texts also restore difficult or obsolete constructions or expressions which had been removed in the course of the seventeenth and eighteenth centuries. The best-known of such restorations is that of 'hugger-mugger', but there are others. Hamlet's exclamation, 'Up, sword, and know thou a more horrid hent' had been found objectionable by earlier eighteenth-century editors (at least in cases where they had done enough collation to become aware of the reading): Rowe and Pope had simply substituted a reading from the 1676 Quarto, 'a more horrid time',[77] whilst Theobald and his successors had followed the reading of the Fourth Folio, 'a more horrid Bent'.[78] Johnson is the first eighteenth-century editor to restore and gloss the reading of the First Folio and early Quartos.[79] Similarly, where earlier editors since Pope had preferred to remove the phrase 'the bore of' from a passage in Hamlet's letter to the King ('I have words to speak in thy ear, will make thee dumb; yet are they much too light for the bore of the matter') rather than to attempt an explanation of it,[80] the phrase reappears in Johnson's text.[81] In Johnson's text of *The*

---

[66] *1714*, i. 9.   [67] *1723–5*, i. 10.   [68] *1747*, i. 11.

[69] *1765*, i. 11. For another example of a metrical emendation silently removed from Johnson's text of *The Tempest*, see *1765*, i. 22: '(Filth as thou art) with humane care, and lodg'd thee'; Hinman, p. 23, l. 486. *1714*, i. 15, and *1747*, i. 15 read 'lodg'd'.

[70] *1723–5*, vi. 397.   [71] *1733*, vii. 282; *1744*, vi. 367; *1747*, viii. 179.

[72] *1765*, viii. 203.   [73] *1723–5*, vi. 430; *1733*, vii. 341; *1744*, vi. 398; *1747*, viii. 219.

[74] *1765*, viii. 251.   [75] *1723–5*, vi. 351; *1733*, vii. 231; *1744*, vi. 325; *1747*, viii. 123.

[76] *1765*, viii. 138.   [77] *1676*, 52; *1714*, vi. 363; *1723–5*, vi. 420.

[78] *1733*, vii. 309; *1744*, vi. 388; *1747*, viii. 205.   [79] *1765*, viii. 236.

[80] *1723–5*, vi. 443; *1733*, vii. 336; *1744*, vi. 410; *1747*, viii. 233.   [81] *1765*, viii. 269.

Tempest 'holp' (as the past tense of 'to help'),[82] 'Scamels' (despite the numerous emendatory offerings from 'sea-mells' to 'shamois'),[83] and 'fellowly drops' (which had been banalized to 'fellow drops' by all editors since Pope)[84] are amongst the First Folio expressions restored to the text.

In the case of *Hamlet* many readings from a series of theatrical Quarto texts of the play published between 1676 and 1718, texts which did not hesitate to revise details of the text which were thought ungrammatical, obsolete, or offensive, had found their way into the eighteenth-century editorial tradition; Johnson was in many instances the first editor to remove readings which had arrived in the eighteenth-century texts by this route. Thus the King's 'A very *riband* in the cap of youth' had in both the 'Players' Quarto' of 1676 and subsequently in all previous eighteenth-century texts become the more conventional 'feather':[85] Johnson restores the reading attested to by the earliest Quarto in his possession, the 1637 text.[86] A similar banalization is removed in Johnson's text of Act 2: a passage which had in the 1676 Quarto and thence in all texts since Rowe's read '*the law of wit*, and the liberty'[87] reads once again in Johnson's text 'the law of *writ*'.[88] Elsewhere, Johnson removes an emendation first quarried from the 1676 Quarto by Theobald and subsequently taken over silently by both Warburton and Hanmer: Theobald had altered 'Confederate season, *else* no creature seeing' to read, more easily for eighteenth-century readers, 'and', following the seventeenth-century text.[89]

In all the cases discussed so far there are clear motives for Johnson's removal of later readings and reinsertions of earlier ones. A better indication of the extent to which Johnson's editorial practice is anti-eclectic on principle, rather than occasionally reviving readings from Elizabethan and Jacobean copies, can be found in cases where the motives for restoration are not so clear. Johnson's text of *The Tempest* makes a point of removing readings which have silently crept into the received text for no apparent reason and have thereby acquired a spurious authority and longevity. Johnson notes that 'In all the later Editions' Ariel's line 'Not a soul | But

---

[82]   *1765*, i. 9. 18th-cent. editors since Pope had read 'help'd': *1723–5*, i. 8; *1733*, i. 8; *1744*, i. 9; *1747*, i. 8.

[83]   *1765*, i. 48; Hinman, p. 28, l. 1216. For previous 18th-cent. readings see *1723–5*, i. 40 ('scamels'); *1733*, i. 39 ('Shamois'); *1744*, i. 40 ('sea-malls'); *1747*, i. 47 ('Shamois').

[84]   *1723–5*, i. 67; *1733*, i. 65; *1744*, i. 63; *1747*, i. 78 all read 'fellow-drops'. *1765*, i. 75 reads 'fellowly drops'. Hinman, p. 34, l. 2020.

[85]   *1676*, 70; *1714*, vi. 384; *1723–5*, vi. 445; *1733*, vii. 339; *1744*, vi. 412; *1747*, viii. 236.

[86]   *1637*, sig. Lɪᵛ; *1765*, viii. 272. Allen and Muir 652.

[87]   *1676*, 32; *1714*, vi. 340; *1723–5*, vi. 391; *1733*, vii. 276; *1744*, vi. 362; *1747*, viii. 173.

[88]   *1765*, viii. 197.

[89]   *1676*, 47; *1733*, vii. 299; *1744*, vi. 381; *1747*, viii. 196. *1765*, viii. 225.

felt a *fever of the mad*' has been read instead 'fever of the *mind*', 'without Reason or Authority, nor is any Notice given of an Alteration'; Johnson accordingly restores 'mad'.[90] On other occasions Johnson silently restores Folio readings which have at one stage or another dropped out of the received text. Rowe's third edition of 1714 first makes Gonzalo tell Sebastian 'you have spoken truer than you *propos'd*',[91] a reading which is then merely inherited by each subsequent text until Johnson's,[92] which silently restores the Folio's 'purposed'.[93] Another instance of the silent restoration of the Folio text of *The Tempest* in an apparently indifferent case is Johnson's reading '*short-grass'd* green' in Ceres' speech to Iris, where eighteenth-century texts had since Rowe's second edition read 'short-grass'.[94] At one point Johnson appears to suggest that, even where the First Folio text cannot now be made sense of, it must be allowed to stand where none of the emendations proposed is of sufficient certainty. Commenting on the famous crux in the First Folio text 'So safely ordered, that there is no *soule*, | No not so much perdition as an hayre | Betid to any creature in the vessell',[95] Johnson suggests an emendation of his own ('Soil') but leaves this possible emendation at the foot of the page and continues to follow the 'apparently [*i.e. evidently*] defective' First Folio reading in his text.[96]

But counter-examples are not lacking of instances in which Johnson takes over from his copy-text a reading not authorized by the First Folio, in many cases without giving notice of the fact in his commentary. Thus in the play's opening scene Gonzalo's expression of faith in the boatswain becomes, as in Warburton's text: 'I'll warrant him *from drowning*'[97] (replacing the reading of the First Folio and all editions until Theobald's, 'for drowning').[98] Johnson later follows Warburton (and Theobald's second edition of 1740) in emending so as to remove what he takes to be the discrepancy of a singular subject governing a plural verb-form.[99] Nor are Pope's metrical emendations always removed. An especially striking instance comes in Gonzalo's description of his ideal commonwealth at the beginning of Act 2, where Pope's 'Letters should not be known: *wealth, poverty*' is allowed to stand in Johnson's text in place of the Folio's

[90] *1765*, i. 15.   [91] *1714*, i. 21.
[92] *1723–5*, i. 25; *1733*, i. 24; *1744*, i. 25; *1747*, i. 30.   [93] *1765*, i. 31.
[94] Ibid. 61; *1714*, i. 48; *1723–5*, i. 57; *1733*, i. 56; *1744*, i. 55; *1747*, i. 64.
[95] Hinman, p. 20, ll. 115–17.   [96] *1765*, i. 8.
[97] *1765*, i. 5; *1733*, i. 5; *1747*, i. 5.
[98] Hinman, p. 19, l. 54; *1714*, i. 4; *1723–5*, i. 5; *1744*, i. 6 read 'for'.
[99] 'this Thing dare not' is taken as a mistaken plural form and becomes in the three texts mentioned 'this thing dares not': *1740*, i. 43; *1747*, i. 53; *1765*, i. 53.

'Riches, poverty'.[100] A more typical example is the reading of Caliban's line in Act 4 'And all be turn'd to Barnacles, or to Apes', which stands in Johnson's text, as in that of all eighteenth-century editors since Pope, as a smooth pentameter: 'And all be turn'd to barnacles, or apes'.[101]

The conclusion that Johnson's emendatory restorations do not in the end amount to a policy of deciding upon the most authoritative text, and using this as the principal source of emendations, is confirmed by an examination of parallel instances in Johnson's text of *Hamlet*. Once more, in many cases Johnson silently reprints the reading of his copy-text even where it has no support from the texts listed in his own bibliographical table. Even such a blatant metrical emendation as Pope's 'Dar'd to the fight. In which, our valiant *Hamlet*' for the reading of both Quarto and Folio 'Dared to the combat' can on occasion be allowed to remain in Johnson's text.[102] Similarly the double negative first removed by Pope from Hamlet's speech to the player is also missing from Johnson's text: the line 'Nor do not saw the air too much with your hand' remains in Johnson's edition, as it had stood in Pope's, 'And do not saw the air too much with your hand'.[103]

Not only does Johnson silently take over such emendations from his copy-texts, but there are also occasions on which he silently adds new emendations of his own. Both the texts under consideration confirm that Johnson did indeed, as his preface suggests, in rare cases consider small details of grammatical construction as legitimate cases for silent emendation. When Horatio tells Hamlet 'I think, I saw him yesternight' Hamlet's astonishment does not in Johnson's text prevent him from remembering to put his pronoun in the accusative case: 'Saw! whom?—'[104] (all previous texts had read 'who?');[105] an accusative is likewise added (on this occasion following Hanmer) to a passage in *The Tempest* in order to correct Ariel's accidence: 'Whom, with a charm join'd to their suffer'd labour | I've left asleep'.[106] Elsewhere, a blatant grammatical emendation made by the earlier eighteenth-century tradition may be removed, but only to be replaced by a less noticeable emendation of Johnson's own. The

---

[100] *1723–5*, i. 29; *1765*, i. 35; Hinman, p. 25, l. 827.

[101] *1723–5*, i. 63; *1733*, i. 62; *1744*, i. 60; *1747*, i. 72; *1765*, i. 71; Hinman, p. 34, l. 1922.

[102] *1723–5*, vi. 348; Hinman, p. 761, l. 101; Allen and Muir 614; *1765*, viii. 133.

[103] Hinman, p. 774, l. 1852; Allen and Muir 636; *1723–5*, vi. 404; *1765*, viii. 213.

[104] *1765*, viii. 147.

[105] Hinman, p. 763, l. 379; Allen and Muir 618; *1723–5*, vi. 357; *1733*, vii. 238; *1744*, vi. 331; *1747*, viii. 131.

[106] *1765*, i. 16, *1723–5*, i. 14, *1733*, i. 14, *1747*, i. 15, all read 'Who'; *1744*, i. 15 reads 'Whom'.

received text of the King's commission to the ambassadors in Act 1 of *Hamlet* had read:

> Giving to you no further personal power
> To business with the King, more than the scope
> Which these dilated articles allow.[107]

'Which' is an emendation of Pope's for 'Of'. Johnson restores 'Of' but dislikes the resulting inconsistency whereby the singular subject 'scope' is made to govern the plural verb-form 'allow' (presumably because 'articles' becomes a false subject for the verb) and therefore tidies the passage up silently by reading 'allows'.[108] On two occasions Johnson even permits himself what appears to be a deliberate removal of oaths: 'Oh God! your only jig-maker'[109] becomes simply 'Oh! your only jig-maker';[110] whilst '*God's bodikins*, man, much better'[111] reads in Johnson's text 'Odd's bodikins'.[112] In neither case does Johnson note the alteration, nor is there any precedent for either alteration in any previous copy.

Nor does Johnson appear in *Hamlet*, any more than in the case of *King Lear*, to be acting on a firm preference for either the Quarto or the Folio text. As Johnson admits, the only Quarto of which he has had sight is that of 1637,[113] but on just one occasion can this be demonstrated to have misled him into reprinting a reading attested by that text but not by the Quarto of 1604–5: in Polonius's catalogue of advice to Laertes, Johnson reads 'Bear't that th'opposer may beware of thee' (a reading first given in the 1611 Quarto but which Johnson would have found in the 1637 text),[114] in place of the reading of his copy-text, of the 1604–5 Quarto, and of the First Folio: 'the opposed'.[115] In all other cases where Johnson departs from his copy-text to insert a reading from the 1637 Quarto the reading is also that of the 1604–5 Quarto. The more significant point here is that Johnson arrives at no decision as to the relative authority of the Quarto and Folio texts but, in cases where either text presents an apparently acceptable reading, chooses freely between them. Thus Johnson feels it necessary to replace the 'What we have two nights seen', which is the reading both of his copy-text and of the Quartos,[116] with the 'What we two nights have seen' of the First Folio;[117] similarly, later, Claudius's 'By letters congruing to that effect', the reading both of the 1757 Theobald reprint and of the

---

[107] *1757*, viii. 110.   [108] *1765*, viii. 139.   [109] *1757*, viii. 164.
[110] *1765*, viii. 218.   [111] *1757*, viii. 152.   [112] *1765*, viii. 201.
[113] Ibid. 128.   [114] Ibid. 154; *1637*, sig. C1ʳ; Furness 67.
[115] *1757*, viii. 119; Hinman, p. 764, l. 532; Allen and Muir 620.
[116] *1757*, viii. 104; Allen and Muir 614; Furness 7.
[117] *1765*, viii. 131; Hinman, p. 760, l. 43.

Quartos,[118] is replaced by the Folio's 'By letters conjuring to that effect'.[119] Yet in the case of other apparently indifferent variants the Quarto is preferred. In the Ghost's speech to Hamlet Johnson replaces the reading of the Folio and of all previous eighteenth-century editions, 'Thy knotty and combined locks to part',[120] with the Quartos' 'Thy knotted and combined locks';[121] in a later speech by Claudius, Johnson reads, following the Quartos, 'It shall as level to your judgment '*pear* | As day does to your eye',[122] where the Folio and previous eighteenth-century editors had read 'pierce'.[123] Such inconsistent decisions, even in cases where either variant would presumably be acceptable, confirm that Johnson has not in the case of *Hamlet* come to any decision as to the principal source for his departures from the received text.

4

Johnson's textual-critical practice, then, does indeed represent a middle way between timidity and presumption: between his insistence that the dull and specialist duty of collation is an indispensable component of competent editing, and his desire that his edition should preserve and add to the accumulated improvements made to Shakespeare's texts by the labours of his predecessors. But this middle way is hardly a settled path, free from inconsistencies. On the one hand, many features of his commentary and editorial practice demonstrate that a serious collation of early Quartos and the First Folio has been accompanied by the beginnings of a recognition that each copy demands independent bibliographical evaluation before being quarried for possible improvements to the copy-text; on the other, a generalized and unfavourable bibliographical assessment of the value of all early copies combines with the remnants of a respect for the received text to allow earlier unauthorized amendments of Shakespeare's style and language to remain intact, and, on rare occasions, to permit new amendments. Given this conclusion, it would be equally mistaken either to salute Johnson as a McKerrow *avant la lettre* or to

---

[118] *1757*, viii. 189; Allen and Muir 647; Furness 321.

[119] *1765*, viii. 254; Hinman, p. 781, l. 2729.

[120] *1757*, viii. 126; Hinman, p. 765, l. 703; *1714*, vi. 321; *1723–5*, vi. 368; *1733*, vii. 251; *1744*, vi. 341; *1747*, viii. 146.

[121] *1765*, viii. 165; Allen and Muir 623; Furness 97.

[122] *1765*, viii. 264; Allen and Muir 650; Furness 147.

[123] *1757*, viii. 196; Hinman, p. 782, l. 2902; *1714*, vi. 379; *1723–5*, vi. 440; *1733*, vii. 333; *1744*, vi. 407; *1747*, viii. 229.

disparage him as the last of the eclectic editors. We should regard neither Johnson's interest in bibliographical evaluation, nor his reliance upon a received text, as accidental aberrations. Instead, it should be recognized that the complexities of Johnson's editorial practice are inseparable from the complex idea of editorial labour which is manifested in his preface and in his discussions of literary production generally. The tensions between Johnson's unprecedentedly blunt refusals to dissimulate the professional character of his work, on the one hand, and the claims to a public authoritativeness which persist, however implicitly or despairingly articulated, both in the *Dictionary* and in the edition of Shakespeare, are not merely contingent to Johnson's working practices, but find expression in the minutest details of his philological and editorial labour.

Conclusion: Textual Criticism and Enlightenment

A CENTRAL argument of this study has been that neither the rise of historicist approaches to the idea of linguistic correctness nor the advent of bibliographically grounded approaches to textual criticism can be understood if they are taken as the inventions of accidentally enlightened pioneers, on the one hand, or as the symptoms of the descent of an 'Enlightenment' epistemological world-view or schema, on the other. Instead, both of these shifts in philological practice are inseparably bound up with the changing representations of literary labour in general, and of the labour of minute criticism in particular, by means of which eighteenth-century editors understood their task and its place in the world of learning. A full discussion of the way in which this process worked in the later years of the century is beyond the scope of this book. But it can be shown that the historicist approach to language and anti-eclectic approach to bibliographical evaluation, which at the beginning of the century had seemed to so many critics to be low and interested incursions upon a public culture, had by the end of the century become the marks of scholarly respectability.

One aspect of Edmond Malone's altercation with Joseph Ritson at the close of the century illustrates this reversal well. Ritson was the son of a servant and a 'friend of liberty', circumstances hinted at in Malone's remark that he will leave Ritson's 'vulgar ribaldry' to 'rest with the low societies among whom it has been picked up'.[1] The contrasting status of the two critics was also alluded to in Ritson's Shakespearian epigraph to his *Cursory Criticisms on the Edition of Shakespeare published by Edmond Malone* (1792): 'A FAULCON, TOW'RING IN HER PRIDE OF PLACE, | WAS BY A MOUSING OWL HAWK'D AT AND KILL'D.'[2] The bibliographical collection and collation which Malone takes for granted as an essential

---

[1] Edmond Malone, *A Letter to the Rev. Richard Farmer, D.D.* (London, 1792; repr. London, 1971), 4.

[2] Joseph Ritson, *Cursory Criticisms on the Edition of Shakespeare published by Edmond Malone* (London, 1971), title-page. Johnson had earlier used the same quotation to describe Heath's attack on Warburton: Samuel Johnson, *Johnson on Shakespeare*, ed. Arthur Sherbo (2 vols., New Haven, Conn., 1968), i. 100.

preliminary to textual criticism are regarded by Ritson as not absolutely indispensable. Malone, unsurprisingly, believes that he has struck a crushing blow when he suggests (not without probability) that Ritson has had no access to any copy of the First Folio and that this explains the resentment which Ritson, as a literary tradesman, expresses at Malone's attack on the Second Folio: 'to depreciate the vitiated folio on which he was generally obliged to depend', Malone writes, 'was to rob him of the only tool with which he could carry on his trade'.[3] But the attitude towards book collection implied in the pamphlet, to which Malone is replying, suggests that Malone's rejoinder would be by no means decisive for Ritson:

'Had he consulted the original quarto,' says Mr. Malone, 'he would have found that the poet wrote'—so and so. Well, but how if he could not get, or never heard of the original quarto? how then? Had he not, in common with every other editor, the right of supplying imperfections or correcting mistakes, according to the best of his judgement?[4]

Ritson goes on to remark that Malone has been 'indebted to chance or favour' for his sight of many of the old Quartos.[5] For Ritson, textual criticism is a public domain in which every scholar has a 'right' to participate, even though the necessary resources may be in private hands. For Malone (who spent over £2,000 in acquiring his Shakespearian library),[6] any scholar without access to the necessary materials is self-evidently disqualified from editing Shakespeare.

One of the most striking aspects of the exchange between Ritson and Malone is the way in which it replicates in reverse so many of the features of the debate between Pope and Theobald. In each case a powerful and respectable literary luminary is attacked by a low and obscure pamphleteer, and in each case this difference in social status features explicitly in the controversy. But on all the central issues—the importance of bibliographical collection and collation, the propriety of removing 'barbarous' or 'corrupt' English—the theory and practice of Malone are far closer to Theobald's and those of Ritson to Pope's, than either of the pairs of contemporaries are to each other. This is especially true of the critics' attitudes towards the place of textual criticism in the public cultural domain. Whilst Pope thought himself justified in complaining that, despite a public advertisement soliciting help from all lovers of Shakespeare

---

[3] Malone, *A Letter*, 16.   [4] Ritson, *Cursory Criticisms*, 8–9.   [5] Ibid. 9.
[6] 'Malone' in *Dictionary of National Biography*, ed. Sidney Lee and Leslie Stephen (21 vols., London, 1908–9), xii. 877–82.

for the forthcoming edition, Theobald had failed to provide assistance or information of any kind, Theobald rejoined that his emendations were his own work and that he was therefore quite entitled to keep them to himself.[7] What Pope presents as a public resource is taken by Theobald as a privately earned professional asset.[8] Later in the century Ritson finds it necessary to fight for his right to participate in this public domain when the resources are in private hands (Malone's, amongst others). Just that insistence on collection and bibliography satirized by Pope as typical of Theobald's meanness later becomes the mark of Malone's respectability, a point tellingly emphasized when Malone is able to quote one of Pope's jibes against Theobald in gentle self-mockery: 'the toil of wading through *all such reading as was never read* has been cheerfully endured, because no labour was thought too great, that might enable us to add one new laurel to the father of our drama'.[9]

If this contrast indicates the way in which what had previously been thought low pedantry had become respectable scholarship by the close of the century, it also suggests the indebtedness of Malone's work to what went before it. The first editor to print a text of Shakespeare abandoning the *textus receptus* as the source of copy-text was Edward Capell. If we are to locate the sudden break between pre-enlightened and enlightened practices of textual criticism implied by both Seary and de Grazia anywhere, it should surely be with Capell's work, rather than with Theobald's or Malone's. But Capell's narrative of his own enlightenment places obstacles in the way of such an interpretation:

he fell immediately to collation,—which is the first step in works of this nature; and, without it, nothing is done to purpose,—first of moderns with moderns, then of moderns with ancients, and afterwards of ancients with others more ancient: 'till, at the last, a ray of light broke forth upon him, by which he hop'd to find his way through the wilderness of these editions into that fair country the Poet's real habitation. He had not proceeded far in this collation, before he saw cause to come to this resolution;—to stick invariably to the old editions (that is, the best of them) which now hold the place of manuscripts, no scrap of the Author's writing having the luck to come down to us; and never to depart from them, but in cases where reason, and the uniform practice of men of the greatest note in this art, tell him— they may be quitted; nor yet in those, without notice.[10]

---

[7] Jones, *Theobald*, 122–3.

[8] A parallel disagreement over the editing of Chaucer can be found in the controversy between Thomas Morell and William Entick: upon Entick's publication of proposals for a new text, Morell protested not only that 'I publish'd Proposals for an Edition of *Chaucer*'s Works in Octavo, about two Years ago' but that 'There is scarce a Gentleman in *Cambridge*, but knows my Design'. William L. Alderson and Arnold C. Henderson, *Chaucer and Augustan Scholarship* (Berkeley, Calif., 1970), 173.

[9] *1790*, i. 262.   [10] *1767–8*, i. 20.

Capell has not decided on the principle of the selection of an authoritative copy-text in advance: it emerges from an editorial practice already under way. What Capell's account makes strikingly clear is that his discovery of the 'resolution' which he must take results from a method of collation which, by the standards of that resolution, has been carried out in an entirely mistaken order, so that moderns are collated with moderns before the best old copies are examined. Moreover, Capell's position is still not entirely free from *receptus*-thinking: 'the uniform practice of men of the greatest note in this art' may justify departures from the copy-text. As in Kuhn's account of scientific revolutions, new theoretical practices do not spring fully formed from the mind of the innovator: they develop from the breakdown of earlier practices, whose mark is left upon the newer methods.

An examination of Malone's editorial practice shows that on the crucial issue, the question of his abandonment of the use of a received text for copy, it is by no means possible to regard even his work as completely free of the eclectic procedures which we have so often found entwined with apparently systematic approaches in the course of this study. Critical attitudes towards the received text surfaced early in the century, both in Shakespearian and in classical and scriptural textual criticism: if an abandonment of the received text for use as copy is to be tied to an 'Enlightenment' epistemological schema dating from the 1790s, as de Grazia suggests, these earlier critical attitudes are hard to explain. In any case, Malone's rejection of the received text as copy was not the black-and-white matter it has sometimes been made to appear. Malone considered but rejected the suggestion of the Chaucer scholar Thomas Tyrwhitt that the First Folio itself should be marked up for the press, pointing out, but not specifying, the 'inconveniences' of such a procedure.[11] Instead, a copy of the Johnson-Steevens 1785 text was collated line by line with the First Folio and those Quartos which Malone regarded as authoritative; the proofs of Malone's text, based on this collation, were then read aloud to him whilst he looked over both the relevant First Folio or Quarto text and a table of variants between Quarto and Folio texts.[12] Despite Malone's undoubted care in collation, this procedure is one which, at a literal level, still takes the received text to provide copy. Moreover, Malone's other remarks about Shakespeare's text often imply that he is thinking of that text as part of a continuing institution rather than simply as a replication of original or authentic copies, as when he remarks that he has added

---

[11] As e.g. in S. K. Sen, *Capell and Malone, and Modern Critical Bibliography* (Calcutta, 1960).

[12] *1790*, i, p. xliv.

1,654 'emendations' to 'the text' by consulting 'authentick' copies: here
'the text' is the 1785 text, and the Quartos and Folios are a source of
emendations to that basic copy.[13]

The implications of such ways of describing editorial procedure are
confirmed by certain aspects of Malone's textual-critical practice itself, as
can be seen in his treatment of *Othello*. Malone argues that where the
Folio text is clearly based on Quarto copy, and even in cases where
the Folio variants might now be thought of as amounting to revision, the
Quartos 'are entitled to our particular attention and examination as *first*
editions', whereas the Folio will in such cases supply 'many valuable
corrections of passages undoubtedly corrupt in the quartos'.[14] Given such
a position, one might at the very least expect that, in the case of apparently
indifferent variants, Malone's text of *Othello* would follow the 1622
Quarto rather than the First Folio. But in a number of such instances,
Malone follows the 1785 text in giving the Folio reading.[15] Since Malone
in these cases opts for a reading given in a text which his introduction
declares to be less authoritative than that whose reading is rejected, there
is a strong presumption that the influence of the received text, the copy
upon which his text is still physically based, can be seen at such points.
Malone's eclecticism in the case of non-indifferent variants also suggests
that the methods and concerns of previous eighteenth-century editors
have by no means been entirely abandoned in favour of the replication of
supposedly 'authentic' copies. Like previous editors, Malone produced a
conflated text not merely in the sense that all available and desirable
material from the relevant Quarto and the First Folio is gathered together
in a single text, but also in that composite lines which appear neither in the
Quarto nor in the First Folio are created from a combination of both. A
typical instance is Malone's text of the dialogue between Iago and
Roderigo at the end of Act 1. In Malone's text Roderigo's parting words
are 'I am changed. I'll sell all my land.' The Quarto's 'I am chang'd' has
been added on to the Folio's 'Ile sell all my Land' to produce a line that
appears in neither.[16]

---

[13]   Malone, *A Letter*, 8.   [14]   *1790*, i, p. xiii.

[15]   Where the Quarto gives 'The Moore howbe't, that I indure him not, | Is of a constant,
noble, louing, nature;' Malone, following the First Folio and the 1785 edn., gives the second
of these lines as 'Is of a constant, loving, noble nature': Allen and Muir 803; Hinman, p. 826,
l. 1072; *1790*, ix. 507; *1785*, x. 609. Where the Quarto reads 'I am to put our Cassio in some
action', Malone, again with the First Folio and the 1785 text, reads, 'Am I to put our Cassio
in some action': Allen and Muir 804; Hinman, p. 827, l. 1173 ('Am I put to our Cassio in
some action'); *1790*, ix. 512; *1785*, x. 615.

[16]   *1790*, ix. 490; Allen and Muir 798; Hinman, p. 823, l. 728.

Moreover, there are points at which Malone follows the reading of the 1785 text in preference to either the 1622 Quarto or the First Folio. Many of these cases concern the regularization of grammar which had been such a prevalent feature of earlier Shakespearian editing. Although it is a central argument of Malone's 'Preface' that editors since the Second Folio editor of 1632 have taken for grammatical mistakes constructions that were the phraseology of Shakespeare's day,[17] and although Malone defends the double negative, for example, on such grounds,[18] there are nevertheless some features of the Quarto and Folio texts which Malone himself finds unacceptable on grammatical grounds, notably disagreement in the number of subject and verb.[19] More noteworthy still are the grounds which Malone gives for his practice in this respect: 'This inaccuracy has been constantly corrected by every editor wherever it occurs'.[20] Elsewhere, Malone silently supplies missing accusatives to pronouns[21] and silently brings the tenses of verbs into conformity,[22] in each case in line with the Johnson and Steevens 1785 text. Once more neither the consensual character of eighteenth-century editing, nor its desire to participate in the polishing of the English tongue and that tongue's most impressive monuments, have been wholly abandoned.

These elements of continuity between earlier eighteenth-century practice and Malone's work suggest that existing maps of the rise of historicist and bibliographically anti-eclectic Shakespearian textual criticism are inadequate. What Peter Seary takes as the achievement of a single pioneer, and what Margreta de Grazia sees as the descent of a Foucaultian episteme, cannot be understood in isolation from changing attitudes towards and circumstances of literary production. The new respectability and dominance which bibliographically and historically based textual criticism had achieved by the 1790s represent no inexplicable epistemological shift but are intimately related to changing attitudes towards the

---

[17] *1790*, i, pp. xix–xliii.   [18] *1790*, i, p. xx.

[19] Where the Quarto reads 'Farewell the plumed troops, and the big warres: | That makes ambition vertue: O farewell', and where the Folio likewise gives a singular verb governed by a plural subject, Malone, like *1785*, silently converts the verb into a plural: 'That make ambition virtue!' Allen and Muir 814–15; Hinman, p. 833, ll. 1992–3; *1790*, ix. 556; *1785*, x. 660.

[20] *1790*, i, p. xlvi.

[21] *1790*, like *1785*, reads 'for the love of his Desdemona: whom let us not therefore blame' in place of the Quarto's and First Folio's 'who': *1790*, ix. 511; *1785*, x. 614; Allen and Muir 804; Hinman, p. 827, l. 1127.

[22] *1790* and *1785* both read 'I heard thee say but now—Thou lik'dst not that' for the 'lik'st' of both Quarto and Folio. *1790*, ix. 536; *1785*, x. 640; Allen and Muir 826; Hinman, p. 841, l. 2911.

division and professionalization of literary labour in the eighteenth century. The deep concern of a work like the *Dunciad* that the division and
professionalization of literary labour would turn all cultural artefacts into
mere things, into mere commodities, that it might, indeed, render the
culture unintelligible, could find no parallel even in the work of Johnson,
let alone in that of Malone. It no longer seemed natural by the end of the
century that editors of Shakespeare should be those who, like Pope,
Warburton, and Johnson, stood at the head of the world of letters as such,
rather than merely at the head of the scholarly community. Historicist
philology, as Margreta de Grazia insists, needs to understand itself as a
historical product, rather than as the inevitable victory of sound method;
but it can only do this by understanding the division of intellectual labour
in which it originated, and by which it continues to be mediated. This is
not the same as reducing philological practice to its conditions of production. The analysis of the history of textual criticism as a history of
intellectual practice (rather than as a history of ideas alone) which has
been undertaken in this study does not wish to reduce eighteenth-century
developments in the theory and practice of textual criticism to these
conditions of production, but shows how the self-representations by
scholars of their work and of the world of learning must be taken into
account if their philological practice is to become intelligible.

It will be clear that the implications of this study are rather implications
for how the history of textual criticism is to be understood than for how
texts are to be edited. Nevertheless, they prompt wider reflection on the
relationship between textual criticism and enlightenment in general.

Enlightenment is the escape of humanity from its self-incurred tutelage. Tutelage is the
incapacity to use one's understanding without the direction of another. This
tutelage is *self-incurred* when its cause is not a defect in the understanding but in
resoluteness and courage to use one's own understanding without the direction of
another. Sapere aude! have the courage to use your *own* understanding! is therefore the maxim of enlightenment.[23]

'Each reader his or her own textual critic' is a maxim which would have
horrified a Fowler Comings or a Conyers Middleton. Yet 'sapere aude'
does not suggest that we should judge for ourselves, however little we
know, but that we should judge *and know* for ourselves. Its corollary in

---

[23] Immanuel Kant, 'Beantwortung der Frage: Was ist Aufklärung?' in *Was ist Aufklärung?
Aufsätze zur Geschichte und Philosophie*, ed. Juergen Zehbe (Göttingen, 1985), 55 (my tr.).
The literal sense of 'sapere aude' is 'dare to know!'

textual criticism would not be a procedure purporting to leave a free choice to the reader, as though choices made in ignorance could properly be described as free, but a wariness about prematurely standing in for the reader so as to decide in advance what he or she does not need to know. Those particulars judged too minute for the general reader to be troubled with—nowadays the historical mutability of typography and orthography, and in the period covered by this study, on some occasions, the historical mutability of syntax and lexicon—may be just those which show to the general reader why he or she is no such thing, but *this* reader entangled in these institutions, histories, and hierarchies; entangled, not immutably, but in an explicable and alterable way. Such minute particulars are an image of the rubble upon which the splendid edifice of the general reader has been elevated. It is a small escape from tutelage, in Kant's sense, to discover for oneself that the obsessive uniformity of modern spelling is a historical product. This is not at all the same as to demand that, say, all editions of Renaissance texts should be old-spelling. Rather, it is to suggest that the division of intellectual labour between textual and literary criticism, between editing and reading, should be seen for the source of 'technically-practical rules'[24] which it is, not misrecognized as an epistemological given. A division of intellectual labour which can no longer understand itself as such, but petrifies into an apparently external and given order, is the very image of tutelary deference. 'Sworn Foe to Myst'ry, yet divinely dark':[25] Pope's horror of a culture gone blind with enlightenment is only half wrong.

The crisis induced in the domain of textual criticism by the arrival of more sophisticated hermeneutic models is not to be wished away. Yet, for so long as technically-practical precepts stand in for epistemological propositions, theory can have no positive prescriptions whatever to make for editing. The idea of specifically deconstructive or feminist or postmodernist or Marxist *methodologies* for editing is for this reason a chimerical one. Any attempt to execute such a methodology would in no way represent a more theoretically enlightened philology, but rather a still more arbitrary truncation of the reader's possible informed autonomy. The history of textual-critical theory and practice conducted at a micrological level in this study should suggest that professionalism in historical scholarship and its concomitant division of intellectual labour is neither a set of mistaken opinions nor a delusory world-view; it cannot

---

[24] The term is Kant's, again: *Critique of Judgment*, tr. Werner S. Pluhar (Indianapolis, 1987), 11.

[25] Alexander Pope, *The Dunciad*, ed. James Sutherland (London, 1963), p. 385, l. 460.

therefore simply be jettisoned and replaced with a more up-to-date model. What theoretical and historical reflection can do is to resist any attempt to naturalize and universalize historically circumscribed categories. For any history of intellectual practice, this implies going beyond both the contented mapping of progress by pioneers supposedly ahead of their time, and the idea of enlightenment as a pit into which we have unluckily and inexplicably tumbled. 'Judge and know for yourself' remains a difficult yet enlightened maxim, by which we might yet come to understand how and why the promises of enlightenment have remained unfulfilled.

The authorship of *An Answer to Mr. Pope's Preface to Shakespear* (1729)

It is indeed 'tempting', as Brian Vickers suggests,[1] to ascribe *An Answer* to Lewis Theobald, not least because so many of the bibliographical arguments with which Peter Seary credits Theobald are first found, in more explicit form, in *An Answer*—for instance, the first suggestion that Quartos may have provided Folio copy.[2] Since Seary argues that Theobald's ideas would have been presented in a more developed account had not that editor feared charges of pedantry,[3] a pamphlet outlining very similar views beneath the shelter of a pseudonym would indeed seem a plausible candidate for ascription to Theobald: perhaps the bibliographical information to be found here might represent material dropped when, worried by the *Dunciad Variorum*'s mock 'Prolegomena', Theobald announced in a letter that 'The whole affair of *Prolegomena* I have decided to soften into *Preface*'?[4] However, there are several possible objections to such an identification of *An Answer*'s author.

First, its references to Theobald are mixed in their tone: although there is an enthusiastic passage eagerly anticipating a new edition of Shakespeare from 'The RESTORER' and accepting that 'That *Gentleman* has fully prov'd his Capacity superior to every *former Editor*',[5] another offers 'a presumptive Observation, that has escaped Mr. *Pope* and Mr. *Theobald*, among all their Guesses',[6] a phrase which suggests some triumph over both editors. Shakespeare's name is persistently spelt as Pope, rather than as Theobald, spelt it: since the very first note to the *Dunciad Variorum* (which had been published the previous April and some verses from which are satirically misquoted on *An Answer*'s title-page) had mocked Theobald at length for his pedantry in this respect, the spelling is not likely to have been accidental, nor is it likely that Theobald wished to retreat from the spelling given in *Shakespeare Restored*, since he later retained it in his edition. Finally, Theobald himself dissents from one of the pamphlet's claims in the preface to his edition of Shakespeare: he mentions its assertion that many Shakespeare manuscripts had

---

[1] Brian Vickers, ed., *Shakespeare: The Critical Heritage, 1733–1752* (London, 1975), 449.
[2] *An Answer*, 33.
[3] Peter Seary, *Lewis Theobald and the Editing of Shakespeare* (Oxford, 1990), 142.
[4] John Nichols, *Illustrations of the Literary History of the Eighteenth Century* (8 vols., London, 1817–58; repr. New York, 1966), ii. 621.
[5] *An Answer*, 26.   [6] Ibid. 24.

passed into the hands of a Warwick baker who had married one of the playwright's descendants, and that they were subsequently lost in a fire, but comments 'I cannot help being a little apt to distrust the authority of this tradition'. It is possible that Theobald came to distrust this story between 1729 and 1733; but his tone in introducing it is sceptical to the point of hostility: 'We have been told, indeed, in print, but not until very lately . . . '.[7]

Furthermore, there is already an alternative attribution available, although the evidence for it is hardly overwhelming. Two of the British Library copies of the pamphlet each have a manuscript note on the title-page identifying the author as 'John Roberts', but giving no further information.[8] The library's general catalogue concurs, describing the author as 'John Roberts, Comedian'. *ESTC* gives Roberts's dates as '1712?–1772'; if the conjectural year of birth is correct, Roberts would have been only 16 or 17 when the pamphlet went to press, which seems unlikely in view of the author's detailed knowledge of Shakespearian bibliography. In the absence of further evidence the matter must remain undecided. It seems impossible that Theobald could have been responsible for the whole pamphlet, although it is possible that information on Shakespearian bibliography was supplied by Theobald to another writer.

[7] *1733*, i, p. xiv.
[8] British Library pressmarks 83 a. 14; 1344 f. 39.

Collations

The table below is a summary of collations made by line-by-line comparisons of five texts of *Hamlet*—Pope's 1723–5 text, Theobald's 1733 text, Hanmer's 1744 text, Warburton's 1747 text, and Johnson's 1765 text—with their respective copy-texts: Rowe's 1714 edition, Pope's 1728 edition, Pope's 1723–5 edition, Theobald's 1733 edition, and Theobald's 1757 edition. *Hamlet* was chosen as a play with both Quarto and Folio textual traditions. For the full collations themselves see Simon Jarvis, 'Scholars and Gentlemen: Shakespearean Textual Criticism and Representations of Scholarly Labour, 1725–1765' (Ph.D. thesis, Faculty of English, University of Cambridge, 1993), 320–432; space did not permit their inclusion here. In that table variations in stage-directions, lineation, and scene-numbering were not recorded; variations in spelling and punctuation were not recorded except where the sense appeared to be materially affected; clear misprints (such as 'wou' for 'you' on p. 202 of Warburton's text) were not recorded. Only readings actually adopted by editors in their texts are recorded: thus, for example, although Warburton remarks that 'We may be sure, then, that *Shakespear* wrote,——*the whips and scorns* OF TH' TIME', his text continues to read 'the whips and scorns of time' (*1747*, viii. 183) and consequently no variation from Theobald's 1740 text (viii. 157) was recorded.

The column headed 'source' recorded all previous occurrences (up until 1676) of the reading given in the right-hand column text; it also recorded the first previous eighteenth-century editor (if any) to suggest or print the reading. It should be noted that the appearance of a given copy in the 'source' column only indicated that the same reading had earlier appeared in that copy; in some cases this may represent coincidence rather than indebtedness. Fortuitous coincidences between readings listed and those of the First, 'Bad' Quarto of 1603 were not listed in the 'sources' column: this Quarto was not rediscovered until the early nineteenth century. A text was only listed as providing a 'source' to an eighteenth-century editor if it gave the same word (variants in spelling have for this purpose been disregarded); it was not possible to record the numerous occasions on which an editor such as Theobald uses the reading of an early text in emended form, and such instances accordingly appeared as 'none'. This indicates the limitations of the list of collations, which is only a necessary, not a sufficient condition of an analysis of editorial practice.

The list of 'sources' was compiled with reference to Furness's Variorum edition. Furness's 'Q2' and 'Q3' are treated as one text by modern editors and are here listed as 'Q2'; consequently, Furness's 'Q4' and 'Q5' become 'Q3' and 'Q4'. The 1637 Quarto was unavailable to Furness, whilst the 1676 Quarto was only occasionally collated by him; these texts were therefore consulted independently in the compilation of the list. Abbreviations for the names of eighteenth-century editors are given, rather than for their texts, because in some cases a reading first appearing in one editor's text was the work of another editor (as with conjectures made by Theobald in *Shakespeare Restored* but not taken up in his own edition, for example; or as with emendations by Warburton used without permission by Hanmer).

The statistical form in which my results are given in this Appendix should be treated with extreme caution. Behind the statistics lies a complex mass of individual editorial decisions and procedures, to which the only reliable guide is the full discussion given in the body of this book itself. They can in no way yield a full account of the textual practice of the editors considered and are given here merely as a broad indication of some of its features.

The abbreviations used in the table of collations are as follows (see *Hamlet*, ed. G. R. Hibbard (Oxford, 1987), 132, for full details):

F_1	First Folio (1623)
F_2	Second Folio (1632)
F_3	Third Folio
F_4	Fourth Folio (1685)
Q_2	Quarto of 1604–5
Q_3	Quarto of 1611
Q_4	undated Quarto (1622?)
Q37	*The Tragedy of Hamlet, Prince of Denmark* (London, 1637)
Q76	*The Tragedy of Hamlet, Prince of Denmark* (London, 1676)
Pope^2	*1728*
Theo	Theobald
Theo^2	*1740*
Han	Hanmer
Warb	Warburton
Thirl	Styan Thirlby

Source	Pope	Theobald	Hanmer	Warburton	Johnson
Q2	6	0	0	0	0
Q3 Q4	1	1	0	0	1
Qq	20	5	1	2	1
Q37	3	1	0	0	0
Q76	6	6	1	0	1
Q37 Q76	5	2	0	0	0
Q2 F1	1	0	0	0	0
Q2 Q76	1	0	0	0	0
Q3 Q4 Q76	1	0	0	0	0
Q2 Q37 Q76	2	0	0	0	0
Q2 Q3 F1 Q37	0	1	0	0	0
Q2 Q3 Ff Q37	0	0	0	0	1
Q2 Q3 Q37 Q76	1	0	0	0	0
Q2 Q4 Q37	0	1	0	0	0
Q2 Q4 Q37 Q76	1	0	0	0	0
Q3 Q4 Q37 Q76	12	2	0	1	0
Q4 Q37 Q76	0	0	0	0	1
Qq Q37	18	6	0	4	3
Qq Q37 Q76	231	47	0	3	7
Qq Q76	5	0	0	0	0
Qq F1	0	1	0	0	0
Qq F1 Q37 Q76	19	7	0	0	0
Qq F1 F2 F3	0	1	0	0	0
Qq F1 F2 Q37 Q76	11	6	0	0	0
Qq F1 F2 Q76	2	0	0	0	0
Qq F1 F4 Q37 Q76	1	0	0	0	0
Qq F1 F2 F3 Q37	0	0	0	0	1
Qq F1 F2 F3 Q37 Q76	1	2	0	0	0
Qq Ff	0	1	0	0	0
Qq Ff Q37 Q76	14	4	0	1	2
Qq Ff Q37	1	2	0	0	1
F1	1	0	0	0	0
F1 F2	1	0	0	0	0
F1 F2 F3	1	2	1	0	0
Ff	1	3	3	1	4
F1 Q4	1	0	0	0	0
F4	0	1	0	0	0
F4 Q37 Q76	1	0	0	0	0
Q2 Ff Rowe	0	1	0	0	0

Source	Pope	Theobald	Hanmer	Warburton	Johnson
Q2 Ff Q37 Rowe	0	0	0	0	1
Qq Ff Rowe	0	2	1	0	2
Qq Ff Q37 Q76 Rowe	0	0	5	4	17
Qq Ff Q37 Rowe	0	2	0	0	3
Qq Ff Q76 Rowe	0	1	0	1	0
Q37 Rowe	0	0	0	1	0
Q76 Rowe	0	0	0	1	0
Ff Rowe	0	20	18	3	11
Ff Q2 Q3 Rowe	0	0	1	0	0
Ff Q37 Q76 Rowe	0	1	2	0	0
Ff Q3 Q4 Q37 Q76 Rowe	0	2	1	0	0
F3 F4 Rowe	0	0	0	0	1
Rowe	0	1	0	1	0
Pope	0	0	0	1	2
Q76 Pope	0	0	0	1	1
Warb	0	3	10	0	4
Han	0	0	0	7	6
Theo	0	0	30	0	3
Qq Theo	0	0	1	0	0
Qq Q37 Q76 Theo	0	0	6	0	0
Qq F1 Q37 Q76 Theo	0	0	1	0	0
Qq F1 F2 Q37 Q76 Theo	0	0	5	0	0
Qq F1 F2 F3 Theo	0	0	1	0	0
Qq F1 F2 F3 Q37 Q76	0	0	1	0	0
Qq Ff Theo	0	0	1	0	0
Qq Ff Q37 Q76 Theo	0	0	1	0	0
Q37 Q76 Theo	0	0	2	0	0
Q76 Theo	0	0	3	0	0
F1 F2 F3 Theo	0	0	1	0	0
Ff Theo	0	0	1	0	0
Theo2	0	0	1	0	0
Qq F1 Pope2	0	0	1	0	0
Qq Q37 Q76 Pope2	0	0	1	0	0
Qq Ff Q37 Thirl	0	0	0	1	0
all	0	0	7	0	0
Qq Ff Q37 Warb	0	0	0	0	1
none	172	37	84	65	32
none [percentile]	31.56%	21.38%	43.52%	66.32%	29.09%
TOTAL	545	173	193	98	110

Bibliography

1. MANUSCRIPT SOURCES

The Poetical Works of Mr. John Milton (London, 1720), with manuscript annotations by Richard Bentley. Cambridge University Library, Adv. b. 52 12.

The Works of Shakespear, ed. William Warburton (8 vols., London, 1747), with manuscript annotations by Samuel Johnson. University College of Wales Library, Aberystwyth, D1388. PR2572 P8 [microfilm].

2. PRIMARY SOURCES: TEXTS OF SHAKESPEARE
(listed in chronological order)

Shakespeare's Plays in Quarto, ed. Michael J. B. Allen and Kenneth Muir (Berkeley, Calif., 1981).

The Norton Facsimile: The First Folio of Shakespeare, ed. Charlton Hinman (New York, 1968).

The Tragedy of Hamlet Prince of Denmark (London, 1637).

The Tragedy of Hamlet Prince of Denmark. As it is now Acted at his Highness the Duke of York's Theatre (London, 1676; repr. 1969).

The Tragedy of Hamlet Prince of Denmark (London, 1703; repr. 1969).

The Works of Mr. William Shakespear, ed. Nicholas Rowe and Charles Gildon (6 vols., London, 1709–10; repr. New York, 1967).

The Works of Mr. William Shakespear, ed. Nicholas Rowe and Charles Gildon, 3rd edn. (8 vols., London, 1714).

Hamlet Prince of Denmark. A Tragedy (London, 1718; repr. 1969).

The Works of Shakespear, ed. Alexander Pope (6 vols., London, 1723–5).

The Works of Mr. William Shakespear. The Seventh Volume, ed. George Sewell (London, 1726).

The Works of Shakespear, ed. Alexander Pope (8 vols., London, 1728).

The Works of Shakespeare, ed. Lewis Theobald (7 vols., London, 1733–4).

The Works of Shakespeare, ed. Lewis Theobald (8 vols., London, 1740).

The Works of Shakespear, ed. Sir Thomas Hanmer (6 vols., London, 1743–4).

The Works of Shakespear, ed. William Warburton (8 vols., London, 1747).

The Works of Shakespeare, ed. Lewis Theobald (8 vols., London, 1757).

The Plays of William Shakespeare, ed. Samuel Johnson (8 vols., London, 1765).

Mr. William Shakespeare his Comedies, Histories, and Tragedies, ed. Edward Capell (10 vols., London, 1767–8).

King Lear. A Tragedy, ed. Charles Jennens (London, 1770).
Hamlet. A Tragedy, ed. Charles Jennens (London, 1773).
Othello. A Tragedy, ed. Charles Jennens (London, 1773).
The Plays of William Shakespeare, ed. Samuel Johnson and George Steevens (10 vols., London, 1773).
The Plays of William Shakespeare, ed. George Steevens and Isaac Reed (10 vols., London, 1785).
The Plays and Poems of William Shakespeare, ed. Edmond Malone (10 vols. in 11, London, 1790).
A New Variorum Edition of Shakespeare: Hamlet, ed. H. H. Furness (Philadelphia, 1877).
A New Variorum Edition of Shakespeare: Henry IV Part 1, ed. S. B. Hemingway (Philadelphia, 1936).
Hamlet, ed. Harold Jenkins (London, 1982).
Hamlet, ed. Philip Edwards (Cambridge, 1985).
Hamlet, ed. G. R. Hibbard (Oxford, 1987).
William Shakespeare: The Complete Works, ed. Gary Taylor and Stanley Wells (Oxford, 1987).

3. OTHER PRIMARY SOURCES

An Account of the Life and Writings of Mr. John Le Clerc (London, 1712).
An Account of the State of Learning in the Empire of Lilliput (London, 1728), repr. in *Gulliveriana V: Shorter Imitations of Gulliver's Travels*, ed. Jeanne K. Welcher and George E. Bush (New York, 1974).
Addison, Joseph, *Dialogues upon the Usefulness of Ancient Medals* (London, 1726; repr. New York, 1976).
An Answer to a Late Pamphlet, Called An Essay concerning Critical and Curious Learning (London, 1698).
An Answer to Mr. Pope's Preface to Shakespear . . . By a stroling Player (London, 1729).
[Atterbury, Francis], *A Short Review of the Controversy between Mr. Boyle, and Dr. Bentley, With Suitable Reflections upon it* (London, 1701).
Bailey, Nathan, *An Universal Etymological English Dictionary* (London, 1721).
Bellum Grammaticale: or, the Grammatical Battel Royal (London, 1712; repr. Menston, 1969).
[Bennet, Thomas,] *An Essay on the Thirty Nine Articles of Religion* (London, 1715).
Bentley, Richard, *The Correspondence of Richard Bentley*, ed. Christopher Wordsworth (2 vols., London, 1842).
—— *A Dissertation upon the Epistles of Phalaris, Themistocles, Socrates, Euripides and Others; And the Fables of Æsop* (London, 1697).
—— *Dissertations upon the Epistles of Phalaris . . .*, ed. Wilhelm Wagner (Berlin, 1874).

—— *Epistola ad Joannem Millium*, ed. G. P. Goold (Toronto, 1962).

—— *Remarks upon a Late Discourse of Free-thinking*, 5th edn. (London, 1716).

—— ed., *Milton's Paradise Lost: A New Edition* (London, 1732).

—— *Dr. Bentley's Proposals for Printing a New Edition of the Greek Testament, and St. Hierom's Latin Version* (London, 1721).

Birch, Thomas, John Peter Bernard, and John Lockman, eds., *A General Dictionary, Historical and Critical* (10 vols., London, 1734–41), ix (1739).

Bolingbroke, Henry St. John, Viscount, *A Letter to the Most Impudent Man Living* (London, 1749; repr. Los Angeles, 1978).

Boswell, James, *Boswell's Life of Johnson*, ed. G. B. Hill, rev. L. F. Powell (6 vols., Oxford, 1934).

—— *The Journal of a Tour to the Hebrides, with Samuel Johnson, LL.D.*, ed. R. W. Chapman (Oxford, 1924).

Bowyer, William, *Critical Conjectures and Observations on the New Testament*, 3rd edn. (London, 1782).

Boyle, Charles, *Dr. Bentley's Dissertations on the Epistles of Phalaris, and the Fables of Æsop, Examin'd*, 3rd edn. (London, 1699).

[Bramston, James,] *The Crooked Six-Pence: With a Learned Preface Found Among Some Papers bearing Date the same Year in which Paradise Lost was publish'd by the late Dr. Bently* (London, 1743).

Brown, Tom, 'Original Letters Lately Written by Mr. Brown', in *The Works of Monsieur Voiture* (2 vols., London, 1705).

Browne, William, *The Works of William Browne*, ed. Thomas Davies (3 vols., London, 1772).

The Builder's Dictionary, or Gentleman and Architect's Companion (2 vols., London, 1734).

Burnet, Gilbert, bishop of Salisbury, *An Exposition of the Thirty-Nine Articles of the Church of England*, 3rd edn. (London, 1705).

[Campbell, Archibald,] *Lexiphanes, A Dialogue Imitated from Lucian, and suited to the present Times* (London, 1767).

[Capell, Edward, ed.,] *Prolusions: or, select Pieces of antient Poetry,—compil'd with great Care from their several Originals, and offer'd to the Publick as Specimens of the Integrity that should be found in the Editions of worthy Authors* (London, 1760).

[Chalmers, George,] *An Apology for the Believers in the Shakespeare-papers* (London, 1797; repr. London, 1971).

—— *A Supplemental Apology for the Believers in the Shakespeare-Papers* (London, 1799; repr. London, 1971).

Chambers, Robert, *A Course of Lectures on the English Law*, ed. Thomas M. Curley (2 vols., Oxford, 1986).

Chesterfield, Philip Dormer Stanhope, 4th Earl of, *Letters*, ed. Bonamy Dobree (6 vols., London, 1932).

Clarendon, Edward Hyde, Earl of, *The History of the Rebellion and Civil Wars in England . . . to which are subjoined the notes of Bishop Warburton* (7 vols., Oxford, 1849).

A Collection of Old Ballads: Corrected from the best and most Ancient Copies Extant (London, 1727).

[Collins, Anthony,] *Priestcraft in Perfection: or, a Detection of the Fraud of Inserting and Continuing this Clause (The Church hath Power to Decree Rites and ceremonys, and Authority in Controversys of Faith) In the Twentieth Article of the Church of England* (London, 1710).

——*An Historical and Critical Essay on the thirty nine Articles of the Church of England* (London, 1724).

Comings, Fowler, *The Printed Hebrew Text of the Old Testament Vindicated* (Oxford, 1753).

[Cruden, Alexander, ed.,] *A Verbal Index to Milton's Paradise Lost* (London, 1741).

Daniel, Samuel, *The Poetical Works of Samuel Daniel, Author of the English History* (London, 1718).

Davies, Sir John, *The Original, Nature and Immortality of the Soul* (London, 1714).

Defoe, Daniel, *An Essay upon Projects* (London, 1697; repr. Menston, 1969).

Dodd, William, *The Beauties of Shakespear* (London, 1752; repr. London, 1971).

Dodsley, Robert, ed., *A Select Collection of Old Plays* (12 vols., London, 1744).

Douglas, Gavin, *Virgil's Aeneis, Translated into Scottish Verse, by the Famous Gavin Douglas, Bishop of Dunkeld. A new Edition. Wherein The many Errors of the Former are corrected and the Defects supply'd, from an excellent Manuscript* (Edinburgh, 1710).

Drummond, William, *The Works of William Drummond of Hawthornden . . . Now Published from the Author's Original Copies* (Edinburgh, 1711).

Dryden, John, *Of Dramatic Poesy and Other Critical Essays*, ed. George Watson (Oxford, 1962).

Edwards, Thomas, *The Canons of Criticism, and Glossary; The Trial of the Letter Y, alias Y, and Sonnets*, 7th edn. (London, 1765; repr. London, 1970).

Elstob, Elizabeth, *An Apology for the Study of Northern Antiquities* (London, 1715; repr. New York, 1956).

F.B., *A Free but Modest Censure On the late Controversial Writings and Debates* (London, 1698).

[Fell, John,] *An Essay towards an English Grammar* (London, 1784; repr. Menston, 1967).

Felton, Henry, *A Dissertation upon Reading the Classicks and Forming a Just Stile* (London, 1713; repr. Menston, 1971).

Five Extraordinary Letters Suppos'd to be Writ to Dr. B——y upon his edition of Horace (London, 1712).

Fleeman, J. D., ed., *The Sale Catalogue of Samuel Johnson's Library: A Facsimile Edition* (Victoria, BC, 1975).

Fortescue, Sir John, *The Difference Between an Absolute and Limited Monarchy; As it more particularly regards the English Constitution*, ed. John Fortescue-Aland (London, 1714).

A Friendly Letter to Dr. Bentley: Occasion'd by his New Edition of Paradise Lost (London, 1732).

Garth, Sir Samuel, *The Dispensary*, 2nd edn. (London, 1699).

Gibbon, Edward, *Critical Observations on the Sixth Book of the Aeneid* (London, 1770).

—— *Memoirs of My Life*, ed. Betty Radice (Harmondsworth, 1984).

[Gildon, Charles, and John Brightland,] *A Grammar of the English Tongue* (London, 1711; repr. Menston, 1967).

Greenwood, James, *An Essay towards a Practical English Grammar* (London, 1711; repr. Menston, 1969).

[Grey, Zachary,] *A Word or Two of Advice to William Warburton; A Dealer in many Words* (London, 1746; repr. New York, 1975).

—— *A Free Familiar Letter to that great Refiner of Pope and Shakespeare, the Rev. Mr. William Warburton* (London, 1750).

—— ed., *Hudibras* (2 vols., Dublin, 1744).

—— *Critical, Historical and Explanatory Notes on Shakespeare* (2 vols., London, 1754).

The Guardian, ed. John Calhoun Stephens (Lexington, Mass., 1982).

Hardinge, George, *Chalmeriana: or a collection of papers, literary and political* (London, 1800; repr. 1971).

[Hare, Francis,] *The Clergyman's Thanks to Phileleutherus for his Remarks on The Late Discourse of Free-thinking* (London, 1712).

Harwood, Edward, *A View of the Various Editions of the Greek and Roman Classics* (London, 1775).

Hawkins, Sir John, *The Life of Samuel Johnson LL.D.* (London, 1787).

Hearne, Thomas, *Remarks and Collections* (11 vols., Oxford, 1885–1921).

—— *The Life of Mr. Thomas Hearne, of St. Edmund's Hall, Oxford* (Oxford, 1772), Mic. (1987), reel 2486, no. 19.

—— ed., *Robert of Gloucester's Chronicle* (2 vols., Oxford, 1724).

—— ed., *A Collection of Curious Discourses Written by Eminent Antiquaries* (Oxford, 1720).

Heath, Benjamin, *A Revisal of Shakespeare's Text* (London, 1765).

Hinman, Charlton, ed., *The Norton Facsimile of the First Folio of Shakespeare* (New York, 1968).

[Holt, John,] *An Attempte to Rescue that Aunciente, English Poet and Playwrighte, Maister Williaume Shakespere, from the Maney Errours, faulsely charged on him* (London, 1749; repr. 1971).

Howard, Henry, earl of Surrey, *Songes and Sonettes . . . Re-printed by E. Curll* (London, 1717).

[Jackson, John, as 'Philocritus Cantabrigiensis',] *A Treatise on the Improvements made in the Art of Criticism: Collected out of the Writings of a celebrated Hypercritic* (London, 1748).

[Johnson, Richard,] *Aristarchus Anti-Bentleianus* (London, 1717).

Johnson, Samuel, *Johnson on Shakespeare*, ed. Arthur Sherbo (2 vols., New Haven, Conn., 1968).

—— *The Rambler*, ed. W. J. Bate and Albrecht B. Strauss (3 vols., New Haven, Conn., 1969).

—— *The Plan of a Dictionary* (London, 1747; repr. Menston, 1970).

—— *Political Writings*, ed. Donald J. Greene (New Haven, Conn., 1977).

—— *Prefaces, Biographical and Critical, to the Works of the English Poets* (10 vols., London, 1779–81).

—— *Samuel Johnson's Prefaces and Dedications*, ed. Allen T. Hazen (New York, 1937).

—— *A Dictionary of the English Language* (2 vols., London, 1755).

—— *A Dictionary of the English Language . . . Abstracted from the Folio Edition* (London, 1756).

—— *A Dictionary of the English Language*, 4th edn. (2 vols., London, 1773).

—— *The Letters of Samuel Johnson*, ed. R. W. Chapman (3 vols., Oxford, 1952).

—— *The Letters of Samuel Johnson*, ed. Bruce Redford (Oxford, 1992–), i–iii (1992).

[Jortin, John,] *Remarks on Spenser's Poems* (London, 1734).

[—— ed.,] *Miscellaneous Observations upon Authors, Ancient and Modern* (2 vols., London, 1731–2).

Kant, Immanuel, 'Beantwortung der Frage: Was ist Aufklärung?' in Jürgen Zehbe, ed., *Was ist Aufklärung? Aufsätze zur Geschichte und Philosophie* (Göttingen, 1985), 55–61.

—— *Critique of Judgment*, tr. Werner S. Pluhar (Indianapolis, 1987).

Kennicott, Benjamin, *The State of the Printed Text of the Old Testament Considered* (2 vols., Oxford, 1753–9).

[Kenrick, William,] *A Defence of Mr. Kenrick's Review of Dr. Johnson's Shakespeare* (London, 1766; repr. New York, 1974).

K[ersey], J[ohn], *A New English Dictionary* (London, 1702).

[King, William], *Dialogues of the Dead: Relating to the Present Controversy Concerning the Epistles of Phalaris* (London, 1699).

Kirkby, John, *A New English Grammar* (London, 1746; repr. Menston, 1971).

Lay-craft exemplified in a discovery of the weakness of the late attempts of the Author of Priestcraft In Perfection and Mr. Benjamin Robinson . . . to Prove the English Clergy Guilty of Forgery (London, 1710).

Le Clerc, Jean, 'Richard Bentley, *A Dissertation on the Epistles of Phalaris*', *Nouvelles de la Republique des Lettres*, June 1699 (Amsterdam, 1699).

—— *Mr. Le Clerc's Judgment and Censure of Dr Bentley's Horace* (London, 1713).

A Letter to the Reverend Master of Trinity-College in Cambridge, Editor of a new Greek and Latin Testament (London, 1721).

The Life and Conversation of Richard Bentley, Delivered in his own Words, for the most part from his own Writings (London, 1712).

The Literary Magazine: or, Universal Review: for the Year MDCCLVII: Vol. II (London, 1757; repr. Newark, 1978).

Lloyd, William, *A Chronological Account of the Life of Pythagoras* (London, 1699).

Locke, John, *The Correspondence of John Locke*, ed. E. S. de Beer (8 vols., Oxford, 1976–89).

—— *An Essay Concerning Human Understanding*, ed. P. H. Nidditch (Oxford, 1975).

—— *An Essay for the Understanding of St. Paul's Epistles: By Consulting St. Paul himself* (London, 1707).

[Mace, Daniel, ed.,] *The New Testament in Greek and English. Containing the Original Text Corrected from the Authority of the most Authentic Manuscripts: And a New Version Form'd agreeably to the Illustrations of the most Learned Commentators* (2 vols., London, 1729).

Mallet, David, *Of Verbal Criticism: An Epistle to Mr Pope. Occasioned by Tibbald's Shakespear, and Bentley's Milton* (London [i.e Edinburgh], 1733).

Malone, Edmond, *A Letter to the Rev. Richard Farmer, D.D. . . . relative to the edition of Shakespeare, published in MDCCXC* (London, 1792; repr. 1971).

—— *An Inquiry into the Authenticity of certain miscellaneous papers and legal instruments . . . Attributed to Shakespeare* (London, 1792; repr. 1970).

Mandeville, Sir John, *The Voiage and Travaile of Sir John Maundevile . . . Now publish'd entire from an Original MS. in the Cotton Library* (London, 1725).

Martin, Benjamin, *Institutions of Language; containing a Physico-grammatical Essay on the Propriety and Rationale of the English Tongue* (London, 1748; repr. Menston, 1970).

Massinger, Philip, *The Dramatic Works of Philip Massinger Compleat*, ed. Thomas Coxeter (London, 1761).

Mathias, Thomas James, *The Pursuits of Literature*, 7th edn. (London, 1798).

[Maynwaring, Arthur,] *The British Academy* (London, 1712; repr. New York, 1967).

Middleton, Conyers, *A Dissertation concerning the Origin of Printing in England* (Cambridge, 1735).

[——] *Remarks, Paragraph by Paragraph, upon the Proposals lately published by Richard Bentley, for a New Edition of the Greek Testament and Latin Version* (London, 1921).

—— *Some Farther Remarks, Paragraph by Paragraph, upon Proposals Lately publish'd for A New Edition of a Greek and Latin Testament, by Richard Bentley* (London, 1721).

[Milner, John,] *A View of the Dissertation upon the Epistles of Phalaris, Themistocles, &c.* (London, 1698).

Milton, John, *The Poetical Works of Mr. John Milton* (London, 1695).

—— *Paradise Lost*, ed. Thomas Newton, 2nd edn. (2 vols., London, 1750).

Milton Restor'd and Bentley Depos'd (London, 1732).

[Morell, Thomas, ed.,] *The Canterbury Tales of Chaucer, in the Original, From the most Authentic Manuscripts* (London, 1740).

Mortimer, John, *The Whole Art of Husbandry: Or, the Way of Managing and Improving of Land*, 5th edn. (2 vols., London, 1721).

Moxon, Joseph, *Mechanick Exercises, or the Doctrine of Handy-Works* (2 vols., London, 1683).

Nichols, John, *Literary Anecdotes of the Eighteenth Century* (9 vols., London, 1812–15; repr. New York, 1966).

—— *Illustrations of the Literary History of the Eighteenth Century* (8 vols., London, 1817–58; repr. New York, 1966).

'Observations on an edition of Milton, publish'd in the Year 1725', *Gentleman's Magazine*, 1 (1731), 55.

[Oldisworth, William, ed.,] *The Odes, Epodes, and Carmen Seculare of Horace, In Latin and English; With a Translation of Dr. Ben-ley's Notes. To which are added, Notes upon Notes* (24 parts, London, 1712).

Oldmixon, John, *Reflections on Dr. Swift's Letter to the Earl of Oxford, about the English Tongue* (London, 1712; repr. Menston, 1970).

[Oldys, William, ed.,] *The Works of Michael Drayton* (London, 1748).

Pearce, Zachary, *A Review of the Text of Milton's Paradise Lost* (London, 1732).

Peck, Francis, *New Memoirs of the Life and Poetical Works of Mr. John Milton* (London, 1740).

Pope, Alexander, *The Dunciad*, ed. James Sutherland (London, 1963).

—— *Pastoral Poetry and an Essay on Criticism*, ed. E. Audra and A. Williams (London, 1961).

—— *Imitations of Horace*, ed. John Butt (London, 1939).

—— *The Correspondence of Alexander Pope*, ed. George Sherburn (5 vols., Oxford, 1956).

—— *The Prose Works of Alexander Pope*, ed. Norman Ault and Rosemary Cowler (2 vols., Oxford, 1936–86).

Proposals for Printing by Subscription . . . a Commentary Critical and Theological upon the learned Mr. Warburton's apologetical dedication to the Reverend Dr. Henry Stebbing . . . by Martinus Scriblerus Junior (London, 1746).

Richardson, Jonathan, father and son, *Explanatory Notes and Remarks on Milton's Paradise Lost* (London, 1734; repr. New York, 1971).

[Ritson, Joseph], *Cursory Criticisms on the Edition of Shakespeare published by Edmond Malone* (London, 1792; repr. 1970).

—— *Remarks, Critical and Illustrative, on the Text and Notes of the Last Edition of Shakespeare* (London, 1783).

Ruffhead, Owen, *The Life of Alexander Pope* (London, 1769).

Rymer, Thomas, *A Short View of Tragedy* (London, 1693; repr. 1971).

[Shaw, William,] *Memoirs of the Life and Writings of Samuel Johnson*, ed. Arthur Sherbo (Oxford, 1974).

Shawcross, John T., ed., *Milton: The Critical Heritage* (London, 1970).

Simon, Richard, *Histoire critique du Vieux Testament* (Rotterdam, 1685).

A Short Account of Dr. Bentley's Humanity and Justice, To those Authors who have written before him, 2nd edn. (London, 1699).

The Spectator, ed. Donald F. Bond (5 vols., Oxford, 1965).

Spence, Joseph, *Observations, Anecdotes and Characters of Books and Men*, ed. James M. Osborn (2 vols., Oxford, 1966).

Spenser, Edmund, *The Works of that Famous English Poet, Mr. Edmund Spenser* (London, 1679).

—— *The Works of Mr. Edmund Spenser*, ed. John Hughes (6 vols., London, 1715).

—— *The Works of Spenser*, ed. John Hughes (6 vols., London, 1750).

—— *The Faerie Queene* (3 vols., London, 1751).

—— *The Works of Edmund Spenser*, ed. Edwin Greenlaw, Charles Grosvenor Osgood, and Frederick Morgan (11 vols., Baltimore, 1932–57).

Sprat, Thomas, *The History of the Royal Society*, ed. Jackson I. Cope and Harold W. Jones (London, 1959).

Stackhouse, Thomas, *Reflections on the Nature and Property of Languages* (London, 1731; repr. Menston, 1969).

Steele, Richard, *The Theatre . . . to which are added, The Anti-theatre . . .*, ed. John Nichols (London, 1791).

The Student or, the Oxford and Cambridge Monthly Miscellany, ed. Donald D. Eddy (New York, 1979).

Swift, Jonathan, *A Proposal for Correcting, Improving and Ascertaining the English Tongue* (London, 1712; repr. Menston, 1969).

Temple, William, *Sir William Temple's Essays on Ancient and Modern Learning*, ed. J. E. Spingarn (Oxford, 1909).

Theobald, Lewis, *Shakespeare Restored* (London, 1726; repr. 1971).

—— *The Cave of Poverty. A Poem. Written in Imitation of Shakespeare* (London, 1715).

—— *The Censor*, 2nd edn. (3 vols., London, 1717).

—— *Double Falshood; or, The Distrest Lovers: A Play . . . Written Originally by W. Shakespeare* (London, 1728; repr. 1970).

—— *The Tragedy of King Richard II . . . Alter'd from Shakespear* (London, 1720; repr. 1969).

[—— ed.,] *The Grove; or a Collection of Original Poems, Translations, etc.* (London, 1721).

—— et al., eds., *The Works of Mr. Francis Beaumont, and Mr. John Fletcher* (10 vols., London, 1750).

T.R., *An Essay Concerning Critical and Curious Learning* (London, 1698; repr. Los Angeles, 1969).

Twells, Leonard, *A Critical Examination of the late New Text and Version of the New Testament* (London, 1731).

Upton, John, *Critical Observations on Shakespeare* (London, 1746).

—— *A Letter concerning a new edition of Spenser's Faerie Queene* (London, 1751).

Urry, John, ed., *The Works of Geoffrey Chaucer, Compared with the Former Editions, and many valuable MSS* (London, 1721).

Vickers, Brian, ed., *Shakespeare: The Critical Heritage* (6 vols., London, 1974–81).

A Vindication of An Essay Concerning Critical and Curious Learning (London, 1698).

Waller, Edmund, *The Works of Edmund Waller Esq' in Verse and Prose Published by Mr. Fenton* (London, 1728).

Wallis, John, *Grammar of the English Language*, tr. and ed. J. A. Kemp (London, 1972).

Warburton, William, *Miscellaneous Translations, in Prose and Verse* (London, 1724).

—— 'Gi. Warburton A.M. in C. Velleii Paterculi, Historias, Emendationes', *Bibliothèque britannique, ou histoire des ouvrages des savans de Grande Bretagne* (n.pl., July–Sept. 1736), 256–94.

—— *A Vindication of Mr. Pope's Essay on Man, from the Misrepresentations of M^r De Crousaz* (London, 1740).

—— *A Letter from an Author, to a Member of Parliament, concerning Literary Property* (London, 1747; repr. New York, 1974).

—— *A Letter to the Editor of the Letters on the Spirit of Patriotism* (London, 1749; repr. Los Angeles, 1978).

—— *An Enquiry into the Nature and Origin of Literary Property* (London, 1762; repr. New York, 1974).

—— *The Divine Legation of Moses Demonstrated, in nine books*, 4th edn. (5 vols., London, 1755–65).

—— ed., *The Works of Alexander Pope ... together with the Commentaries and Notes of Mr. Warburton* (9 vols., London, 1751).

Wells, Edward, *A Specimen of An Help for the More Easy Understanding of the Holy Scriptures* (Oxford, 1709).

Whalley, Peter, *An Enquiry into the Learning of Shakespeare* (London, 1748; repr. New York, 1970).

—— ed., *The Works of Ben Jonson* (7 vols., London, 1756).

Wheare, Degory, *The Method and Order of Reading both Civil and Ecclesiastical Histories ... The Third Edition, with Amendments. With Mr. Dodwell's Invitation to Gentlemen, to acquaint themselves with ancient history*, 3rd edn. (London, 1710).

Whitehead, Paul, *The State Dunces* (London, 1733).

Wotton, William, *Reflections upon Ancient and Modern Learning*, 3rd edn. (London, 1705).

4   SECONDARY SOURCES

Aarsleff, Hans, *From Locke to Saussure* (Minneapolis, 1982).

Abbott, John L., 'The Making of the Johnsonian Canon', in Paul Korshin, ed., *Johnson after Two Hundred Years* (Philadelphia, 1986), 127–39.

Adorno, Theodor, 'On the Fetish Character in Music and the Regression of Listening', in J. M. Bernstein, ed., *The Culture Industry: Selected Essays on Mass*

Culture (London, 1991), 26–52.

—— and Horkheimer, Max, *Dialectic of Enlightenment*, tr. John Cumming (New York, 1972).

Alderson, William L., and Henderson, Arthur C., *Chaucer and Augustan Scholarship* (Berkeley, Calif., 1970).

Alston, R. C., *A Bibliography of the English Language from the Invention of Printing to the Year 1800* (12 vols., Menston, 1965–73).

Atkinson, A. D., 'Notes on Johnson's Dictionary', *Notes and Queries*, 194 (1949), 443–5; 195 (1950), 36–7, 55–6, 164–7, 249–50, 338–41, 516–19, 541–6, 561–3.

—— 'Donne Quotations in Johnson's Dictionary', *Notes and Queries*, 196 (1951), 387–8.

Ayres-Bennet, Wendy, 'Usage and Reason in Seventeenth-Century French Grammar: A Fresh look at Vaugelas', in Hans Aarsleff *et al.*, eds., *Papers in the History of Linguistics* (Amsterdam, 1987).

Balderston, Katherine C., 'Dr. Johnson's Use of William Law in the Dictionary', *Philological Quarterly*, 39 (1960), 379–88.

Barnard, John, ed., *Pope: The Critical Heritage* (London, 1973).

Barrell, John, *English Literature in History, 1730–1780: An Equal, Wide, Survey* (London, 1983).

Basker, James G., 'Minim and the Great Cham: Smollett and Johnson on the Prospect of an English Academy', in James Engell, ed., *Johnson and his Age* (Cambridge, Mass., 1984), 137–62.

—— 'Scotticisms and the Problem of Cultural Identity in Eighteenth-Century Britain', *Eighteenth-Century Life*, 15 (1991), 81–95.

Bate, Jonathan, *Shakespearean Constitutions: Politics, Theatre, Criticism 1730–1830* (Oxford, 1989).

Bate, Walter Jackson, *Samuel Johnson* (London, 1984).

Belanger, Terry, 'Tonson, Wellington and the Shakespeare Copyrights', in *Studies in the Book Trade in Honour of Graham Pollard* (Oxford, 1975), 195–209.

Bevington, David, 'Determining the Indeterminate: The Oxford Shakespeare', *Shakespeare Quarterly*, 38 (1987), 501–24.

Black, Matthew W., and Shaaber, Matthias A., *Shakespeare's Seventeenth-Century Editors, 1632–1685* (New York, 1937).

Bloom, Lillian D., 'Pope as Textual Critic: A Bibliographical Study of his Horatian Text', *Journal of English and Germanic Philology*, 47 (1948), 150–5.

Bourdette, Robert E., jun., ' "To *Milton* Lending Sense": Richard Bentley and *Paradise Lost*', *Milton Quarterly* 14/2 (1980), 37–49.

Bowers, Fredson, *On Editing Shakespeare and the Elizabethan Dramatists* (London, 1955).

Boyce, Benjamin, 'Pope's Yews in Shakespeare's Graveyard', *Notes and Queries*, 199 (1954), 287.

Branam, G. C., *Eighteenth Century Adaptations of Shakespearean Tragedy* (Berkeley, Calif., 1956).

Brownell, Morris R., *Alexander Pope and the Arts of Georgian England* (Oxford, 1978).

Butler, Marilyn, 'Oxford's Eighteenth-Century Versions', *Studies in the Eighteenth Century*, 12 (1988), 128–36.

Butt, John, *Pope's Taste in Shakespeare* (London, 1936).

Cherpack, Clifton, 'Warburton and the *Encyclopédie*', *Comparative Literature*, 7 (1955), 226–39.

Cohen, Michael M., and Bourdette, Robert E., jun., 'Richard Bentley's Edition of *Paradise Lost* (1732): A Bibliography', *Milton Quarterly*, 14/2 (1980), 49–54.

Coldwell, David F. C., ed., *Virgil's Aeneid Translated into Scottish Verse by Gavin Douglas, Bishop of Dunkeld* (4 vols., Edinburgh, 1957–64).

Collins, A. S., *Authorship in the Days of Johnson* (London, 1927).

Copley, Stephen, 'Polite Culture in Commercial Society', in Andrew E. Benjamin, Geoffrey N. Cantor, and John R. R. Christie, eds., *The Figural and the Literal: Problems of Language in the History of Science and Philosophy, 1630–1800* (Manchester, 1987), 176–201.

Cuming, A., 'A Copy of Shakespeare's Works which Formerly Belonged to Dr. Johnson', *Review of English Studies*, 3 (1927), 208–12.

Dane, Joseph A., 'The Reception of Chaucer's Eighteenth-Century Editors', *Text*, 4 (1988), 217–36.

Dawson, Giles E., 'Warburton, Hanmer, and the 1745 Edition of Shakespeare', *Studies in Bibliography*, 2 (1949–50), 35–48.

Dearing, Vinton A., 'Pope, Theobald, and Wycherley's *Posthumous Works*', *Publications of the Modern Languages Association*, 68 (1953), 223–36.

De Grazia, Margreta, 'The Essential Shakespeare and the Material Book', *Textual Practice*, 2 (1988), 69–86.

—— *Shakespeare Verbatim* (Oxford, 1991).

De Maria, Robert, *Johnson's 'Dictionary' and the Language of Learning* (Oxford, 1986).

Dixon, Peter, 'Pope's Shakespeare', *Journal of English and Germanic Philology*, 63 (1964), 191–203.

Dobree, Bonamy, 'How to edit Shakespeare', in D. W. Jefferson, ed., *The Morality of Art* (London, 1969), 33–40.

Dobson, Michael, ' "Remember/First to possess his Books": The Appropriation of *The Tempest* 1700–1800', *Shakespeare Survey*, 43 (1991), 99–108.

—— *The Making of the National Poet* (Oxford, 1992).

Douglas, Desmond, *English Scholars, 1660–1730*, 2nd edn. (London, 1951).

Eastman, Arthur M., 'The Texts from which Johnson Printed his Shakespeare', *Journal of English and Germanic Philology*, 49 (1950), 182–6.

—— 'In Defence of Dr. Johnson', *Shakespeare Quarterly*, 7 (1957), 493–500.

Evans, A. W., *Warburton and the Warburtonians* (London, 1932).

Evans, G. B., 'The Text of Johnson's *Shakespeare* (1765)', *Philological Quarterly*, 28 (1949), 425–8.

Feather, John, 'The Publishers and the Pirates: British Copyright law in Theory and Practice, 1710–1755', *Publishing History*, 22 (1987), 5–32.

Fleeman, J. D., *A Preliminary Handlist of Documents and Manuscripts of Samuel Johnson* (Oxford, 1967).

—— *A Preliminary Handlist of Copies of Books Associated with Dr. Samuel Johnson* (Oxford, 1984).

Fleming, Lindsay, 'Dr. Johnson's Use of Authorities in Compiling his Dictionary of the English Language', *Notes and Queries*, 199 (1954), 254–6, 94–7, 343–7.

Ford, H. L., *Shakespeare 1700–1740: A Collation of the Editions and Separate Plays* (Oxford, 1935).

Fox, Adam, *John Mill and Richard Bentley: A Study of the Textual Criticism of the New Testament 1675–1729* (Oxford, 1954).

Fox, Christopher, *Locke and the Scriblerians: Identity and Consciousness in Early Eighteenth-Century Britain* (Berkeley, Calif., 1988).

Foxon, D. F., *Thoughts on the History and Future of Bibliographical Description* (Los Angeles, 1970).

—— *Pope and the Early Eighteenth-Century Book Trade*, rev. and ed. James McLaverty (Oxford, 1991).

Franklin, Colin, *Shakespeare Domesticated* (Aldershot, 1991).

Frazier, Harriet C., *A Babble of Ancestral Voices: Shakespeare, Cervantes and Theobald* (The Hague, 1974).

Fuller, Reginald, *Alexander Geddes, 1737–1802: A Pioneer of Biblical Criticism* (Sheffield, 1984).

Gascoigne, John, *Cambridge in the Age of the Enlightenment: Science, Religion and Politics from the Restoration to the French Revolution* (Cambridge, 1989).

Gibson, Strickland, 'Thomas Bennet, a Forgotten Bibliographer', *The Library*, 5th ser. 6 (1951), 43–7.

Gilmore, Thomas B., jun., 'Johnson's Attitudes toward French Influence on the English Language', *Modern Philology*, 78 (1980–1), 243–60.

Goldberg, Jonathan, 'Textual Properties', *Shakespeare Quarterly*, 37 (1986), 213–17.

Goldstein, Malcolm, *Pope and the Augustan Stage* (Stanford, Calif., 1958).

Grafton, Anthony, 'The Origins of Scholarship', *American Scholar*, 48 (1979), 236–61.

—— *Joseph Scaliger: A Study in the History of Classical Scholarship* (Oxford, 1983).

—— *Defenders of the Text: The Traditions of Scholarship in an Age of Science* (London, 1991).

Greene, Donald J., *The Politics of Samuel Johnson* (New Haven, Conn., 1960).

—— *Samuel Johnson's Library: An Annotated Guide* (Victoria, BC, 1975).

Greetham, D. C., '[Textual] Criticism and Deconstruction', *Studies in Bibliography*, 44 (1991), 1–30.

Greg, W. W., 'The Rationale of Copy-Text', in *Collected Papers*, ed. J. C. Maxwell (Oxford, 1966).

Griffith, Philip Mahone, 'Samuel Johnson and Charles the Martyr: Veneration in the Dictionary', *The Age of Johnson: A Scholarly Annual*, 2 (1989), 235–61.

Griffith, R. H., *Alexander Pope: A Bibliography*, i/2 (Austin, Tex., 1927).

Grundy, Isobel, ed., *Samuel Johnson: New Critical Essays* (London, 1984).

Hale, John K., 'Notes on Richard Bentley's Edition of *Paradise Lost* (1732)', *Milton Quarterly*, 18 (1984), 46–50.

Hammond, Brean, 'Scriblerian Self-Fashioning', *Yearbook of English Studies*, 18 (1988), 108–24.

Hart, John A., 'Pope as Scholar-Editor', *Studies in Bibliography*, 23 (1970), 45–9.

Hay, Louis, 'Does "Text" Exist?', *Studies in Bibliography*, 41 (1988), 64–76.

Hedrick, Elizabeth, 'Locke's Theory of Language and Johnson's Dictionary', *Studies in English Literature*, 20 (1987), 422–44.

Hill, G. B., *Johnsonian Miscellanies* (2 vols., Oxford, 1897; repr. New York, 1966).

Hogan, C. B., *Shakespeare in the Theatre, 1701–1800* (2 vols., Oxford, 1952).

Horkheimer, Max, 'Traditionelle und kritische Theorie', *Zeitschrift für Sozialforschung*, 6 (1937), 245–94.

—— *Critical Theory: Selected Essays*, tr. Matthew J. O'Connell *et al.* (New York, 1972).

Housman, A. E., 'The Application of Thought to Textual Criticism', *Proceedings of the Classical Association*, 18 (1921), 67–84.

Howard-Hill, T. H., 'Theory and Praxis in the Social Approach to Editing', *Text*, 5 (1991), 31–46.

Hudson, Nicholas, *Samuel Johnson and Eighteenth-Century Thought* (Oxford, 1988).

Hughes, Geoffrey, 'Johnson's Dictionary and Attempts to "Fix the Language"', *English Studies in Africa*, 28 (1985), 99–107.

Hurlebusch, Klaus, 'Conceptualisations for Procedures of Authorship', *Studies in Bibliography*, 41 (1988), 100–35.

Ioppolo, Grace, '"Old" and "New" Revisionists: Shakespeare's Eighteenth-Century Editors', *Huntington Library Quarterly*, 52 (1989), 347–61.

Jackson, MacDonald P., 'Editions and Textual Studies', *Shakespeare Survey*, 42 (1990), 200–13.

—— 'Editions and Textual Studies', *Shakespeare Survey*, 43 (1991), 255–70.

Johnston, Shirley White, 'Samuel Johnson's Text of *King Lear*: "Dull Duty" Reassessed', *Yearbook of English Studies* (1976), 80–91.

—— 'From Preface to Practice: Samuel Johnson's Editorship of Shakespeare', in Paul J. Korshin and Robert R. Allen, eds., *Greene Centennial Studies* (Charlottesville, Va., 1984), 250–70.

Jones, R. F., *Lewis Theobald, his Contribution to Scholarship* (New York, 1919).

Kaminski, Thomas, *The Early Career of Samuel Johnson* (Oxford, 1987).

Keast, W. R., 'The Two *Clarissas* in Johnson's *Dictionary*', *Studies in Philology*, 54 (1957), 429–39.

Kenney, E. J., *The Classical Text* (Berkeley, Calif., 1974).

Kernan, Alvin, *Printing Technology, Letters and Samuel Johnson* (Princeton, NJ, 1987).

Klinkenborg, Verlyn, 'Johnson and the Analogy of Judicial Authority', *The Eighteenth Century: Theory and Interpretation*, 28 (1987), 47–59.

Kolb, Gwin J., and Sledd, James H., *Dr. Johnson's Dictionary: Essays in the Biography of a Book* (Chicago, 1955).

Korshin, Paul, 'Johnson and the Earl of Orrery', in W. H. Bond, ed., *Eighteenth-Century Studies in Honour of Donald F. Hyde* (New York, 1970), 29–44.

—— 'Johnson and the Scholars', in *Samuel Johnson: New Critical Essays*, ed. Isobel Grundy (London, 1984), 51–67.

Kowalk, Wolfgang, *Popes Shakespeare-Ausgabe als Spiegel seiner Kunstauffassung* (Berne, 1975).

Kroll, Richard W. F., 'Mise-en Page, Biblical Criticism, and Inference during the Restoration', *Studies in Eighteenth-Century Culture*, 16 (1988), 3–40.

Kristeller, Paul Oskar, 'The Lachmann Method: Merits and Limitations', *Text*, 1 (1984), 11–20.

Kuhn, Thomas S., *The Structure of Scientific Revolutions*, 2nd edn. (Chicago, 1970).

Landon, Richard, ed., *Editing and Editors: A Retrospect* (New York, 1988).

Leonard, Sterling A., *The Doctrine of Correctness in English Usage, 1700–1800* (Madison, Wis., 1929).

Leranbaum, Miriam, *Alexander Pope's 'Opus Magnum' 1729–1744* (Oxford, 1977).

Levine, Joseph M., *The Battle of the Books: History and Literature in the Augustan Age* (London, 1991).

Lounsbury, Thomas R., *The First Editors of Shakespeare* (London, 1906).

McGann, Jerome J., *A Critique of Modern Textual Criticism* (Chicago, 1983).

—— ed., *Textual Criticism and Literary Interpretation* (Chicago, 1985).

—— 'Response to Howard-Hill', *Text*, 5 (1991), 47–8

—— 'What is Critical Editing?', *Text*, 5 (1991), 15–30.

Mack, Maynard, *Collected in Himself: Essays Critical, Biographical and Bibliographical on Pope and Some of His Contemporaries* (Newark, NJ, 1982).

—— *Alexander Pope: A Life* (New Haven, Conn., 1985).

—— and Winn, James A., eds., *Pope: Recent Essays by Several Hands* (Brighton, 1980).

McKane, William, *Selected Christian Hebraists* (Cambridge, 1989).

McKenzie, D. F., *Bibliography and the Sociology of Texts* (London, 1986).

—— 'Printers of the Mind: Some Notes on Bibliographical Theories and Printing-House Practices', *Studies in Bibliography*, 22 (1969), 1–75.

McKerrow, R. B., 'The Treatment of Shakespeare's Text by his Earlier Editors (1709–1768)', in Peter Alexander, ed., *Studies in Shakespeare: British Academy Lectures* (Oxford, 1964), 103–31.

McLachlan, H., 'An Almost Forgotten Pioneer in New Testament Criticism', *Hibbert Journal*, 37 (1938–9), 617–25.

McLaverty, James, *Pope's Printer, John Wright: A Preliminary Study* (Oxford, 1976).
—— 'Lawton Gilliver: Pope's Bookseller', *Studies in Bibliography*, 32 (1979), 101–24.
—— 'The Concept of Authorial Intention in Textual Criticism', *The Library*, 6th ser. 6 (1984), 121–38.
—— 'The Mode of Existence of Literary Works of Art: The Case of the *Dunciad Variorum*', *Studies in Bibliography*, 37 (1984), 82–105.
McLeod, Randall (as 'Random Cloud'), 'Information on Information', *Text*, 5 (1991), 241–82.
McNair, Arnold, *Dr. Johnson and the Law* (Cambridge, 1948).
Marsden, Jean, ed., *The Appropriation of Shakespeare* (London, 1991).
Merk, Otto, 'Anfänge neutestamentlicher Wissenschaft im 18. Jahrhundert', in Georg Schwaiger, ed., *Historische Kritik in der Theologie* (Göttingen, 1980).
Metzger, Bruce M., *Chapters in the History of New Testament Textual Criticism* (Leiden, 1963).
—— *The Text of the New Testament: Its Transmission, Corruption and Restoration* (Oxford, 1964).
Miller, Aura, 'The Sources of the Text of *Hamlet* in the Editions of Rowe, Pope, and Theobald', *Modern Language Notes*, 22 (1907), 163–8.
Milne, Drew, 'The Function of Criticism: A Polemical History', *Parataxis: Modernism and Modern Writing*, 1 (1991), 30–50.
Monk, James Henry, *The Life of Richard Bentley, D.D.*, 2nd edn. (2 vols., London, 1833).
Morison, Stanley, *Politics and Script: Aspects of Authority and Freedom in the Development of Graeco-Latin Script from the Sixth Century B.C. to the Twentieth Century A.D.* (Oxford, 1972).
Moyles, R. G., 'Edward Capell (1713–1781) as Editor of Paradise Lost', *Transactions of the Cambridge Bibliographical Society*, 6/4 (1975), 252–61.
—— *The Text of 'Paradise Lost': A Study in Editorial Procedure* (Toronto, 1985).
Nicoll, Allardyce, 'The Editors of Shakespeare from First Folio to Malone', in Israel Gollancz, ed., *Studies in the First Folio* (London, 1924), 157–78.
Parker, G. F., *Johnson's Shakespeare* (Oxford, 1989).
Pasquali, Giorgio, *Storia della tradizione e critica del testo*, 2nd edn. (Florence, 1952).
Pocock, J. G. A., *The Machiavellian Moment* (Princeton, NJ, 1975).
Rajan, Tillotama, 'Is there a Romantic Ideology? Some Thoughts on Schleiermacher's Hermeneutic and Textual Criticism', *Text*, 4 (1988), 57–76.
Read, Allen, 'The Contemporary Quotations in Johnson's Dictionary', *English Literary History*, 2 (1935), 246–51.
Reddick, Allen, *The Making of Johnson's Dictionary, 1746–1773* (Cambridge, 1990).
Reed, Joel, 'Restoration and Repression: The Language Projects of the Royal Society', *Studies in Eighteenth-Century Culture*, 19 (1989), 399–412.

Reedy, Gerard, SJ, *The Bible and Reason: Anglicans and Scripture in Late Seven-teenth-Century England* (Philadelphia, 1985).

Rendall, Vernon, 'Johnson and Scaliger on Dictionary-Making', *Notes and Queries*, 194 (1949), 161–2.

Reventlow, Henning Graf, 'Richard Simon und seine Bedeutung für die kritische Erforschung der Bibel', in Georg Schwaiger, ed., *Historische Kritik in der Theologie* (Göttingen, 1980).

Rizzo, Betty, 'The English Author-Bookseller Dialogue', *The Age of Johnson: A Scholarly Annual*, 2 (1989), 353–74.

Rose, Gillian, *Hegel contra Sociology* (London, 1981).

Rosslyn, Felicity, *Alexander Pope* (London, 1990).

Ruml, Treadwell II, 'The Younger Johnson's Texts of Pope', *Review of English Studies*, NS 36 (1985), 180–98.

Ryley, Robert M., *William Warburton* (Boston, Mass., 1984).

Salmon, Vivian, and Burness, Edwina, eds., *A Reader in the Language of Shakespearean Drama* (Amsterdam, 1987).

Saunders, J. W., *The Profession of English Letters* (London, 1964).

Scholes, Robert E., 'Dr. Johnson and the Bibliographical Criticism of Shakespeare', *Shakespeare Quarterly*, 11 (1960), 163–71.

Seary, Peter, 'The Early Editors of Shakespeare and the Judgements of Johnson', in Paul Korshin, ed., *Johnson after Two Hundred Years* (Philadelphia, 1986), 175–86.

—— *Lewis Theobald and the Editing of Shakespeare* (Oxford, 1990).

Segar, Mary, 'Dictionary-Making in the Early Eighteenth Century', *Review of English Studies*, 7 (1931), 210–13.

Sen, S. K., *Capell and Malone, and Modern Critical Bibliography* (Calcutta, 1960).

Shapiro, F. R., 'Earlier Uses of *Bibliography* and Related Terms', *Notes and Queries*, 31 (1984), 30.

Sherbo, Arthur, 'Dr. Johnson Marks a Book List', *Notes and Queries*, 197 (1952), 519.

—— 'Warburton and the 1745 "Shakespeare" ', *Journal of English and Germanic Philology*, 51 (1952).

—— *Samuel Johnson, Editor of Shakespeare* (Urbana, Ill., 1956).

—— 'Dr. Johnson's "Dictionary" and Warburton's "Shakespeare" ', *Philological Quarterly*, 33 (1959), 71–82.

—— 'Johnson's Shakespeare Criticism and the Dramatic Criticism in the *Lives of the English Poets*', in G. B. Evans, ed., *Shakespeare: Aspects of Influence* (Cambridge, Mass., 1976).

—— *The Birth of Shakespeare Studies* (East Lansing, Mich., 1986).

—— *Isaac Reed, Editorial Factotum* (Victoria, BC, 1989).

Shillingsburg, Peter L., 'Text as Matter, Concept and Action', *Studies in Bibliography*, 44 (1991), 31–82.

Siebert, Donald T., '*Bubbled, Bamboozled* and *Bit*: "Low Bad" Words in

Johnson's *Dictionary*', *Studies in English Literature*, 26 (1986), 485–96.

Smith, David Nichol, *Shakespeare in the Eighteenth Century* (Oxford, 1928).

Spencer, Hazelton, '*Hamlet* under the Restoration', *Publications of the Modern Languages Association*, 38 (1923), 770–91.

Starnes, DeWitt T. and G. E. Noyes, *The English Dictionary from Cawdrey to Johnson* (Chapel Hill, NC, 1946).

Stillinger, Jack, 'Multiple Authorship and the Question of Authority', *Text*, 5 (1991), 283–93.

Tanselle, G. Thomas, *Textual Criticism since Greg: A Chronicle 1950–1985* (Charlottesville, Va., 1987).

—— 'Bibliographical History as a Field of Study', *Studies in Bibliography*, 41 (1988), 33–63.

—— *A Rationale of Textual Criticism* (Philadelphia, 1989).

—— 'Textual Criticism and Literary Sociology', *Studies in Bibliography*, 44 (1991), 83–143.

Taylor, Gary, *Reinventing Shakespeare: A Cultural History from the Restoration to the Present* (London, 1989).

—— and Warren, Michael, eds., *The Division of the Kingdoms: Shakespeare's Two Versions of* King Lear (Oxford, 1983).

Timpanaro, Sebastiano, *La genesi del metodo del Lachmann* (Florence, 1963).

Tinkler, John F., 'The Splitting of Humanism: Bentley, Swift, and the English Battle of the Books', *Journal of the History of Ideas*, 49 (1988), 453–72.

Trousdale, Marion, 'A Second Look at Critical Bibliography and the Acting of Plays', *Shakespeare Quarterly*, 41 (1990), 87–96.

Tucker, Susie I., 'Dr. Watts Looks at the Language', *Notes and Queries*, 199 (1959), 274–9.

Urkowitz, Steven, 'The Base shall to th' Legitimate: The Growth of an Editorial Tradition', in Gary Taylor and Michael Warren, eds., *The Division of the Kingdoms: Shakespeare's Two Versions of* King Lear (Oxford, 1983).

—— 'Reconsidering the Relationship of Quarto and Folio Texts of Richard III', *English Literary Renaissance*, 16 (1986), 442–65.

—— '"If I Mistake in Those Foundations Which I Build Upon": Peter Alexander's Textual Analysis of Henry VI Parts 2 and 3', *English Literary Renaissance*, 18 (1988), 230–56.

Vander Meulen, David, 'The *Dunciad in Four Books* and the Bibliography of Pope', *Publications of the Bibliographical Society of America*, 83 (1989), 293–310.

Walder, Ernest, *Shakespearian Criticism: Textual and Literary, from Dryden to the End of the Eighteenth Century* (Bradford, 1895; repr. New York, 1982).

Warren, Austin, *Alexander Pope as Critic and Humanist* (Princeton, NJ, 1929).

—— 'Pope and Ben Jonson', *Modern Language Notes*, 45 (1930), 86–8.

—— 'Pope's Index to Beaumont and Fletcher', *Modern Language Notes*, 46 (1931), 515–17.

Wasserman, Earl, *Elizabethan Poetry in the Eighteenth Century* (Urbana, Ill., 1947).

Watkins, W. B. C., *Johnson and English Poetry before 1660* (Princeton, NJ, 1936).

Weinbrot, Howard D., 'Johnson's *Dictionary* and *The World*: The Papers of Richard Owen Cambridge', *Philological Quarterly*, 50 (1971), 663–9.

—— ed., *New Aspects of Lexicography: Literary Criticism, Intellectual History, and Social Change* (Carbondale, Ill., 1972).

Wells, Stanley, *Re-editing Shakespeare for the Modern Reader* (Oxford, 1984).

—— and Taylor, Gary, *William Shakespeare: A Textual Companion* (Oxford, 1987).

Werstine, Paul, 'The Textual Mystery of *Hamlet*', *Shakespeare Quarterly*, 39 (1988), 1–26.

—— 'Narratives about Printed Shakespearean Texts: "Foul Papers" and "'Bad' Quartos"', *Shakespeare Quarterly*, 41 (1990), 65–86.

Wheeler, David, 'Eighteenth-Century Adaptations of Shakespeare and the Example of John Dennis', *Shakespeare Quarterly*, 36 (1985), 438–49.

Wilamowitz-Moellendorf, Ulrich von, *History of Classical Scholarship*, tr. Alan Harris (London, 1982).

Williamson, William L., 'Thomas Bennet and the Origins of Analytical Bibliography', *Journal of Library History*, 16 (1981), 177–86.

Wilson, F. P., *Shakespeare and the New Bibliography*, rev. and ed. Helen Gardner (Oxford, 1970).

Wimsatt, W. K., jun., 'Samuel Johnson and Dryden's *Du Fresnoy*', *Studies in Philology*, 48 (1951), 126–39.

—— and Wimsatt, M. H., 'Self-Quotations and Anonymous Quotations in Johnson's Dictionary', *English Literary History*, 15 (1948), 60–8.

Woodhouse, J. R., 'Dr. Johnson and the Accademia della Crusca', *Notes and Queries*, 32 (1985), 3–6.

Woudhuysen, H. R., 'Editions and Textual Studies', *Shakespeare Survey*, 44 (1992), 244–56.

Wurtsbaugh, Jewel, *Two Centuries of Spenserian Scholarship* (Baltimore, 1936).

Zeller, Hans, 'A New Approach to the Critical Constitution of Literary Texts', *Studies in Bibliography*, 28 (1975), 231–64.

Zionkowski, Linda, 'Territorial Disputes in the Republic of Letters: Canon Formation and the Literary Profession', *The Eighteenth Century: Theory and Interpretation*, 31 (1990), 3–22.

Index